CAMBRIDGE
UNIVERSITY PRESS

UNIVERSITY *of* CAMBRIDGE
ESOL Examinations

CAMBRIDGE OFFICIAL PREPARATION MATERIAL

Cambridge English

Compact First

D1997415

Student's Book with answers

Peter May

CAMBRIDGE
UNIVERSITY PRESS

University Printing House, Cambridge CB2 8BS, United Kingdom

One Liberty Plaza, 20th Floor, New York, NY 10006, USA

477 Williamstown Road, Port Melbourne, VIC 3207, Australia

4843/24, 2nd Floor, Ansari Road, Daryaganj, Delhi – 110002, India

79 Anson Road, #06–04/06, Singapore 079906

Cambridge University Press is part of the University of Cambridge.

It furthers the University's mission by disseminating knowledge in the pursuit of education, learning and research at the highest international levels of excellence.

www.cambridge.org
Information on this title: www.cambridge.org/9781107428447

First published 2014
20 19 18 17 16 15 14 13 12 11 10 9 8 7 6

Printed in Malaysia by Vivar Printing

A catalogue record for this publication is available from the British Library

ISBN 978-1-107-42842-3 Student's Book without answers with CD-ROM
ISBN 978-1-107-42844-7 Student's Book with answers with CD-ROM
ISBN 978-1-107-42857-7 Teacher's Book
ISBN 978-1-107-42855-3 Workbook without answers with Audio
ISBN 978-1-107-42856-0 Workbook with answers with Audio
ISBN 978-1-107-42845-4 Student's Book Pack
ISBN 978-1-107-42848-5 Student's Pack
ISBN 978-1-107-42852-2 Class Audio CDs (2)

CONTENTS

Map of the units 4

Introduction 6

Exam overview 7

1 Yourself and others 8

2 Eating and meeting 16

3 Getting away from it all 24

4 Taking time out 32

5 Learning and earning 40

6 Getting better 48

7 Green issues 56

8 Sci & tech 64

9 Fame and the media 72

10 Clothing and shopping 80

W Writing guide 88

L Listening guide 94

S Speaking guide 97

Visual materials 101

G Grammar reference 103

Wordlist 114

Answer key 122

Writing guide answer key 159

Acknowledgements 160

MAP OF THE UNITS

UNIT	TOPICS	GRAMMAR	VOCABULARY	READING
1 Yourself and others	Daily life People	Review of present tenses Present simple in time clauses	Adjectives ending in *-ed* and *-ing* Character adjectives Adjective prefixes and suffixes: *-able*, *-al*, *dis-*, *-ful*, *-ic*, *im-*, *-ish*, *-itive*, *-ive*, *-ous*, *un-*, *-y*	Part 7: multiple matching
2 Eating and meeting	Food and drink Restaurants Relationships	Review of past tenses	Fixed phrases	Part 6: gapped text
3 Getting away from it all	Travel and tourism Transport Festivals and customs	Review of modal verbs Adverbs of degree	Dependent prepositions	Part 5: multiple-choice questions + long text
4 Taking time out	Entertainment (film, music, arts) Leisure	Verbs followed by *to* + infinitive or *-ing* *too* and *enough* Review of present perfect	Phrasal verbs with *on*	Part 6: gapped text
5 Learning and earning	Education, study and learning Careers and jobs	Review of future forms Countable and uncountable nouns	Phrasal verbs with *take* Noun suffixes: *-or*, *-ist*, *-ian*, *-er*, *-ant*	Part 7: multiple matching
6 Getting better	Health and fitness Sport	Relative clauses (defining and non-defining) Purpose links	Medical vocabulary Phrasal verbs with *up* Sports vocabulary	Part 5: multiple-choice questions + long text
7 Green issues	The environment The weather	Review of conditionals 1–3 Mixed conditionals Comparison of adjectives and adverbs Contrast links	Phrases with *in*	Part 6: gapped text
8 Sci & tech	Science Technology	Review of passive forms Articles	Communications vocabulary Science vocabulary Collocations	Part 5: multiple-choice questions + long text
9 Fame and the media	The media Celebrities	Review of reported speech and reporting verbs	Media vocabulary Noun suffixes	Part 7: multiple matching
10 Clothing and shopping	Shopping and consumer goods Fashion	Position of adverbs of manner and opinion Review of *wish* and *if only* Review of causative *have* and *get*	Clothing and shopping vocabulary Phrasal verbs with *out* Extreme adjectives	Part 6: gapped text

USE OF ENGLISH	WRITING	LISTENING	SPEAKING
Part 3: word formation	Part 2 informal letter: getting ideas, informal language	Part 1: multiple-choice questions + short texts	Part 1: describing people, home
Part 2: open cloze	Part 2 article: narrative linking expressions	Part 2: sentence completion	Part 2: giving opinions, comparing
Part 1: multiple-choice cloze	Part 1 essay: linking expressions, for and against	Part 3: multiple matching	Part 3: turn taking, suggesting, speculating
Part 4: key word transformations	Part 2 review: descriptive adjectives, recommendations	Part 4: multiple-choice questions + long text	Part 4: asking for and justifying opinions
Part 3: word formation	Part 2 formal letter of application: formal expressions, achieving aims	Part 2: sentence completion	Part 1: talking about future plans
Part 2: open cloze	Part 2 letter: informal language, purpose links	Part 1: multiple-choice questions + short texts	Part 3: agreeing and politely disagreeing
Part 4: key word transformations	Part 1 essay: contrast links, for and against	Part 3: multiple matching	Part 2: comparing: *-er*, *more*, *(not) as ... as*, etc.
Part 1: multiple-choice cloze	Part 2 article: reason and result links, involving the reader	Part 2: sentence completion	Part 4: adding more points
Part 3: word formation	Part 2 report: recommending and suggesting	Part 4: multiple choice questions + long text	Part 2: keeping going
Part 4: key word transformations	Part 1 essay: extreme adjectives, for and against	Part 3: multiple matching	Parts 3 and 4: decision-making

INTRODUCTION

Who *Compact First Second Edition* is for

Compact First is a short but intensive final preparation course for students planning to take the *Cambridge English: First* exam, also known as First Certificate of English (FCE). The course provides B2-level students with thorough preparation and practice of the grammar, vocabulary, language skills, topics and exam skills needed for success in all four papers of the exam: Reading and Use of English, Writing, Listening and Speaking. The course can be used by classes of any age, but it is particularly suitable for students over 17.

What the Student's Book contains

- *Compact First Second Edition* Student's Book has ten units for classroom use. Each unit covers all four papers, focusing on one part of each paper in each unit. The Reading and Listening texts cover all core *Cambridge English: First* topics. Writing tasks include both sample and model answers and follow a step-by-step approach. The Speaking activities are designed to improve fluency and accuracy, and to help students express themselves with confidence.
- Grammar pages provide additional focus on grammar and each unit ends with a revision page to check how well students have learned the grammar and vocabulary. The Vocabulary input is at B2 level and is based on English Vocabulary Profile. Grammar and vocabulary work is integrated in exam practice, including exercises based on research from the Cambridge Learner Corpus.
- *Quick steps* with advice on how to approach each part of all the exam papers.
- Exam tips with useful advice on exam strategies.
- Cross-references to the Writing, Listening and Speaking guides, and Grammar reference.

Writing, Listening and Speaking guides
These guides explain in detail what students can expect in Papers 2, 3 and 4, and give suggestions on how best to prepare and practise in each case. The guides include a summary of the strategies, advice and tips focused on in the units of the Student's Book with additional tasks and model answers in the Writing guide, and lists of useful expressions in the Speaking guide.

The **Grammar reference** gives clear explanations of all the main areas of grammar students need to know for *Cambridge English: First*.

Wordlist
The wordlist includes approximately 30 key words with definitions for each unit.

CD-ROM
The CD-ROM accompanying the Student's Book contains interactive exercises, including listening exercises that help students prepare for the exam, as well as an electronic version of the wordlist, and a link to the *Online Cambridge Advanced Learner's Dictionary.*

Student's Book with answers: this component includes all the answer keys and recording scripts for the Student's Book.

Other course components

Audio: with listening material for the ten units of the Student's Book. The icon used with listening activities indicates the CD and track numbers.

Teacher's Book including:
- A list of aims for each unit.
- Step-by-step guidance for presenting and teaching all the material in the Student's Book. In some cases, alternative treatments and extension activities are suggested.
- Complete answer keys with recording scripts for both the Student's Book and Workbook. The keys include sample and model answers for Writing tasks.
- Five photocopiable progress tests, one for every two Student's Book units. The tests use a variety of non-exam task types.

Workbook without answers with Audio including:
- Ten units for homework and self-study corresponding to the Student's Book units. Each unit has four pages of exercises providing further practice and consolidation of the language and exam skills presented in the Student's Book. Exercises are based on research from the Cambridge Learner Corpus. Vocabulary is based on the English Vocabulary Profile.
- The Audio CD includes listening material for the Workbook.

Workbook with answers with Audio: this component includes all the answer keys and recording scripts for the Workbook.

Website
Two complete *Cambridge English: First* practice tests with accompanying audio as MP3 files are available on the website at www.cambridge.org/compactfirst.

Cambridge English: First

Overview
The *Cambridge English: First* examination has four papers.

Reading and Use of English 1 hour 15 minutes
Parts 1 and 3 mainly test your vocabulary; Part 2 mainly tests grammar. Part 4 often tests both. Answers are marked on a separate answer sheet.
Reading texts in Parts 5, 6 and 7 are about 550–650 words each. They are taken from newspaper and magazine articles, fiction, reports, advertisements, correspondence, messages and informational material such as brochures, guides or manuals. Answers are marked on a separate answer sheet.

Part	Task type	Questions	Format
1	Multiple choice gap-fill	8	You choose from words A, B, C or D to fill in each gap in a text.
2	Open gap-fill	8	You think of a word to fill in each gap in a text.
3	Word formation	8	You think of the right form of a given word to fill in each gap in a text.
4	Key word transformations	6	You complete a sentence with a given word so that it means the same as another sentence.
5	Multiple choice	6	You read a text followed by questions with four options: A, B, C or D.
6	Gapped text	6	You read a text with sentences removed, then fill in the gaps by choosing sentences from a jumbled list.
7	Multiple matching	10	You read 4–6 short texts and match the relevant sections to what the questions say.

Writing 1 hour 20 minutes
You have to do Part 1 plus **one** of the Part 2 tasks. In Part 2 you can choose one of questions 2–4. Answers are written in the booklet provided.

Part	Task type	Words	Format
1	Question 1 Essay	140–190	You write an essay giving your opinion on a given topic. You can use the ideas given and any of your own.
2	Questions 2–4 possible tasks: article, email/ letter, report or review	140–190	You do a task based on a situation. The topic, reader and reason you are writing will be explained.

Listening about 40 minutes
You both hear and see the instructions for each task, and you hear all four parts twice.
If one person is speaking, you may hear information, news, instructions, a commentary, a documentary, a lecture, a message, a public announcement, a report, a speech, a talk or an advertisement. If two people are talking, you might hear a conversation, a discussion, an interview, part of a radio play, etc.
Answers are marked on a separate answer sheet.

Part	Task type	Questions	Format
1	Multiple choice	8	You hear one or two people talking for about 30 seconds in eight different situations. For each question, you choose from answers A, B or C.
2	Sentence completion	10	You hear one person talking for about three minutes. For each question, you complete sentences by writing a word or short phrase.
3	Multiple matching	5	You hear five extracts, of about 30 seconds each, with a common theme. For each one, you choose from a list of six possible answers.
4	Multiple choice	7	You hear two people talking for about three minutes. For each question, you choose from answers A, B or C.

Speaking 14 minutes
You will probably do the Speaking test with one other candidate, though sometimes it is necessary to form groups of three. There will be two examiners, but one of them does not take part in the conversation.

Part	Task type	Minutes	Format
1	The examiner asks you some questions.	3–4	You talk about yourself.
2	You talk on your own for one minute.	3–4	You talk about two pictures and then comment on the other candidate's pictures.
3	You talk to the other candidate.	3–4	You discuss some prompts together.
4	You talk about things connected with the topic of Part 3.	3–4	You take part in a discussion with both the other candidate and the examiner.

Further information
For a full description of *Cambridge English: First*, including information about task types, testing focus and preparation for the exam, see the *Handbook*, which can be obtained from Cambridge English at: www.cambridgeenglish.org

1 Yourself and others
LISTENING

Part 1

L Page 94

1 Look at the photos. What are the people doing? How much time each day do you spend: a) studying or working, b) travelling, and c) relaxing?

2 Look at question 1 in the exam task. Answer these questions.

1 How many speakers will you hear? Are they female or male? What is the situation?
2 Part 1 questions may focus, for instance, on opinion, purpose or place. What is the focus of *Where is he?*

3 Read the recording script for question 1. Which is the correct answer (A, B or C)? Why? Why are the other two wrong?

I'm standing here in Church Avenue with about thirty other media people, but by the look of the place there isn't anybody in. Nobody's quite sure if ← C
he'll be back later this afternoon – or whether he's spending the weekend away, perhaps at a luxury hotel in the city centre. What does seem clear, ← B
though, is that he's unlikely to play in Sunday's big match – otherwise these TV crews would be waiting at the gates of the club's training ground to film him, not here. ← A

4 1.02 Work in pairs. For each of questions 2–8, ask and answer the questions in Exercise 2. Then listen and do the exam task.

Quick steps to Listening Part 1
- Don't choose an answer until you've heard the whole extract.
- You can always change your mind about an answer while you're listening or when you listen again.

Exam task

You will hear people talking in eight different situations.
For questions **1–8**, choose the best answer (**A**, **B** or **C**).

1 You hear a reporter talking on the radio.
Where is he?
A outside a training ground
B outside an expensive hotel
C outside somebody's house

2 You hear a woman talking about travelling to work every day. How does she feel about the daily train journey?
A It is often quite tiring.
B It is a good opportunity to talk to people.
C It is a relaxing way to begin the day.

3 You overhear a woman talking on the phone.
Why is she calling?
A to apologise for a mistake
B to refuse to do something
C to deny she did something

4 You hear a man talking about reading books.
Why does he enjoy reading at home?
A It helps him pass the time.
B It enables him to spend time alone.
C It makes a change from his job.

5 You overhear a conversation in a holiday resort.
Who is the woman?
A a waitress
B a tourist
C a café owner

6 You hear a man talking about staying healthy.
What is he doing to improve his fitness?
A eating less food
B going to the gym
C walking to work

7 You hear a woman talking about her home.
Where does she live?
A in a city-centre flat
B in a house in the suburbs
C in a country cottage

8 You overhear two people talking about finding something.
How does the woman feel?
A grateful
B relieved
C concerned

5 Have you chosen an answer for every question? Even if you're not sure, you could be right.

1 GRAMMAR

Review of present tenses (G) *Page 103*

1 Match extracts a–g from the recording in Listening with rules 1–7.

a *I'm standing here in Church Avenue.*
b *I live a long way out in the suburbs.*
c *Whenever I can, I go into the study.*
d *The traffic into town is getting worse all the time.*
e *Somebody is always pushing.*
f *A south-facing room gets lots of sunshine.*
g *This month I'm working particularly hard.*

We use the present simple to talk about:
1 a routine or habit
2 a permanent situation
3 something which is always true

We use the present continuous to talk about:
4 something happening right now
5 a temporary situation
6 a situation that is changing or developing
7 something irritating or surprising, using *always*

Note: verbs which describe states, e.g. *think*, *own*, *have*, *understand*, are normally used in simple tenses, but some can be continuous when they describe something we do, e.g. *I'm thinking of buying a bike.*

See Grammar reference page 103: stative verbs.

2 Correct the mistakes in these sentences written by exam candidates.

1 I suppose that you are understanding my situation.
2 This evening, people are playing music and have fun.
3 I know that you are liking your job, but in my opinion you are working too hard.
4 I wait for your answer to my letter.
5 Nowadays, I'm preferring to go to work by bicycle.
6 In summer it's nice to go on a boat and having dinner on the lake.
7 'Sara, can you hear me? I stand on your left, by the bridge.'

3 Complete the sentences with the correct form of the verbs in brackets.

1 Katie's in, but she .... (write) an email to someone at the moment.
2 Scientists believe that sea levels .... (rise) because of global warming.
3 My brother Oliver .... (quite often / go) mountain biking on Sundays.
4 My neighbours .... (always / shout) early in the morning. It's really annoying.
5 That notebook on the table .... (belong) to me.
6 I .... (stay) with my friends this week while my family are away.
7 In every continent on Earth, the sun .... (set) in the west.
8 Listen! Ellie .... (have) an argument with her boyfriend.

Present simple in time clauses (G) *Page 103*

4 Look at these extracts from the recording in Listening. Do all the verbs refer to the future? What tense do we use after time expressions like *when*?

I'll move back into my place when they finish repainting it on Friday.
Next time I want things like that, I'll buy them online instead.

5 Choose the correct option.

1 I *get* / *'ll get* some more milk when I *go* / *'ll go* shopping tomorrow.
2 I *wait* / *'ll wait* here until you *come* / *'ll come* back later on.
3 As soon as the film *ends* / *will end* tonight, I *catch* / *'ll catch* the bus home.
4 I *don't* / *won't* move house before I *start* / *'ll start* my new job next month.
5 By the time you *arrive* / *'ll arrive* at 8.30, I *am* / *'ll be* ready to go out.
6 I *talk* / *'ll talk* to my flatmates tonight once I *get* / *'ll get* home.

6 Complete the sentences about yourself. Then tell your partner.

1 I'll have a meal as soon as …
2 I'll spend less money the next time …
3 I'm going to buy a house when …
4 I don't think I'll have children before …
5 I won't stop studying English until …
6 I think I'll watch TV after …

1 READING AND USE OF ENGLISH

Part 7

1 Look at photos 1–4. What do you think a typical day is like for each person? Think about:

- when they do things like having meals
- where they go and how they travel
- who they see
- what they do to relax
- how they feel at various times of the day

2 Look at the exam task. Answer these questions.

1 How many people are there?
2 Is it one text in sections, or is it several short texts?
3 What's the topic?
4 What must you find? (e.g. *Which place … ?*)
5 How many questions are there?
6 Can you use letters A, B, C and D several times each?

3 Look quickly at the text and match parts A–D with photos 1–4. Which person starts working earliest? Who finishes latest?

4 Look at this Part 7 example question and the underlined words in the text. There are references to this in parts A, B and D. Why is B right? Why are A and D wrong?

Example:
Which person never has breakfast? B

> **Quick steps to Reading and Use of English Part 7**
> - Look at the instructions, title and layout, then read quickly through the questions.
> - Remember that the information you need may not be in the same order as the questions.
> - Be careful with words that only *seem* to say the same as a particular question, but in fact mean something quite different.

5 Do the exam task. Underline the words or sentences that tell you the right answers.

Exam task

You are going to read an article about four people's daily lives. For questions **1–10**, choose from the people (**A–D**). The people may be chosen more than once.

Which person

sometimes sleeps in the early afternoon?	**1**	
thinks they ought to do more frequent exercise?	**2**	
says they have their best ideas late in their working day?	**3**	
has to hurry to catch the train to work?	**4**	
does not always get up at the same time every day?	**5**	
dislikes working later than they should do?	**6**	
believes exercise helps them prepare for the day ahead?	**7**	
is now more relaxed at work?	**8**	
chooses not to follow local tradition?	**9**	
enjoys answering questions from customers?	**10**	

Different *lives*

A University student **Jake Harris** is in his first year. 'Assuming I don't oversleep, which can happen, I'm out of bed by 7.45. If there's time, I have some tea and toast, then set off. I used to aim for the 8.25 train, but I kept missing it so nowadays I do the uphill walk into town, which wakes me up and enables me to plan what I'm going to do in the morning and afternoon. From nine till one it's lessons and a group activity, with a quick break at eleven to grab something to keep me going till lunch. The afternoon is similar to the morning, really. After that I sometimes head for the gym, but not as often as I should. Once I get home I work for a few hours and later – if I'm not feeling too exhausted – I go out with friends. I've met some fascinating people here!'

C Website Designer **Oliver McShane** works at home and, unsurprisingly, is a late riser: 'rolling out of bed,' as he puts it, 'at 9 a.m.' Switching on his laptop, his first task is to answer any early-morning emails, and then he carries on from where he left off the previous evening. 'If I have a creative peak,' he says, 'that's when it is, and it takes me a while to get going again the next day. Whenever I've stayed up working very late, I make up for it by having a 20-minute lie-down after lunch. Then, when I wake up, I feel refreshed and ready for another long working session. Occasionally I pack my laptop and sit in a café for a while, although I can get distracted from work if I run into someone I know.'

B For Assistant Sales Manager **Julia Anderson**, each day begins at 6.30 a.m. with a quick shower, a few minutes to get ready, and then a dash to the station to catch the 7.15 into Manhattan. By eight o'clock she's at her workstation. 'I need to be there then, before the salespeople start arriving. I spend the rest of the morning in meetings and dealing with client queries, which for me is one of the most interesting, challenging and worthwhile aspects of the job. Then it's out for a quick lunch – my first meal of the day – and back to work at 1 p.m., followed by more of the same up to 5 p.m. That's how things are here: you have to keep to a tight schedule. At first I found working here pretty stressful, but I'm used to it now and it doesn't bother me.'

D **Anita Ramos** is a Tourist Guide who works mornings and evenings. 'It's just too hot to walk around the city in the afternoon,' she says, 'so I spend it at home. It's the custom here to have a sleep after lunch, but I haven't got time for that. In any case, I'm not tired then because I don't get up particularly early. When I do, I usually skip breakfast, though sometimes I have cereal or something. Then it's off to the office before heading downtown to wherever I'm meeting the first group. I take four or five groups out before lunch and I'm supposed to finish around 2 p.m., though there always seems to be someone in the last group who asks lots of questions, which can be a bit irritating if I end up doing unpaid overtime. It also means I risk missing the 2.15 train home.'

Exam tip ›

When you have finished, make sure you have answered all ten questions.

Adjectives ending in *-ed* and *-ing*

6 Find these words in the text and complete the rules with *-ed* and *-ing*.

exhausted, fascinating (A)	interesting, challenging (B)
refreshed, distracted (C)	tired, irritating (D)

1 We use adjectives with .... to describe how somebody feels about something.
2 We use adjectives with .... to describe the thing or person which causes the feeling.

7 Complete these sentences with *-ing* and *-ed* adjectives formed from the verbs in brackets. Then answer the questions about yourself.

1 At what time of day do you feel most .... (relax)?
2 What's the most .... (amuse) film you've ever seen?
3 When do you sometimes feel a little .... (worry)?
4 What's the most .... (depress) news item you've heard recently?
5 When do you feel most .... (motivate) to study?
6 Are you .... (terrify) of anything, such as spiders or heights?
7 What's the most .... (astonish) story you've ever heard?
8 What's the most .... (puzzle) thing about the English language?

8 Compare a typical day in your life with those of the four people in the text. What are the different times in your day like, and how do you feel? Use words from Exercises 6 and 7.

1 SPEAKING

Part 1

S Page 97

1 In Part 1, the examiner may ask you questions like these. What are they about? Which verb tense would you mainly use to reply?

1 Where are you from?
2 What do you like about living there?
3 Tell me a little about your family.
4 Which time of the year is your favourite? Why?
5 What do you enjoy doing when you are on holiday?
6 What do you use the Internet for?

2 In pairs, read this example conversation from Part 1. What is wrong with Nico's and Lena's replies (1–6)? Correct two mistakes. Then study the *Quick steps* for ways of improving the other four replies.

Examiner: Is your routine at weekends different from your daily routine in the week?
Nico: (1) Yes.
Examiner: In what ways?
Nico: (2) I am staying in bed later, of course. I go out with friends after lunch.
Examiner: And what about your routine at weekends, Lena? Is it different from your daily routine?
Lena: (3) Not really. I have to get up at about the same time.
Examiner: Why?
Lena: (4) Well, I have a job in a shop and I'm going to work early. It's a long way from my house. And I arrive home late every day.
Examiner: Now tell me, Nico. How often do you read newspapers or magazines?
Nico: (5) Repeat.
Examiner: How often do you read newspapers?
Nico: (6) Not often. I don't like them much.

Quick steps to Speaking Part 1

- Be friendly to the examiners and to the other candidate.
- Don't just reply *yes*, *no* or *I don't know*. Give reasons (*because … , so …*) or examples (*such as … , like …*).
- You can politely ask the examiner to repeat a question. Ask: *Pardon? Could you say that again, please? Sorry?*

3 Lena says *I arrive home late every day*. Look at these expressions and answer the questions.

every hour or so   from time to time   most weekends   five times a week   hardly ever   now and then

1 Where do frequency expressions like *every day* go in the sentence?
2 Which one means 'almost never'?
3 Which two mean 'occasionally'?

Exam tip ›

Use as wide a range of grammar and vocabulary as you can.

4 Work with a different partner. Ask and answer the examiner's questions in Exercises 1 and 2.

5 How well did you answer the Part 1 questions? How good were your partner's answers? Tell each other what you think.

Character adjectives

6 Find out what kind of person your partner is by asking them questions 1–12. Give examples, using expressions like *now and then* and *nearly always* in your replies.

WHAT ARE YOU LIKE?

1 Do you think about what other people need or want?
2 Do you usually expect good things to happen?
3 Do you behave in a way that is silly and not adult?
4 Do you like telling other people what to do?
5 Are you good at dealing with problems?
6 Do you get annoyed if things happen too slowly?
7 Do you want to be very successful in life?
8 Are you easily upset and do you know when others are upset?
9 Do you find it easy to make up your mind quickly?
10 Do you do things that nobody expects?
11 Are you sensible and fair with other people?
12 Do you find it difficult to plan things well?

7 Match the adjectives with questions 1–12. Do you think they describe your character correctly? Then use some of these adjectives to say what you think each person in the pictures might be like.

ambitious   bossy   childish   decisive   disorganised   impatient   optimistic   practical   reasonable   sensitive   thoughtful   unpredictable

Forming adjectives

1 Underline these prefixes and suffixes in the words in Speaking Exercise 7. One word has both a prefix and a suffix

-able -al dis- -ful -ic im- -ish -itive -ive -ous un- -y

2 Form character adjectives from these words with the prefixes and suffixes in Exercise 1. Be careful with spelling changes.

adventure aggression anxiety artist caution cheek compete emotion energy enthusiasm fool greed help honest pessimist polite popular rely respect sympathy

Part 3

3 Correct the mistakes in these sentences written by exam candidates.

1 You were a charmful host, as always.
2 Joey can be quite rude and unpolite.
3 I think that going to work or to school by bike is very healthful.
4 We really enjoyed the festival in spite of the disorganising programme.
5 I'm helpful and sociality, so I'd like a job working with people.
6 Sometimes shopping can be a stressing experience.

4 Complete the sentences with the correct form of the words in brackets. In each case add a prefix and/or a suffix.

1 Amelia thinks she'll win, and her family are quite .... (optimism), too.
2 Question 9 in the quiz was quite .... (challenge), but I got it right.
3 The team has lost every game, so their fans are feeling .... (depress).
4 The staff disliked the boss and they were .... (sympathy) when he lost his job.
5 It was a hot day, but Chloe felt .... (refresh) after having a cool shower.
6 People seem .... (enthusiasm) about the TV show. Few are watching it.

5 Look at the exam task. Answer these questions.

1 How many gaps are there in the text?
2 What do you have to put in each of them?
3 Does this task mainly test grammar or vocabulary?

Quick steps to Reading and Use of English Part 3

- Read the text quickly to find out its purpose and main points.
- Look at each word in capitals, then the words next to the gap. Do you need a noun, an adjective, or another part of speech?
- Does the word in capitals need more than one change?

6 Quickly read the text, ignoring the gaps for now. What is the purpose of the text? What is each paragraph about?

7 Look at the example (0). Answer the questions. Then do the exam task.

1 What kind of word probably goes between *the* and *thing*?
2 Does it describe how someone feels, or what causes a feeling?
3 What suffix do we use for this?
4 If this suffix begins with a vowel, how does *fascinate* change?

Exam task

For questions **1–8**, read the text below. Use the word given in capitals at the end of some of the lines to form a word that fits in the gap **in the same line**. There is an example at the beginning (**0**).

Example: 0 FASCINATING

Same family, different people

The three children grew up in the same home, but for friends of the family the **(0)** .... thing is that now, as young adults,	**FASCINATE**
they all have very different **(1)**	**PERSONAL**
Grace, 23, always has to be busy. Ever since she was a young girl, she has been highly **(2)** .... to succeed, and now that	**MOTIVATE**
she is working in a business environment she makes no secret of how **(3)** .... she is: her aim is to be Managing Director before she is 30.	**AMBITION**
Whereas Grace can sometimes appear rather **(4)** .... ,	**EMOTION**
even cold, her 21-year-old sister Evie can be quite **(5)** .... to what others say, particularly if their	**SENSE**
comments are unfair. But she is always kind to her friends, and **(6)** .... whenever anyone wants to talk about their problems.	**SYMPATHY**
Daniel, just 19, is the **(7)** .... one. He's mad about sports like rock climbing, snowboarding and motorcycling.	**ADVENTURE**
He takes too many risks and he gives his family some **(8)** .... moments, but somehow he always manages to get home safely.	**ANXIETY**

Part 2 informal letter

W Page 90

1 Look at the exam task and answer these questions.

1 Who has written to you?
2 What does this person want you to do?
3 What style is the extract from the letter written in? Find examples of the following:
  a contracted forms, e.g. *I'm*
  b short, common words, e.g. *got*
  c simple linking words, e.g. *because*
  d informal punctuation, e.g. dash (–)
  e friendly expressions, e.g. *tell me*

Exam task

This is part of an email from an English friend, Alex.

> I'm lucky because I've got really good friends – especially those I've known since I was a kid. I don't know what I'd do without them! So tell me, how important are friends to you? Who's your best friend and what do you like about him or her?
>
> Looking forward to hearing from you soon.

Write your **email** to Alex in **140–190** words. Do not write any addresses.

Quick steps to writing a Part 2 informal letter

- Look at the task, including any text, and decide who you are writing to, why, and which points to include.
- Note down ideas and decide how many main paragraphs you will need. Then put your ideas under paragraph headings.
- Begin *Dear (friend's first name)* and thank them for their last message.
- Keep to your plan and use informal language throughout.
- Close in a friendly way, asking them to write back. End *Lots of love*, *Best wishes*, etc.

2 Read the model letter and answer these questions.

1 Is Lydia's letter the right length?
2 Has she made any language mistakes?
3 How does she open and close her message?
4 What does she talk about in her introduction and conclusion?
5 Does she answer all of Alex's questions? In which main paragraphs?
6 What examples of informal language can you find?
7 What character adjectives does she use?
8 Which phrases of hers might be particularly useful when you write other letters?

> Dear Alex,
>
> Many thanks for your message. It was great to hear from you!
>
> The first thing I want to say is that I completely agree with you about friends. I see some of mine almost every day and I really miss them when they're away.
>
> My closest friend is Nicole, who's also a student, is the same age as me and lives just down the road. We've been best mates for many years and we tell each other everything, but I think we've got quite different personalities.
>
> For instance, I can be a bit indecisive at times, but she's very practical and gets everything done quickly. She's not bossy, though. In fact she's really thoughtful. Whenever I get upset she's always sympathetic and then she finds a way to cheer me up – she's got a wonderful sense of humour!
>
> I hope one day you can get to know her, and that I have the chance to meet your friends, too. Please tell me more about them in your next letter. Write soon!
>
> Best wishes,
>
> Lydia

3 Think about these questions and note down some ideas for your own letter to Alex.

1 What does friendship mean to you?
2 How often do you see your friends?
3 Who are you going to write about?
4 How long have you known each other?
5 Which character adjectives best describe your friend?

4 Make a plan for your letter. Put your best ideas from Exercise 3 under these headings: 1 *Friends in general*, 2 *Best friend: who*, 3 *Best friend: why*. Then add some details, such as the person's age or job. You could put the points under each heading into main paragraphs 1, 2 and 3.

Exam tip ›

Make sure you leave enough time at the end to check your letter for mistakes.

5 Write your letter. When you have finished, check it for the following:

- correct length
- all the content asked for in the instructions
- good organisation into paragraphs
- correct grammar, spelling and punctuation
- suitable style of language

1 REVISION

1 Complete the sentences with the present simple or present continuous form of the verbs in brackets.

1 This summer, I .... (stay) at the seaside and I .... (work) in a local shop in the mornings.
2 My friends .... (usually eat) at home, but this evening they .... (have) dinner in a restaurant.
3 Hi, I .... (wait) to get onto the plane, but there .... (seem) to be a delay.
4 The climate .... (change) all the time and the temperatures here .... (get) higher every year.
5 Natalie .... (be) quite annoying. She .... (always complain) about something.
6 My grandparents .... (own) a house in the village, though they .... (not live) there any more.
7 This far north, it .... (get) dark very early at this time of year, so I .... (think) of spending the winter in Australia.

2 Add a prefix or suffix to these words and complete the sentences.

artist caution energy greed honest pessimism polite

1 Martin always eats too much food. He's really ....
2 It's .... to take things from a shop without paying for them.
3 The quality of these drawings and paintings shows how .... Alexia is.
4 If someone helps you, it's .... not to say 'thank you'.
5 Paola is usually quite .... , but she doesn't feel like doing sports today.
6 Jerry likes to take risks, but his brother Anton is a much more .... boy.
7 I'm sorry to be so .... , but I just know we're going to lose this game.

See the CD-ROM for more practice.

3 Complete the sentences with the correct form of the words in brackets.

1 Terry is quite .... (predict). You never know what he's going to do next.
2 I thanked my friends for being so .... (sympathy) when I had to go into hospital.
3 It's .... (reason) to expect people to do all your work for you.
4 Going up that mountain is quite .... (challenge), even for an expert climber.
5 It was .... (thought) of you to remember my mother's birthday.
6 To succeed in business, you have to be .... (decision) and not keep changing your mind.

4 Read the text below. Use the word given in capitals at the end of some of the lines to form a word that fits in the gap in the same line.

In the morning I normally take the underground. At that time of day it's crowded, you have to stand, and it's certainly not a (1) .... way to travel. But the service is quick, frequent and (2) .... , which makes it by far the most (3) .... way to get across the city in the rush hour.

RELAX
RELY
PRACTICE

Occasionally, though, I travel into town in a friend's car to go shopping and, quite honestly, I often find it an absolutely (4) .... experience. Every time we get onto the ring road, I'm (5) .... by the way people behave when they drive a car. Some are extremely (6) .... , driving straight at you to make you get out of their way, while others are (7) .... , trying to have races with other drivers all the time. They just seem (8) .... to me.

TERRIFY
ASTONISH
AGGRESSION
COMPETE
CHILD

What I find most (9) .... about this is the fact that by the time they actually get to their offices, they're probably too (10) .... to do a proper day's work.

PUZZLE
EXHAUST

Part 6

1 Many people start cooking for themselves if they move away from their family home to study. Look at the pictures and discuss these questions with a partner.

1 Which picture (A or B) probably shows a student's kitchen? Why? Which is more like the kitchen in your home?
2 Do you often make your own meals? If so, what meals do you cook? What meals cooked by your family do you like most?
3 Which of the objects in the pictures, e.g. pots and pans, oven, freezer, do you or your family use? How?

2 Look at the exam task instructions. Answer these questions.

1 What kind of text do you have to read?
2 What do you have to put in gaps 1–6?
3 Do you have to use all of sentences A–G?

3 Quickly read the text, ignoring sentences A–G for now. Answer these questions.

1 Why did Matthew change his cooking and eating habits?
2 What was the result of this change?

4 Question 1 has been done as an example. Look at sentence C and the first two paragraphs of the main text. How do the underlined words link sentence C to gap 1? Why can't sentence C fit gap 2?

5 Do the exam task, underlining the words and phrases in sentences A–G and in the main text which are linked to each other in some way.

Quick steps to Reading and Use of English Part 6
- Study the instructions, read the main text for gist, then look quickly at sentences A–G.
- Study the words next to each gap, then look for similar or contrasting ideas in sentences A–G.
- Look for: vocabulary links; grammatical links, such as verb tenses; reference words, e.g. *these*; and linking expressions, e.g. *but*, *after*, *too*, *ones*, so.

6 Make sure you have chosen an answer to every question. There will be one letter you haven't used.

7 Find words and phrases in the text that mean the following.

1 make food hot so that you can eat it (paragraph 1)
2 eating small amounts of food (paragraph 2)
3 food which is unhealthy but is quick and easy to eat (paragraph 2)
4 not having your usual breakfast, lunch or dinner (paragraph 2)
5 eating only a particular type of food (paragraph 2)
6 healthy mixture of different types of food (paragraph 5)
7 amounts of food for one person (paragraph 5)
8 very hungry (paragraph 5)
9 making you feel full after you have eaten only a little of it (paragraph 5)
10 find and buy something on sale for less than its usual price (sentence G)

Exam task

You are going to read an article about a student who learns to cook for himself. Six sentences have been removed from the article. Choose from the sentences **A–G** the one which fits each gap (**1–6**). There is one extra sentence which you do not need to use.

Cooking at university

For university student Matthew, getting to grips with cooking for himself on his first time away from home was a real learning curve. Now totally at ease in the kitchen, he looks on the experience as literally life-changing.

'To be honest,' Matthew says, 'when I left home for university, I didn't give a great deal of thought to how I would feed myself. At that time I was more concerned with all the other challenges ahead of me, particularly the academic ones, and anyway I knew how to heat up ready meals. **1** C Especially as I was trying to keep up with difficult new work, and socialising into the small hours with new friends.

'At first I couldn't believe that snacking on nothing but junk food and sometimes skipping meals altogether could have serious effects. **2** ____ I had much less energy than before.' And, worryingly, he was in bad shape. 'That did it,' he admits. 'After a lifetime of healthy home cooking, I was suddenly living on junk food. My diet and lifestyle were harming my system and I desperately needed to turn things round.'

He returned to university equipped with a new pan or two and some cooking lessons from Mum under his belt. 'I decided to eat as much fresh food as possible – not difficult, since I've always enjoyed fruit and vegetables,' says Matthew. 'I took time to seek out the best and cheapest places to shop. **3** ____

'These changes, though, didn't cut me off from student life. I wanted to enjoy everything about my experience of university – the friends, the new interests and the social side as well as the study that would hopefully mark out my career. But it took some reorganising and a commitment to set aside time to eat more healthily. **4** ____

'Within weeks of changing to a balanced diet of healthy, freshly cooked food, my concentration powers, my energy and my appearance were all improving. Getting organised brings benefits. I got into the habit of preparing double portions for the fridge or freezer. I would buy fish or chicken portions, add vegetables and throw the whole thing in the oven. **5** ____ It's also good to keep a stock of frozen vegetables to save time and to eat wholegrain foods which fill you up for longer. At exam time, when time is really short, and I'm starving, I can make a filling omelette in minutes.'

What were the reactions to his new lifestyle? Matthew explains: 'Well, these days it's cool for guys to be interested in cooking. True, there were jokes that I'd let the side down and abandoned student traditions. **6** ____ But I learned that if you are on an intensive course – I'm doing engineering – you need to have the strength for study and, hopefully, a social life too.'

A I hadn't, of course.
B Cooking it that way saves on pots and washing up, and it's an easy, tasty meal.
C Before long, though, I was getting pretty fed up with eating those and I started to think cooking for myself might be important after all.
D Eating out like that quite often also made a considerable difference.
E On the more positive side, doing all this became easier as time went on.
F But after a few months I made my first visit home, and the family's comments on my unhealthy appearance made me realise it was true.
G In the same way, I got to know the best times to find the freshest items and when to pick up a bargain.

Exam tip ›

Make sure the extra sentence doesn't fit any of the gaps.

Part 2

L Page 95

1 Look at the photo. Tell your partner what you think might be happening in this kitchen, using some of these expressions.

> catering (to) chop (to) consume delicious dish
> (to) go off ingredients in season ripe (to) slice
> tough vegetarian

Quick steps to Listening Part 2

- Quickly read the instructions and all the sentences, including any words after the gaps.
- Decide what type of information, e.g. noun, verb, you need for each gap.
- Wait to hear all the information about each point before you decide on your answer.

2 1.03 Look at the exam task and answer these questions. Then listen and do the exam task.

1 In question 1, what kind of word probably goes before the verb *cooking*? What does the word *his* indicate?
2 What kind of word – adjective, adverb, noun, verb, number or date – do you need for each of questions 2–10?

Exam task

You will hear a restaurant chef talking about his work. For questions **1–10**, complete the sentences.

Max decided to become a professional chef when he saw his ____________ **1** cooking.

His father wanted him to become ____________ **2** instead of a chef.

He started his first job in late ____________ **3** .

The worst thing about working in the hotel was the ____________ **4** .

He went to work in France because he knew a ____________ **5** in Paris.

In Paris he sometimes cooked meals for ____________ **6** and other famous people.

In his own restaurant, Max always aims to use ____________ **7** products.

Max is particularly proud of the ____________ **8** of meals available at his restaurant.

He says that everything in his restaurant is ____________ **9** cooked for the customer.

On one occasion, all the ____________ **10** was stolen on its way to the restaurant.

3 Read all your completed sentences. Do they make sense? Are your grammar and spelling correct?

Giving your opinion

4 Now that you have heard Max talking about being a chef, do you think it is a good job to have? Use some of these expressions and give reasons.

> Actually, I'm convinced that ... I'd say that ...
> Personally, I think ... In my opinion, ...
> It seems to me ... Well, my own feeling is that ...

Exam tip ›

Write your answers exactly as you hear them – don't try to use other words that mean the same.

2 GRAMMAR

Review of past tenses

G Page 103

1 Look at these extracts from the recording in Listening and answer the questions about the underlined verb forms.

a He was very impressed by the meal I'd made for him.
b As a child I used to watch my parents preparing meals at home …
c … and I would imagine myself cooking something delicious.
d First I went to catering college, in the autumn of 2001.
e I was working very long hours when I was there.
f I'd been thinking of going to Paris for some time before I actually went.

Which verb form do we use:

1 for actions or events in the past?
2 to talk about something that was going on when something else happened?
3 when we are already talking about the past and we want to talk about an earlier event?
4 to talk about how long something went on up to a point in the past?
5 to talk, without using time expressions, about things we did regularly in the past but don't do anymore?
6 like 5, but only for actions, not states?

2 Correct the mistakes in these sentences written by exam candidates. In some cases more than one answer is possible.

1 He started walking back to the shop where he left his bike the day before.
2 People saw that Anita cried, but nobody could help her.
3 The street party was something that we organised for weeks before the holidays.
4 I used to be a member of a swimming club for about ten years.
5 We were very surprised as we knew that the house was empty for nearly thirty years.
6 I listened, and it was clear that someone walked across the floor.
7 When you look back, people didn't used to worry about what they ate.
8 I wanted to go to Egypt because I used to decide that I wanted to be an archaeologist.

3 Choose the correct form of the verb (A, B or C) to complete each sentence.

1 I don't think I .... Holly before last week's party.
A was meeting B met C 'd met

2 My aunt and uncle had no children of their own, so they .... a baby girl last year.
A adopted B used to adopt C were adopting

3 When I got home last night I felt quite tired because I .... at the club all evening.
A used to dance B 'd been dancing C danced

4 Sean .... with somebody else all last summer, but now he's my sister's boyfriend.
A used to go out B had gone out C was going out

5 I was born in July 1983. My mother .... a widow only two months earlier.
A became B had become C was becoming

6 When I arrived at Micky's house, everyone .... a film on TV.
A watched B used to watch C was watching

4 Use the given verb form to complete the sentences.

1 This morning I saw my cousin Emilia while I … (past continuous)
2 Nowadays I go on holiday with friends, but when I was younger I … (*used to*)
3 My stepbrother was upset and his eyes were red because he … (past perfect continuous)
4 I made friends with lots of people when I … (past continuous)
5 When we were kids, we often went to birthday parties where we … (*would*)
6 I had a date with Zyta, but I was late and by the time I arrived she … (past perfect)

2 SPEAKING

Part 2 S Page 98

1 We can use sentences a–g to compare two pictures. Fill in gaps 1–10 with these words. You can use some of them more than once.

> both difference different other same similar similarity

a In (1) ....both........ of these pictures there are some people eating, but in this one they're also watching TV.
b In this picture there are four people, a family, but in the (2) .... one there are just two.
c These two are (3) .... in age, about 18, unlike the family.
d One (4) .... between the pictures is that (5) .... show people eating together in the (6) .... place: at home.
e And in (7) .... pictures it looks as if they're enjoying their meal.
f But in some ways the situation in the two pictures is completely (8) ....
g The biggest (9) .... between them is that this one shows people talking and laughing together, but in the (10) .... one they're looking at the TV, not at each other.

2 Look at photos 1 and 2. Which of points a–f are the same or similar in the two photos, and which are different?

a the room
b the food and drinks
c the number of people
d the people's age
e the people's appearance
f what the people are doing

3 Look at photos 3 and 4 and note down as many points of similarity and difference as you can.

> **Quick steps to Speaking Part 2**
> - Think about what you are going to say before you start speaking.
> - Mention as many similarities and differences as you can.
> - When your partner is speaking, listen to what they say but don't interrupt.

4 Look at the exam instructions. What does Candidate A have to do? What does Candidate B have to do?

5 Work in pairs and do the exam task.

Exam task

Each of you will be given two photographs. You have to talk about your photographs on your own for about a minute, and also to answer a short question about your partner's photographs.

Candidate A: It's your turn first. Look at photographs 1 and 2. They show people in restaurants. Compare the photographs, and say what you think could be enjoyable about having a meal there. Talk about your photographs on your own for about a minute.
Candidate B: Do you like to eat in restaurants?

1

2

Candidate B: Look at photographs 3 and 4. They show people ordering meals. Compare the photographs, and say why you think people choose to eat there. Talk about your photographs on your own for about a minute.
Candidate A: Which of these two kinds of place do you prefer to go to?

3

4

6 Change roles and repeat the exam task.

> **Exam tip ›**
> Don't try to describe everything in the pictures. Just say what's similar and different about them.

7 How well did you and your partner speak in Part 2? Tell each other what you think.

2 READING AND USE OF ENGLISH

Fixed phrases

1 Replace the underlined words with these fixed phrases.

at first sight	keep me company
at ease	propose to her
break my heart	leave me alone
get on my nerves	lose touch
is attracted to	takes me for granted

1. When I'm with my best friend Sophie, I feel <u>completely relaxed</u>.
2. He keeps sending me silly text messages and it's starting to <u>annoy me</u>.
3. It's sad when a friend moves away and you <u>stop communicating</u> with them.
4. Louis doesn't seem very intelligent <u>the first time you see him</u>, but he is.
5. From the way Zoe looks at Mark, I think she <u>really likes</u> him.
6. I love Carla and I'm going to <u>ask her to marry me</u>.
7. Those people are annoying me. I want them to <u>stop talking to me</u>.
8. I don't want to be on my own this evening. Will you <u>stay here with me</u>, please?
9. It'll <u>make me very, very sad</u> if you marry somebody else.
10. Sometimes I think Jeff <u>forgets how lucky he is to have me as a friend</u>.

Part 2

2 Look at the exam task. Answer the questions.

1. How many gaps are there?
2. How many words must you put in each gap?
3. Are you given a choice of words to use?

Quick steps to Reading and Use of English Part 2

- Read the title and the example, then quickly read the text.
- For each gap, decide what kind of word you need, e.g. auxiliary verb, preposition.

3 Without filling in any gaps, quickly read the text and answer these questions. Then do the exam task.

1. What does the title mean? Why is it appropriate?
2. What kind of text, e.g. a news item, is it?

Exam task

For questions **1–8**, read the text below and think of the word which best fits each gap. Use only **one** word in each gap. There is an example at the beginning (**0**).

Example: 0 HAD

A BRIEF ENGAGEMENT

Before she became famous in the 1880s, Emily **(0)** .... been engaged to wealthy businessman William Davies. In **(1)** .... days, parents often chose their future son-in-law, and when they introduced William to her it was certainly not love at **(2)** .... sight.

Although tall and handsome, he was twelve years older than her and, she suspected, rather arrogant. In fact she was not really attracted **(3)** .... him at all, but when he proposed to her she accepted rather than upset her parents.

She soon realised what a huge mistake she **(4)** .... made. His bossy, impatient manner quickly started **(5)** .... on her nerves, and even when they were out walking together she never felt **(6)** .... ease with him. She tried her best to make the relationship work, but he made no effort at all and she felt he was **(7)** .... her for granted.

Eventually she decided to break **(8)** .... her engagement. Some years later, Emily would write that it was the best decision she had ever made.

4 Make sure you have given one word for every question and that your spelling is correct. Which answers complete fixed phrases from Exercise 1, and which complete past tenses?

Exam tips

- Don't use abbreviations such as *etc.*, or contracted forms like *won't* – these count as two words.
- Use the correct verb form with the subject given, e.g. *people were going* (not *was*).
- Remember to fill in the answer sheet or your answers won't count!

2 WRITING

Linking expressions

1 Match the underlined linking words with their meanings.

as soon as
at first
at the same time
between those two times
immediately
very surprisingly

1 Initially, Jeff thought he was alone. But then he realised there was someone else there.
2 It was 8.30 and the train left at 9.15. In the meantime, I had a coffee.
3 Once Sonia had woken up, she put the light on.
4 The door opened, but to my amazement there was nobody there.
5 The thief broke the car window. Instantly, a loud alarm went off.
6 There was a flash of light and simultaneously a loud noise.

Part 2 article

W Page 91

2 Look at the exam task and answer these questions.

1 Who are you writing the article for?
2 Should you write mainly about the past, the present or the future?
3 How many words must you write?

Exam task

You have seen the following announcement on an international website for young people:

Had a great night out? If so, tell us about it!

Write an article about the best evening or night out you've ever had. We will put the best articles on our site next week. Send us your article, and you could have readers all over the world!

Write your **article** in **140–190** words.

3 Quickly read the model article and answer these questions.

1 Is the article about the right length?
2 Is the style very formal or very informal – or somewhere in between? Give examples.
3 Why will readers want to continue reading after the first paragraph?
4 Which part of the article does the ending refer back to?
5 Find and correct one mistake in each paragraph.

Out at night

Have you ever felt that birthdays were more fun when you were a kid? I certainly did on my 18th as I sat at home watch TV. Sure, people had given me some nice presents, but somehow the old excitement was missing. Then, to my surprise, the doorbell rang.

The moment I opened the door and saw my friends standing there my mood changed. 'We're taking you downtown!' they said, laughing. You can imagine how delighting I was!

I quickly got ready and before long we were in a taxi. First they took me shopping, buying me any clothes I wanted, and after that we went bowling. For once I actually won! Then we had a delicious pizza before going to a fashionable nightclub, where we spent hours dancing and meeting with people, some of them quite famous.

Eventually I arrived home, but just as I was going to bed I received a text message. It was from one of the celebrities I had been talking to earlier, inviting me out for a dinner the next day. I think you will agree it had been quite an evening!

4 Read the article more carefully and find the following:

1 expressions the writer uses to speak directly to the reader
2 examples of the past continuous, the past perfect and the past perfect continuous
3 linking expressions that mean the following:
a immediately b after a while c in the end

Quick steps to writing a Part 2 article

- Plan your article, noting down points for all parts of the task.
- Think of a title that will attract the readers' attention, and also an interesting first paragraph to keep them reading.
- Involve your readers by using expressions like *Do you ever … ?*, *You might think … but* or *How would you feel if … ?*

5 Read the exam task again and write your own article. When you have finished, check your work as in Unit 1 Writing Exercise 5 on page 14.

Exam tip ›

In an article, you can give your own opinions using expressions from Exercise 4 on page 18.

2 REVISION

1 Choose the correct options to complete the text.

Meeting at the station

It was quite late in the evening when I walked into the Central café, and everybody else there (1) *ate / was eating* while they talked to their friends.

We (2) *arranged / had arranged* to meet there as it was close to the station, and also because we (3) *used to go / were going* there when we were at the local school. In those days we (4) *had spent / would spend* hours chatting over a cup of coffee, but then we both (5) *were going / went away* to university and sadly we lost touch with each other.

Until last Friday, when quite by chance we (6) *would meet / met* on the train. She (7) *gave / was giving* me her phone number and on Saturday morning I called her and we decided to meet at the Central.

By ten o'clock, though, I (8) *'d been waiting / 'd waited* for nearly an hour, and I (9) *was starting / used to start* to worry. I checked my mobile phone to see if she (10) *'d sent / sent* me a text message and, to my horror, I realised that I (11) *forgot / 'd forgotten* to switch it on.

As soon as I (12) *had / did* so, I saw there were two messages from Sophie. In the first, at 8 p.m., she (13) *used to suggest / suggested* meeting at the station instead of the café; in the second she said she (14) *gave up / 'd given up* waiting for me and she had to go home. Instantly I forgot about dinner and (15) *ran / had run* out of the café towards the station.

2 Correct the mistakes in the fixed phrases.

1 As soon as Lara and Tim saw each other, it was love at first heart.
2 Sadly, I lost company with Lucas when he went to live in Australia.
3 Elisa is worried and she doesn't look at all on ease.
4 I know you're missing your family, so I'll stay and keep you companion.
5 It broke Josef's feelings when his girlfriend ended their relationship.
6 The boss depends on you, so don't let him leave you for granted.
7 Carl is always making stupid jokes and it keeps on my nerves.
8 I don't want to see anyone. Please go away and leave me only.

See the CD-ROM for more practice.

3 Complete the sentences with these words.

amazement eventually long meantime moment once

1 .... the waiter brought our food, after we'd been waiting for over an hour.
2 It'll take a while for dinner to cook, so in the .... let's have a drink.
3 .... we'd climbed over the hill, we could at last see the lights of the town.
4 The .... I first met Carmen, I knew we would be good friends.
5 The kitchen looked terrible, but before .... we were making good progress tidying it up.
6 I looked up at the desert sky and, to my .... , I saw snow starting to fall.

4 Complete the crossword with words from Unit 2.

Across
5 part of a meal, or container for serving food
6 that makes you feel full
8 ask someone to marry you
9 miss (a meal)
14 food that's difficult to cut or eat
15 quantity of food for one
16 eat or drink something

Down
1 cut into thin, flat pieces
2 become the parents of someone else's child
3 cut into small pieces
4 eat a small amount of food
7 ready to be eaten (especially fruit)
9 extremely hungry
10 woman whose husband has died
11 something bought for a low price
12 end a marriage
13 unhealthy, fast (food)

3 Getting away from it all

LISTENING

Part 3

L Page 95

1 Put these words into the correct group, a, b or c. Some words can go into more than one group.

cruise	expedition	explore	flight	hiking
hitchhiking	journey	sailing	sightseeing	
tour	travel	trekking	trip	voyage	wander

a to *travel*......

b to go *hiking*......

c to go on a/an *journey*......

2 The photos show places the speakers in the exam task went to. Answer these questions.

1 Which photo shows each of the following?
The salt flat of Uyuni, Bolivia
Uluru (Ayers Rock), Australia
Petra: the city cut from stone, Jordan
The Masai Mara National Reserve, Kenya
The Forbidden City, China

2 What do you think the speakers might say about each place?

3 Which three places do you think are the most impressive? Why?

4 Which other places would you add to a list of the world's top sights? Why?

3 1.04 Look at option A in the exam task. The key words are *not permitted* and *walk*. These words have similar or opposite meanings: *can* / *can't* / *mustn't* / *have to* and *on foot* / *drive*. For each of options B–H, underline the key words and note down some expressions with similar or opposite meanings. Then listen and do the exam task.

Quick steps to Listening Part 3

- Quickly read the instructions and options A–H, and think about what you're going to hear.
- Underline the key words in each option. Before you listen, think of words or phrases that the speakers might use.
- The first time you hear the extracts, get a general idea of what each speaker says. Then, the second time you listen, check that options A–H match exactly what they say.

Exam task

You will hear five different people talking about going to famous places. For questions **1–5**, choose from the list (**A–H**) what each speaker says about their visit to each site. Use the letters only once. There are three extra letters which you do not need to use.

A Visitors are not permitted to walk inside the site.

B We did not take enough water on our trip.

C A very large animal tried to attack us.

D Motor vehicles are not allowed to enter the site.

E It was very expensive to enter the site.

F We respected the wishes of the local people.

G The guidebook I was carrying was very useful.

H All the people we met or saw there were tourists.

Speaker 1		**1**
Speaker 2		**2**
Speaker 3		**3**
Speaker 4		**4**
Speaker 5		**5**

Exam tip

Be careful if words in one option are mentioned by more than one speaker. Only one of them can be the correct answer.

4 Make sure you have chosen one letter for each answer.

3 GRAMMAR

Review of modal verbs

G Page 104

1 Study Modal verbs on page 104. Then choose the correct option in these sentences. Say why it is right and why the other one is wrong.

1. We *could walk / could have walked*, but it was hot so we decided to go by camel.
2. Aircraft *mustn't / don't have to* take off at night. It's against the law.
3. I can't find my ticket. I *had to drop / might have dropped* it on the platform.
4. You *have to / must* make less noise, children, while I'm driving.
5. You *shouldn't / don't have to* wear a seat belt on the train.
6. There *may have been / must have been* an accident, but it's more likely that roadworks caused the traffic jam.
7. I was at the airport by 6 a.m. but *I didn't need to get / needn't have got* there so early because my flight was delayed.
8. The waves were huge and Mark realised he *can't have / shouldn't have* sailed his small yacht into the storm.

2 Say what the mistakes are in these sentences written by exam candidates. Correct the mistakes.

1. So, before I took the bus to school, I must buy a new notebook.
2. I could find Juan's number and I phoned him the next day.
3. That day must have been a great day for us, but it was not.
4. We don't have to drive too fast, or do anything against the law.
5. We needn't to call you before we arrived because we knew that you were expecting us.
6. Bicycles are cheaper than cars, and you mustn't spend any money on petrol.
7. If there are a lot of people on the airport bus, you can have to stand all the way.
8. You might already heard that there is a robot that can clean floors.

3 Complete this phone conversation between two friends with the correct form of the verbs in brackets.

Amy: Hi, I'm at the station but I can't see Stella. She (1) …………………… (must / miss) the 9.15 train.
Lisa: Are you sure? It (2) …………………… (could / get in) early, and she (3) …………………… (might / leave) the station before you got there.
Amy: No, she (4) …………………… (can't / do). I think I saw the 9.15 pulling out just as I arrived, and all the passengers getting off (5) …………………… (have to / walk) past where I was standing, so I would've seen her.
Lisa: Have you tried phoning her?
Amy: Yes, but there's no reply. She (6) …………………… (must / switch off) her phone, or she (7) …………………… (might / even / forget) to take it with her.
Lisa: Hang on, I've just had a text from her, saying she's sorry but she fell asleep on the train.
Amy: She (8) …………………… (must / have) a very late night last night!

4 Use the correct form of the modal in brackets to reply to these comments. More than one answer is possible, and in some cases negative forms are needed.

1. That girl looks exactly like her sister. (must)
2. I felt really sleepy this morning. (should)
3. At my school, it was compulsory to wear a uniform. (have to)
4. I left my bike in the street and now it's gone. (must)
5. I took the train as I didn't know the bus was so cheap. (could)
6. I sometimes go horseriding without wearing a helmet. (should)
7. I've just seen the Prime Minister waiting at the bus stop. (can)
8. I'm sure I had some money on me, but I can't find it. (might)

5 Look at the photos and talk about what *might*, *may*, *could*, *must* or *can't* have happened.

3 READING AND USE OF ENGLISH

Part 5

1 How important are the following when choosing a holiday?

- the harm to the environment caused by the journey itself
- the effect of tourism on the local environment
- the benefit to the local people and the local economy that tourism can bring

2 Look at the exam task. Answer the questions.

1 What kind of text do you have to read?
2 What different kinds of question are there?
3 For each question, how many options are wrong?

3 Quickly read the text. What is the writer's main purpose?

A to explain how green the hotel industry is now
B to show there is no demand for green holidays
C to advertise particular travel organisations
D to encourage people to take greener holidays

Quick steps to Reading and Use of English Part 5

- Quickly read the text, ignoring questions 1–6 for now, to see what it's about.
- For each question, look only at the first part of the question or unfinished statement and read what the text says about it.
- Think about the answer in your own words, then decide which option (A–D) is closest to your own answer.

4 Read the first two paragraphs of the text and answer question 1. Why are the other options wrong? Then do the rest of the exam task.

Exam tip ›

If a question asks about a particular word or phrase, work out the meaning by looking for examples, explanations, and similar or contrasting expressions in the text around the chosen word.

Exam task

You are going to read an article about travelling. For questions **2–6**, choose the answer (**A**, **B**, **C** or **D**) which you think fits best according to the text.

Leave only your footprints

Today's travellers have a range of responsible holiday choices. Aoife O'Riordain reports.

With the increasing awareness of global warming and the overuse of the Earth's natural resources, it would seem that the travelling public has never been so conscious of the effects and impact that their holidays have, not just on the environment but also on local communities the world over.

That said, Justin Francis, the co-founder of the website Responsible Travel, still feels there is a long way to go so far as the public's awareness of green travel issues is concerned. Francis believes that although some consumers are now actively seeking out these types of holidays, the majority are still not aware of the growing number of choices. 'I wish that people were springing out of bed in the mornings thinking that they must select a holiday that does a better job of protecting environments and communities. Sadly it does not happen, and the main factors are still the right experience, the right price and convenient departure schedules,' says Francis.

Despite a major airline's recent announcement that it plans to fly jets on fuel made from rubbish to shrink their carbon footprint, most people are aware that air travel is a controversial issue in the environmentally friendly travel debate. While many insist that the only truly green option is not to fly or to stay at home, those who still want to get away have an increasing number of choices available to help them lessen the environmental impact and give more to their host community.

The Green Traveller website promotes holidays that can be reached by land, as well as offering plenty of tips about having a greener holiday wherever you decide to go. Its managing director, Richard Hammond, agrees that interest in this kind of travel has grown. 'Very few holidays are 100 per cent green, so it's really about having a greener holiday. The most basic choice is looking at low-pollution forms of transport, or, if you are going somewhere really distant, minimising your impact at the destination,' says Hammond.

While many of the properties it features already have certification from a growing range of international and national schemes, Green Traveller's team of writers also personally assess each property and apply their own standards to the selection process, such as how waste is dealt with, to what extent local agricultural products are used, and whether visitors are encouraged to arrive by rail.

Older-established tour operators have also realised that a growing number of clients are beginning to include this new set of factors when making their decision on where to holiday. Last year, First Choice added a Greener Holidays brochure into its programme, and tour operators now often list accommodation-only or activity-only prices so people can choose their own means of transport, such as travelling by rail rather than by air.

Hotels are increasingly keen to talk up their ecological achievements. One of the biggest criticisms of international hotel chains is their overuse of the Earth's resources, and in response many have implemented measures they claim will reduce this. While these are no doubt based on good environmental principles, schemes like planting a tree for every five towels reused, for instance, are unlikely to make much difference overall.

Francis believes that consumers are becoming more aware of such tokenism from hotels and tour operators that may not have the best interests of the community or the planet true to their hearts. 'My real hope is that we get much more curious and more questioning, and there are rebellious tourists who see through this and ask increasingly tough questions,' he says.

5 Make sure you have chosen one answer for every question.

6 Find words and phrases in the text that mean the following.

1 people going somewhere
2 the days and times when particular flights leave
3 operate aircraft
4 go somewhere on holiday to have a rest
5 the place where you are going
6 firms that organise travel for people
7 thin book with photos that advertises something
8 transport not included
9 way of travelling

7 Which of the ideas in the text for greener holidays would you like to try? Can you think of some others?

1 What does Justin Francis say about attitudes to holidays?
A Everyone's top priority these days is to have greener holidays.
B Most people's reasons for choosing holidays remain the same.
C Tourists are only interested in finding the cheapest travel deals.
D Nowadays, more people who travel know about global warming.

2 What does the writer say about going on holiday by plane?
A A lot of people believe that it is harmful to the environment.
B Few people realise there is discussion about the harm it may do.
C There is no way of making it less harmful to the environment.
D The public think that new technology is making it harmless.

3 What does Richard Hammond suggest to people going a long way for their holiday?
A Take a train or a bus to get there instead of a plane.
B Do as little environmental damage as you can there.
C Make sure your holiday there is completely green.
D Look elsewhere for advice on greener holidays.

4 What does 'it' in line 36 refer to?
A the destination
B the team of writers
C the selection process
D the website

5 Some firms believe that people are now more likely to choose a holiday
A which includes the cost of travel in the price.
B in a place that serves food from that area.
C somewhere that produces no waste material.
D that is organised by a traditional travel company.

6 What is meant by 'tokenism' in line 60?
A taking steps with the result that the problem is solved
B appearing to show concern but in practice doing very little
C setting a good example which others are now following
D doing as much as possible but without achieving success

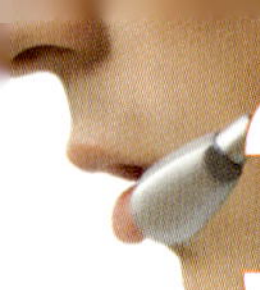

3 SPEAKING

Adverbs of degree G Page 105

1 Look at the rules for adverbs of degree on page 105. Then choose the correct options to complete the dialogue.

Lucas: So how was the trip to the coast?
Sarah: It was (1) *totally / pretty* good, overall. The bus was (2) *slightly / really* late, though only ten minutes, and I was (3) *rather / completely* tired after (4) *quite / fairly* a long day, but once we got out of town I (5) *slightly / really* started to relax.
Lucas: Yes, sometimes I'm (6) *absolutely / a bit* surprised to find that I (7) *rather / very* enjoy bus journeys, though the train's much quicker.
Sarah: Yes, you're (8) *a bit / quite* right, but it was (9) *totally / extremely* impossible to get a cheap ticket.
Lucas: I know what you mean. I was (10) *absolutely / slightly* astonished to see how much the train costs on a Friday evening. But, anyway, it sounds like the bus was (11) *fairly / a bit* comfortable.
Sarah: Actually, it was (12) *completely / extremely* comfortable! I slept most of the way.

2 1.05 Listen to the dialogue to check your answers. Which other adverbs of degree are possible in each case except item 5?

Part 3 S Page 99

3 Look at the exam task. Answer the questions. Then check your answers in the Speaking guide on page 99.

1 Who do you talk to in Part 3?
2 For how long?
3 What kind of thing do you look at?

4 Read the instructions in detail. What is the situation? What do you have to do?

Exam task

You're going to talk about something together for about two minutes.

Imagine that your town wants to attract more tourists. Here are some things that may help make a town more attractive to visitors.

Look at the task and talk to each other about how these things could help bring in more tourists.

How could these things help bring in more tourists?

- theatre
- street carnival
- boat rides on the lake
- open-top bus tour
- city marathon
- art gallery

Now you have a minute to decide which two things would attract most visitors to the town.

5 1.06 You will hear Laura and Jonas, two strong students, doing this task. The first time you listen, answer these questions.

1 Do they discuss all the prompts?
2 Do they take turns speaking?
3 Which two things do they choose?

6 1.06 Complete the expressions used to make suggestions and speculate. Then listen again to check your answers.

Right, (1) .... start?
I think (2) .... quite a good one.
So (3) .... the next one – the carnival?
Talking about summer, (4) .... have the boat rides, too.
Yes, maybe. And (5) .... including the bus tour?
Either way, (6) .... very popular.
OK, that's five of them done. (7) .... the last one.
Which two shall we choose? (8) .... the art gallery.

7 Work in pairs. Do the exam task, using expressions from Exercise 6.

8 Did you both speak for the same amount of time? Discuss this with your partner.

Quick steps to Speaking Part 3
- Take turns with your partner as you talk about each of the prompts.
- Make suggestions, using expressions like *Let's …* and *Why don't we … ?*
- Use modals to speculate, e.g. *It may be … , It couldn't be … ,* and adverbs of degree.

3 READING AND USE OF ENGLISH

Dependent prepositions

1 Look at the underlined words in the extracts from the recording in Speaking Part 3. Then decide which preposition (*to*, *with*, *of*) follows each of the expressions below.

Things that may help make a town more attractive to visitors.
It might not be very popular with visitors.
Instead of the art gallery, I'd choose the boat rides.

ashamed	capable	conscious	familiar
fed up	in connection	in need	in place
in relation	in response	in terms	
in view	informed	involved	
(have) nothing to do	obliged	obsessed	
prepared	required	sensitive	sort
supposed	the trouble	with regard	

2 For each of these sentences written by exam candidates, choose the correct preposition (A, B, C or D).

1 Excuse me, I would like to have a word .... you.
A to B for C at D with
2 My job wasn't hard: I was responsible .... the decorations on the tree.
A to B over C for D upon
3 Last summer, I joined a camp which was aimed .... teenagers.
A at B to C over D below
4 I'd like to welcome you on behalf .... the hotel manager.
A for B by C off D of
5 Working in a museum is a less tiring job compared .... working in a restaurant.
A by B to C of D on
6 Cameras enable the police to keep an eye .... everyone.
A on B over C to D about

Part 1

3 Look at the exam task. Answer the questions.

1 How many words are missing?
2 How many possible words are there for each gap?
3 What do these words have in common?

4 Quickly read the title, the example and the text without filling in any gaps. Decide what the text is about. Then do the exam task.

Quick steps to Reading and Use of English Part 1
- For each gap, decide what kind of word, e.g. adjectives, the four options are.
- Study the words either side of the gap, underlining any dependent prepositions.
- Try each word in the gap, checking whether it fits the grammar of the sentence.

Exam task

For questions **1–8**, read the text below and decide which answer (**A**, **B**, **C** or **D**) best fits each gap. There is an example at the beginning (**0**).

Example: 0 A declared **B** claimed **C** pretended **D** announced

CARNIVAL IN COLOMBIA

The Barranquilla Carnival, **(0)** ....B.... to be the biggest in the world after Rio's, is held annually on Colombia's Caribbean coast. For four days and nights, normal city life is **(1)** .... by music and dancing, mixing European, African and Latin American influences in what is possibly the most culturally **(2)** .... carnival on Earth.

Many thousands of people from all over the Caribbean **(3)** .... there every February or March to enjoy an event that **(4)** .... back to the 19th century. With them they bring a huge range of musical and dance styles, and some **(5)** .... amazing costumes.

Anyone **(6)** .... with Barranquilla at that time will know how exciting the atmosphere can be. From the moment the mayor officially opens the Carnival, the action never stops, with events **(7)** .... from colourful parades to lively street theatre. By night there are spectacular firework displays and many of the younger people seem **(8)** .... of dancing round the clock.

	A	B	C	D
1	A ceased	B suspended	C cancelled	D interrupted
2	A diverse	B differing	C disguised	D distinguished
3	A join	B concentrate	C gather	D encounter
4	A takes	B dates	C calls	D sends
5	A slightly	B extremely	C very	D absolutely
6	A familiar	B informed	C conscious	D knowledgeable
7	A ranging	B spreading	C stretching	D extending
8	A skilled	B capable	C qualified	D expert

5 Read through the completed text. Does it all make sense?

6 Tell another student about a carnival or special event in your country. In what ways is it similar or different to the one in Barranquilla?

3 WRITING

Part 1 essay

W Page 88

1 Which of these linking expressions do we use in an essay for: a) the first point, b) more points, c) the final point, d) the conclusion?

First of all,	Lastly,
For another thing,	Next,
For one thing,	On balance,
In the first place,	To conclude,

2 Look at the exam task instructions and answer these questions.

1 What is the situation and the topic?
2 Who will read your essay?
3 What question must you answer?
4 What points must you include?
5 What must you add to those points?

Exam task

In your English class you have been talking about the advantages and disadvantages of taking holidays near home rather than travelling abroad. Now, your English teacher has asked you to write an essay.

Write an essay using all the notes and give reasons for your point of view.

Is it better to have holidays near home rather than travel abroad?

Notes
Write about:
1 which is cheaper
2 which is better for the environment
3 your own idea

Write your **essay** in **140–190** words. You must use grammatically correct sentences with accurate spelling and punctuation in an appropriate style.

3 Read the model essay and answer these questions.

1 Which kind of holiday does the writer say is better?
2 Which paragraph covers each of the points?
3 Which addition links, e.g. *firstly,* are used?
4 What other addition links do you know?

Some people believe we should not travel long distances for our holidays, that we ought to spend our free time in our own country, enjoying the local countryside. I, however, disagree.

To begin with, budget flights and package holidays enable ordinary people to travel to exotic locations that previous generations could only have dreamt of visiting. Inexpensive student railcards also make it possible to take trains to exciting international destinations. In fact, it often costs less to travel abroad than at home.

Secondly, green holidays in distant countries are now widely available. Much of the journey can be done by ship, train or bus. Once there, accommodation may be in tents or in country houses that use little energy, with local travel by horse, by bicycle or on foot.

Finally, it is natural for young people to want to see more of the world, meet people in different cultures and understand the problems that other societies face. They cannot do this by staying in their home town.

To sum up, I am absolutely convinced that holidays abroad are positive experiences that can be both economical and environmentally friendly.

4 Read the essay again and find formal expressions that mean the same as these words and expressions (1–7).

1 shouldn't	5 you can do
2 though	6 can't
3 places	7 I'm quite sure
4 cheap	

Quick steps to writing a Part 1 essay
- Read the question or statement in the instructions and decide what your opinion is.
- Write in a fairly formal style if the intended reader is a teacher.
- Connect your points with addition links.

5 Follow the exam task instructions and write your essay.

Exam tip ›

Always plan your essay, but don't try to write a draft. There won't be time in the exam to write the essay twice.

6 When you have finished, check your work as in Unit 1 Writing Exercise 5 on page 14.

3 REVISION

1 Complete the sentences with the correct form of the modals and verbs in brackets.

1 I'm not sure when Julia was going. She ....may have left.... (may / leave) on Saturday.
2 You .... (must / hit) your brother's computer, or you'll break it!
3 Ethan cycled round the island in under an hour. He .... (must / ride) very fast.
4 Your face is red. You .... (should / spend) so long lying in the sun!
5 Gemma is away in Australia all summer. You .... (can / see) her here yesterday!
6 Carlos hasn't replied to my text message. He .... (might / take) his phone with him.
7 I made food for six people, but only four came to dinner. I .... (need / cook) so much.

2 Complete the second sentence so that it means the same as the first sentence. Use modal verbs.

1 There's a possibility of heavy snow later today.
Later today it ....might snow heavily.... .
2 It isn't necessary to check in if you already have a boarding pass.
If you already have a boarding pass, you don't ....
3 I'm certain that Simon went home early.
Simon ....
4 It wasn't necessary to go to college yesterday so I stayed at home.
I stayed at home yesterday because I ....
5 It was compulsory for passengers on the small boat to wear life jackets.
Passengers on the small boat ....
6 It's a pity you didn't put petrol in the car before you set off.
Before you set off, you ....
7 It's possible that the taxi driver had the wrong address.
The taxi driver ....

3 Decide which answer (A, B, C or D) best fits each gap.

1 I'm going on a long rail .... from Moscow to Beijing.
A trip B travel C voyage D journey
2 We went .... across the fields and up a narrow mountain track.
A hiking B travelling C touring D hitchhiking
3 To go on holiday, the most environmentally friendly .... of transport is the train.
A way B means C method D system
4 Are you .... sure we're going the right way?
A slightly B quite C extremely D rather
5 We will shortly be landing at Barajas Airport, ten minutes ahead of ....
A timetable B forecast C schedule D programme
6 Some tour .... organise holiday cruises around Antarctica.
A dealers B supervisors C operators D controllers

4 Fill in the gaps with suitable prepositions.

Blog

After nearly a year working non-stop for not much pay, I was fed up (1) .... my job and I was feeling in need (2) .... a good break. The sort (3) .... holiday I had in mind was a week on a sunny beach somewhere, so I booked myself a cheap flight along (4) .... six nights in a bed and breakfast next to the sea. On the day of the journey, I was aiming (5) .... catching the 8.30 bus to the aiport, but I ended up leaving the house rather late and when I got to the stop there was no sign (6) .... the bus. I knew I was supposed (7) .... check in two hours before the flight, so instead (8) .... waiting any longer and probably missing it, I jumped into a taxi. That was much quicker than going by bus, but the trouble (9) .... taking taxis to the airport is that they are incredibly expensive. So when I got to check-in and was informed (10) .... a three-hour delay to my flight, I realised I had wasted quite a lot of my hard-earned cash.

See the CD-ROM for more practice.

4 Taking time out
READING AND USE OF ENGLISH

1

2

3

4

Part 6

1 What's happening in the photos? Use some of these words.

abstract audience cast contemporary entertaining exhibition gallery gig live lyrics performance portrait scene script set shot solo soundtrack venue work

2 Discuss these questions.

1 In what ways are the people in the four photos similar? In what ways are they different?
2 What can people do while they are in each of these places? What *shouldn't* they do?

3 Look at the exam task, but not at options A–G. Quickly read the text and answer this question. What does the writer dislike about going to pop concerts?

A the quality of the music nowadays
B the way some members of the audience behave
C the attitude of the performers to the audience
D the poor organisation of these events

4 Read the second paragraph of the text. Answer the questions. Then do the exam task.

1 Which of options A–G has a word with a similar meaning to *response*?
2 What reference word does it follow?
3 What is the link in meaning between that sentence and the sentence beginning *Who hasn't been to?*

Quick steps to Reading and Use of English Part 6
- Look quickly at sentences A–G, choosing any that clearly fit particular gaps.
- Underline any vocabulary links, grammatical links and linking expressions in the main text and/or sentences A–G.

Exam task

You are going to read an article about going to pop concerts. Six sentences have been removed from the article. Choose from the sentences **A–G** the one which fits each gap (**1–6**). There is one extra sentence which you do not need to use.

Quiet, please: rock gig in progress

Talking loudly at a pop concert these days can get you told off – and don't even think of spilling your drink. Fiona Sturges welcomes this change in attitudes.

Last week a well-known singer is reported to have shouted at an audience member in response to their talking loudly throughout his performance, after which he is said to have emptied a glass of water on their head. **1** ____ Who hasn't been to a gig at some point and had their night ruined by the behaviour of a stranger?

People's enjoyment of a concert relies on the good manners of others. At its best, live music can be a life-changing experience. When everything goes right, the music coming from the stage can lift the soul and make you forget your surroundings. **2** ____

Something like that happened when I went to see one of my favourite bands. It was a sit-down gig and I had a seat about ten rows from the front. Despite being so near the stage, I couldn't hear a thing thanks to a group of people sitting in front of me, who kept on gossiping and laughing all the way through the show. **3** ____ And that's when I leaned forward and asked, as politely as I could, if they could keep it down. They were absolutely shocked. 'How dare you!' replied one of them.

When it comes to audience interaction, every art form requires a certain amount of appropriacy although there are no formal rules. **4** ____ For instance, it's acceptable to move around and talk in art galleries but wild dancing is, as a general rule, not tolerated.

In the theatre you can sit down and fall asleep and no one will care, but anyone who talks at anything louder than a whisper or answers their mobile phone is asking for trouble. Actually, at one city-centre venue, posters on the walls forbid gig-goers from talking during performances altogether. But generally, when it comes to pop concerts it's more a case of attitudes starting to change. **5** ____ Singing along loudly is unreasonable unless the artist specifically requests it. And drinks should be consumed by their owner and not spilt down the back of the person in front of them.

The habits of gig-goers vary according to the type of music being performed. From the hard-rocking gigs of my teenage years, I frequently emerged soaked in drinks and sweat, and thought nothing of standing in the middle of a crowd for hours. **6** ____ Happily, I have learned that the further back you stand in a crowd, the less likely you are to be pushed or have someone step on your foot. As for the talkative ones in the audience, I say pour cold water on the lot of them.

Exam tip ›

Before choosing one of the sentences A–G, make sure that verbs and nouns agree in tense, person or number with the main text.

A This noise went on for around twenty minutes before my patience ran out.
B But there are also times when the greatest performers in the world can't compete with the idiot in the crowd who decides to sing along, spill drinks and casually push people.
C These days, though, I am much less keen on all this.
D If this reaction was a bit strong, the emotion behind it was understandable.
E I always walk out whenever they start doing that.
F Some unwritten ones, however, do exist.
G Talking, for example, is acceptable but not to the point where the strangers next to you are forced to listen to details of your private life.

5 When you have chosen all your answers, read the complete text. Does it all make sense? Have you chosen a letter for every question?

Phrasal verbs with *on*

6 Look at these verbs in the text and sentences A–G. What does each one mean?

1 relies on (line 9)
2 kept on (line 16)
3 step on (line 39)
4 went on (sentence A)

7 Complete the sentences with phrasal verbs. Use the correct form of these verbs + *on*.

base carry count depend focus ~~jump~~ log play sit turn

1 During the concert, somebody from the audience ...jumped on... the stage.
2 I'll .... to my computer to find out more about the composer of that music.
3 At the cinema I asked some people to be quiet, but they just .... talking.
4 The success of a film often .... the amount of publicity it gets and what the critics say.
5 There's nothing to .... at that art gallery, and standing up all the time gets tiring.
6 The gig was supposed to finish at 10.30, but the band .... until after midnight.
7 At the cinema, they always .... all the lights after the film has finished.
8 The film is .... real events in a small town in southern USA.
9 'You're a good friend and I know I can always .... your support,' he said.
10 The story begins by looking at her childhood while the second half .... her adult life.

4 LISTENING

Part 4

L Page 96

1 Why are online videos so popular? Which have you enjoyed the most?

> **Quick steps to Listening Part 4**
> - Quickly read the instructions. These may include information such as the main speaker's name, occupation or hobby, and the setting, e.g. a radio interview.
> - For each question, study the stem only and underline the key words. When you listen, think of an answer in your own words.
> - Choose the option (A, B or C) most like your answer.

2 1.07 Look at the exam task instructions and read question 1. Then listen to the first part of the recording and answer these questions.

1 Which expressions have similar meanings to the key words *most want* and *girl*?
2 Which is the correct answer (A, B or C)? Why?
3 Why are the other two answers wrong?

Exam tip ›

Remember that the questions follow the order of the information that you hear, and each part of the recording relates to a particular question.

3 1.08 Look at the stem of questions 2–7 and underline the key words. Then listen and do the exam task. When you hear the recording, listen for expressions with similar or opposite meanings to these words.

Exam task

You will hear part of a radio interview with Sonia Evans, an artist whose work first became popular on the Internet. For questions **1–7**, choose the best answer (**A**, **B** or **C**).

1 What did Sonia most want to do when she was a girl?
A create sculptures
B paint using colours
C draw with a pencil

2 What disappointed Sonia about the exhibition in the art gallery?
A not enough people saw her drawings
B there was a bad review of her drawings
C nobody bought any of her drawings

3 Sonia decided to use the Internet to show her drawings because
A she did not want to go and live somewhere else.
B the gallery refused to hold another exhibition of her work.
C her friend had already promoted his photos that way.

4 What made Sonia's video different from the others?
A Her work had more artistic quality.
B The film was more professionally made.
C It did not show a completed picture.

5 How did Sonia feel when she found out how many people had looked at her video?
A rather uncomfortable
B highly delighted
C quite relieved

6 What happened as a result of the success of her videos?
A She drew more and more pictures.
B She began sleeping less at night.
C She started to forget what time it was.

7 How did she react to negative comments about her work?
A She replied angrily to them.
B She started to become depressed.
C She stopped reading them.

4 Make sure you have chosen one of the options (A, B or C) for each of questions 1–7. Then check your answers.

4 GRAMMAR

Verbs followed by *to* + infinitive or *-ing*

G Page 106

1 Look at extracts a–f from the recording in Listening. Answer these questions.

1 Which verbs are followed by *to* + infinitive, and which by *-ing*?
***Example:* a** *tend + to + infinitive*
2 Which verb can be followed by either *to* + infinitive or *-ing*? Does the meaning change?

a *I tended to see it as just the first step.*
b *They agreed to show some of my drawings.*
c *I didn't bother trying to have anything else shown.*
d *He never actually got round to doing it.*
e *I started going to the opposite extreme.*
f *I started to become a bit too obsessed.*

2 Decide which of these verbs are followed by *to* + infinitive, and which by *-ing*.

appear avoid dislike enjoy expect finish imagine insist on keep (on) learn manage mind miss offer promise refuse seem suggest threaten want

3 Match the sentence halves and explain the difference in meaning.

1 a I went on watching
b I went on to watch
i another DVD after that one had ended.
ii the same DVD for another hour.

2 a He tried working in theatre
b He tried to work in theatre
i but he never managed to get a job.
ii but he earned very little money.

3 a I regret saying that
b I regret to say that
i you have not been chosen to appear in the new film.
ii you had no talent at all.

4 a I'll remember watching
b I'll remember to watch
i that film for many years.
ii that film on TV tonight!

5 a We stopped talking to
b We stopped to talk to
i the neighbours in the street last night.
ii the neighbours because they were so rude.

6 a I won't forget visiting
b I won't forget to visit
i the film studios last year.
ii my grandmother next week.

4 Correct the mistakes in these sentences written by exam candidates.

1 When I arrived home I could not stop thinking about why I had agreed helping him.
2 My fellow students have suggested to buy her a DVD or a book.
3 I forgot asking you whether you have an email address.
4 It was my first time at primary school and I remember to be very frightened.
5 I don't mind to work hard sometimes.
6 You will get into trouble if you go on to behave like that.

5 Complete the news story with the *to* + infinitive and the *-ing* form of the verbs in brackets.

Cinema audiences still rising

The latest cinema audience figures, which appear (1) .... (show) an increase of twelve per cent on the same period last year, seem (2) .... (indicate) that the economic downturn has not stopped people (3) .... (go) to watch their favourite films. Film critic Nick Kaminski says: 'These days people are trying (4) .... (spend) less money, and as an evening out at the cinema is much cheaper than, say, going to a restaurant, many of them are choosing (5) .... (see) a film rather than have a meal out. I expect the figures will keep on (6) .... (rise).'

6 Work in pairs. Ask your partner about the following:

- the kinds of film their local cinema tends to put on
- the kinds of film they enjoy watching, and dislike watching
- a film they particularly remember seeing
- a film they don't want to see
- a film they regret missing
- a film they must remember to see

7 Tell your partner about a film you have enjoyed watching. Use as many verbs as you can from Exercises 1–3.

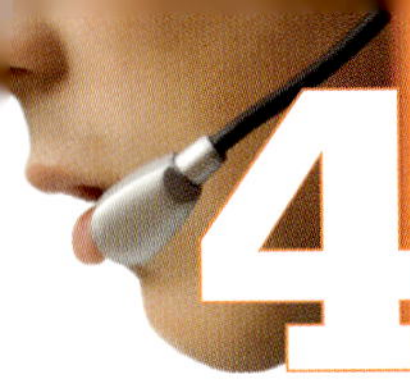

4 SPEAKING

too and *enough*

G Page 106

1 Complete extracts a–e from the recording in Listening on page 34 with *too* and *enough*. Then answer the questions below.

a *There were .... many to count.*
b *I had the uneasy sensation that there were .... many hits.*
c *I got over it quickly ....*
d *I started to become a bit .... obsessed.*
e *I didn't have .... time to do my work properly.*

1 Does *too* go before or after adjectives and adverbs? Does it mean the same as 'very'?
2 Does *enough* usually go before or after adjectives and adverbs? What about nouns?
3 Can *too* and *enough* be followed by *to* + infinitive, or the *-ing* form of the verb?

2 Correct the mistakes in these sentences written by exam candidates.

1 I'm too much lazy to ride a bicycle.
2 When you go shopping, there are too much people everywhere.
3 Students don't have leisure time enough.
4 If you don't get up enough early, you can't have breakfast.
5 Here are too narrow streets, which means a lack of parking spaces.
6 Television shows us a lot of too bad news from around the world.

3 Look at the examples. Then rewrite sentences 2–5 using *too* and *enough* with *for* in the same ways.

1 The DVD was so expensive that I couldn't buy it.
The DVD was too expensive for me to buy.
The DVD wasn't cheap enough for me to buy.
2 I can't watch films on this computer because it is so slow.
3 It was so noisy that we couldn't hear what was going on.
4 I couldn't read that book in a week because it was so long.
5 That bed was so uncomfortable that I couldn't sleep on it.

Part 4

S Page 100

4 Put these expressions into four groups: 1 *Asking for opinions*, 2 *Asking for reasons*, 3 *Giving reasons*, 4 *Giving examples*.

because ...	What's your opinion?
for example ...	What do you think?
for instance ...	Is that because ... ?
for one thing ...	The main reason is that ...
like ...	Could you tell me why?
so ...	What are your feelings about this?
such as ...	Any particular reason?
Why do you think so?	How do you feel about ... ?

Quick steps to Speaking Part 4
- Support your opinions by giving reasons and examples.
- Listen carefully to what your partner says, adding to their ideas or encouraging them to say more.

5 1.09 You will hear Julian and Daniela, two strong students, practising Part 4. Which of questions 1–6 does the teacher ask? Which student do you think does this part of the Speaking test better? Why?

1 What are the advantages and disadvantages of having lots of leisure time?
2 How important do you think it is to have hobbies and interests in your free time?
3 Do you think it is necessary to spend money in order to relax and have a good time? (Why? / Why not?)
4 Which hobby or interest would you most like to take up? (Why?)
5 Which leisure activities do you think are becoming more popular these days? (Why?)
6 Do you think people these days read fewer books than previous generations did? (Why? / Why not?)

6 1.09 Listen again, and tick the expressions in Exercise 4 that Daniela uses.

Exam tip ›
The questions in Part 4 are not written down, so listen to the examiner carefully.

7 Work in a group of three: one 'examiner' and two 'candidates'. The examiner asks the candidates some of the questions in Exercise 5. The candidates answer, using some of the following:

- expressions from Exercise 4
- verbs followed by *to* + infinitive and *-ing*, e.g. *tend, enjoy*
- *too* and *enough* to give reasons

8 The examiner tells the candidates how well he/she thinks they did the task. Examiners should be polite and helpful in their comments.

4 READING AND USE OF ENGLISH

Review of present perfect

G Page 106

1 Look at these extracts from the recording in Speaking and answer the questions.

I've wanted to have a dog for a while.
We've just moved to a smaller flat.
I haven't asked my parents yet.
My eyes have been getting sore since I began reading a lot of texts online last year.
I've already had to start using reading glasses.

1 Which tense is used for something:
  a that happened in a period of time that is finished?
  b that started changing or developing in the past and is still happening now?
  c that started in the past and is permanent or has a result now?

2 Match the underlined words with uses a–e.
  a for something that has happened sooner than expected
  b to say how long something has been happening
  c for an event that is expected to happen
  d to say when something that is happening started
  e for something that happened a short time ago

2 Correct the mistakes in these sentences written by exam candidates.

1 I'm living in this nice, small town for one year now.
2 Let me tell you more about what I've done last month.
3 I have been living here since a month.
4 I already have printed my boarding pass for my flight.
5 We've waited all this time. Did you miss the bus?
6 I'm at the beach because my holiday has ended yet.

Part 4

3 Look at the exam task example. Answer these questions.

1 What adverb is used in the second sentence instead of *since*?
2 What change is there in verb form?
3 Which word is not needed in the second sentence?
4 Which two parts of the answer do you get marks for?

Quick steps to Reading and Use of English Part 4
- Decide whether the word in capitals is a noun or verb, for example, and what often goes with it, e.g. an adverb.
- Look at any verb in the second sentence to see whether you need a singular or plural noun in your answer.

4 Do the exam task. Note down the changes you make.

Exam task

For questions **1–6**, complete the second sentence so that it has a similar meaning to the first sentence, using the word given. **Do not change the word given**. You must use between **two** and **five** words, including the word given. Here is an example (**0**):

Example:
0 It's a long time since we last went there.
BEEN
We ...HAVE NOT (or HAVEN'T) BEEN THERE FOR... a long time.

1 By eight o'clock I couldn't read because it was so dark.
ENOUGH
By eight o'clock it wasn't .... read.

2 Despite his poor eyesight, my grandfather continued to read books.
CARRIED
Despite his poor eyesight, my grandfather .... books.

3 I stopped doing ballet when I was at primary school.
DONE
I .... I was at primary school.

4 The plot was so complicated that none of us could follow it.
TOO
The plot was .... us to follow.

5 I've had Chinese lessons since this time last year.
LEARNING
I .... exactly a year.

6 You can't be sure you'll win the prize, you know.
COUNT
You can't .... the prize, you know.

5 When you have finished, check all your answers for correct grammar and spelling.

Exam tips
- Use no more than five words. Contracted forms like *I'd* or *it's* count as two words, except *can't* – which counts as one.
- If more than one answer is possible, give only one of them.

4 WRITING

Part 2 review

W Page 93

1 Look at the exam task and answer these questions.

1 Who will read your review?
2 What should it contain?
3 How many words must you write?

Exam task

You see this notice in an international English-language magazine.

> Have you read a good novel recently? If so, would you like to write a review of it? Include information on the setting, story and main characters, and say whether you would recommend the book to other readers.

Write your **review** in **140–190** words.

2 Read the model review and answer these questions.

1 Match the headings a–d with the four paragraphs of the review.
 a conclusion and recommendation
 b comments on various aspects of the book
 c introduction and setting
 d outline of the story and main characters
2 Is the review written in a style that is quite formal or very informal? Give examples.
3 Find words in the review that mean the following:
 a things that happen in the story (noun)
 b moves along quickly (adjective)
 c completely holds your attention (adjective)
 d can make you believe they are real (adjective)
 e makes you admire it (adjective)
 f subjects of a book, film, play, etc. (noun)
 g that makes it difficult to relax (adjective)
4 Does the reviewer recommend the book to other readers? If so, in which sentence?

The Sugar Glider

Rod Neilsen's novel *The Sugar Glider* is an adventure story set in Australia, moving from the modern coastal city of Brisbane to the wild uninhabited interior.

When a cargo plane crashes in the outback, pilot Don Radcliffe and his teenage daughter Judy quickly realise it was no accident. They then face a struggle to survive in the desert as a criminal gang tries to find the illegal cargo – and them. It is a struggle in which Judy soon finds herself having to take the lead.

The plot is well constructed and as the story develops it becomes fast-paced and quite gripping. The main characters, particularly Judy, are convincing, and for such a short book there is an impressive mixture of themes that range from dishonesty, greed and selfishness, to courage, family values and concern for native culture.

This is a book that I could not put down, and I read it right through in a few hours. If you enjoy a tense thriller which is quick and easy to read, I suggest you choose this one.

3 Which of these descriptive adjectives usually have a negative meaning?

absurd bizarre breathtaking delightful dreadful exceptional fine moving mysterious outstanding poor predictable remarkable slow-moving superb tremendous

4 Which of these expressions do we use to recommend something, and which to say not to do something?

My advice is to avoid this … and instead …
This ... is really worth … because …
This is one of the best … I have ever … , so I suggest …
I would advise everyone to … a better … than this, such as …
Anyone who likes … will really enjoy this …

Quick steps to writing a Part 2 review
- Think about who your readers are and what they want to know.
- Make a plan that includes description, explanation and conclusion.
- Try to include some interesting facts and lively comments.
- Recommend or advise readers against the subject of your review.

5 Write your own book review. Include some descriptive adjectives.

6 When you have finished, check your work as in Unit 1 Writing Exercise 5 on page 14.

4 REVISION

1 Complete the second sentence so that it has a similar meaning to the first sentence, using the word given. Do not change the word given. You must use between two and five words, including the word given.

1 I should have gone to that concert.
REGRET
I .... to that concert.

2 Maria took up gymnastics last autumn.
BEEN
Maria .... last autumn.

3 Nathan was determined to pay for all our drinks.
INSISTED
Nathan .... all our drinks.

4 Unfortunately, the heating in that theatre regularly breaks down.
ON
Unfortunately, the heating in that theatre .... down.

5 That piece is so difficult that only the very best pianists can play it.
TOO
That piece is .... except the very best.

6 The last time Phil sang here was two years ago.
SUNG
Phil .... two years.

2 Put the words in the correct order to form questions. Then write your answers in full sentences.

1 been / how long / you / English / learning / have ?
2 have / the theatre / you / how many times / to / been ?
3 evening meal / yet / your / had / have / you ?
4 the radio / listening to / the last hour / you / been / have / for ?
5 spoken / you / to / just / your partner / have ?

3 Complete the questions with the *to* + infinitive or the *-ing* form of the verbs in brackets. Then answer the questions about yourself.

1 What kind of music do you enjoy .... (listen) to?
2 Is there anything you've tried .... (do) recently, but failed?
3 What have you managed .... (do), even though it was difficult?
4 What do you most dislike .... (have to) do every day?
5 What mustn't you forget .... (do) next week?
6 Which musical instrument would you like to learn .... (play)?
7 Which song do you first remember .... (hear) when you were a child?
8 Is there anything you regret .... (not do) last week?

4 Complete the crossword with words from Unit 4.

Across
1 short part of a film or play
2 played to an audience
4 painting, book, piece of music, etc.
5 of very high quality
7 marvellous
8 subject of a book
10 all the things which happen in a story
12 photograph, or picture in a film
13 person who reviews books, films, etc.
14 words of a song
15 pop concert (informal)

Down
1 words of a film or play
3 place where music is performed
6 holding your attention completely
7 place where a film is recorded
9 causing strong feelings
11 of very low quality
12 performed by one person only
13 all the actors in a film or play

See the CD-ROM for more practice.

5 Learning and earning

LISTENING

1

2

3

4

Part 2

L Page 95

1 Look at the photos. Which university is in the UK, the USA, Australia and New Zealand? Why do you think so?

2 1.10 Complete the text with these words. Then listen to check your answers.

academic Bachelor's graduate lectures Master's postgraduate qualify secondary seminars thesis tutor undergraduates

The higher education systems in some English-speaking countries such as the UK, Australia and New Zealand are similar in some ways. Pupils at (1) .... school take examinations at the age of 18, and those who (2) .... for university then usually begin their (3) .... degree courses, which normally last three or four years. At this stage students are known as (4) .... , and they learn about their subject by attending (5) .... in large groups. These are often followed by discussion in (6) .... , involving a much smaller group of students and a (7) .... who asks questions and encourages them to talk about the topic. When they successfully finish their first degree, students (8) .... and may then go on to do a (9) .... course such as a (10) .... degree. For most students, the highest (11) .... achievement is to obtain a doctoral degree by writing a (12) .... based on research.

3 Look at the exam task instructions and answer these questions.

1 What is the topic of the recording?
2 Why do you think Alba went to New Zealand to study?
3 What do you think are the advantages and disadvantages of doing that?

4 1.11 Read exam questions 1–10. What kind of word, e.g. date, noun, do you need for each question? Then listen and do the exam task.

Quick steps to Listening Part 2

- Try to predict what you will hear by reading the instructions and the sentences.
- The first time you listen, write your answer lightly in pencil, in case you want to change it later.

Exam task

You will hear European student Alba Ortega talking about going to university in New Zealand. For questions **1–10**, complete the sentences.

Alba decided to go to New Zealand because her
__________ **1** had studied there.

One reason Alba chose Christchurch was that she could go
__________ **2** when she was there.

Alba likes the fact that the __________ **3**
is quite different from that in her home country.

At first she found it difficult to call some people by their
__________ **4** .

She is impressed by the fact that most of the staff write
__________ **5** .

She believes she is now a lot better at
__________ **6** than she was.

After she graduates, Alba intends to
__________ **7** in Christchurch.

When she first came to New Zealand, Alba was surprised by the distance from __________ **8** .

Her summer holidays start on __________ **9** .

In December, Alba hopes to see __________ **10**
when she goes away.

Exam tip ›

Sometimes you need to write three words, but often one or two words are enough.

Review of future forms

Page 107

1 Look at extracts a–f from the recording in Listening and match them with uses 1–6. What is the name, e.g. future simple, future continuous, of each of these future forms?

a *I think I'll give skiing a try sometime.*
b *I will have graduated, I hope, by the end of this year.*
c *I'm meeting my personal tutor on Wednesday.*
d *I've already made up my mind I'm going to teach.*
e *I'll be doing that for about a year.*
f *My exams started on October 28th and they finish a week from now.*

1 for a definite future arrangement with someone
2 for an action in progress in the future
3 for a decision about the future or a prediction based on evidence
4 for a prediction, something that's not certain or a sudden decision
5 for a future event fixed by a timetable or schedule
6 for something that will be finished before a particular time

2 Which of these sentences written by exam candidates contain mistakes? Correct the mistakes. In some cases more than one answer is possible.

1 On the ticket it says that my plane is arriving at 22.30 on Friday.
2 The new teacher is meeting the college students later today.
3 I would only like to travel in late June because I've just finished my course at that time.
4 I also know English and French quite well, which I believe are going to help me a great deal.
5 I'll tell you everything, with all the details, when we meet again.
6 I'm sorry but I can't do the course in August because I'll go camping with my friends then.
7 Visiting you in July is just perfect because the schools will have closed and I will already have sat my exams.
8 I need a new dictionary. I think I will have gone to Foyles Bookshop next Monday.

3 In pairs, ask and answer the questions using future forms. Use full sentences.

1 Where / you spend / your summer holidays?
A: *Where will you be spending your summer holidays?*
B: *I'll be spending them at the seaside.*
2 When / you do / your homework?
3 Who / you meet / next weekend?
4 In which month / the next school term / start?
5 By what age / you think / you / finished studying?
6 How many children / you think / you have?
7 Where / you probably work / ten years from now?

Noun suffixes: *-or, -ist, -ian, -er, -ant*

4 Match these suffixes with groups 1–5 to form words for jobs, then write each word. What spelling changes are needed for some of the words in each group?

-or -ist -ian -er -ant

1 assist, attend, consult, account, serve
2 music, politics, electricity, history, mathematics
3 novel, guitar, economics, physics, psychology
4 invent, operate, inspect, investigate, invest
5 deal, lecture, bank, philosophy, research

5 Look at these pairs of nouns. In each case, which means 'the person who gives something', and which means 'the person who receives something'?

trainee/trainer employee/employer payee/payer interviewee/interviewer examinee/examiner

6 What do we call somebody who:

1 participates in something?
2 instructs other people?
3 works in chemistry, or studies it?
4 presents a TV show?
5 specialises in something?
6 works in a library?
7 survives an accident?
8 drives a motor vehicle?
9 supplies something?
10 seeks refuge from a disaster?

5 READING AND USE OF ENGLISH

Part 7

doctor

engineer

financial adviser

legal assistant

1 Look at the photos. Answer the questions.

1 What do you think these young trainees will be doing in twenty years' time?
2 Which of them will have the biggest salary?
3 Which will enjoy their work the most? Why?

2 Read the exam task instructions and the title of the text, and look at its layout. Answer these questions.

1 What is the topic of the text and how many parts are there?
2 Who are the people?
3 What kind of information do you need to find?

3 For each of questions 1–10, underline (or note down) the key words as in the example (1).

4 Do the exam task. As you read, look for words, phrases and sentences that express the same ideas as the key words in the questions. Underline the words, phrases or sentences that tell you the right answers.

Exam tip ›

You don't have to begin by reading the whole text. You may find it helpful to read the questions first, then scan each part of the text.

Quick steps to Reading and Use of English Part 7

- Before you make your mind up about an answer, read the question again and look carefully at the evidence in the text.
- For some questions, you may be able to choose more than one option. If so, there will be extra spaces next to these questions.

Exam task

You are going to read an article in which four people talk about their careers. For questions **1–10**, choose from the people (**A–D**). The people may be chosen more than once.

Which person

did not go to university?	**1**	
has heard the company might be bought by a bigger organisation?	**2**	
was pleasantly surprised by the working conditions?	**3**	
says that enthusiasm and determination will bring great success for the employee?	**4**	
found it difficult at first to complete work on time?	**5**	
is confident they will be able to carry out their extra duties?	**6**	
says the way they are paid makes financial planning simpler?	**7**	
liked their job as soon as they started it?	**8**	
had to understand a lot of new things very quickly?	**9**	
is unsure exactly how much they will earn in the future?	**10**	

Training for the future

Four young trainees talk about their jobs.

A **Jessica**

After leaving school, I had a gap year working in Africa before I did my medical degree. I'm now a Junior Doctor in training at a local hospital, where the work is demanding but very rewarding with lots of advice and support from senior colleagues. Before I started here I'd expected to have to work very long hours, but nowadays there's a maximum of 48 hours per week for doctors. There is of course shift work, but the days of junior doctors having to live in and be on call all night are, I was happy to find, long gone. There's also a clearly laid-down salary structure in this profession, and that makes it easier to think ahead – for instance, if you're intending to take out a loan for house purchase, you know roughly what you'll be able to afford.

B **Stefan**

I'm a Trainee Financial Advisor with a leading Financial Services firm. I came here after I graduated in Economics and took to the work straightaway. Once I've finished my training, I'll be working with an established team of specialist advisors. That will mean taking on a lot of added responsibilities such as building lasting business relationships with clients, but I'm sure I'll manage. And although the basic salary is possibly a little below average, from next year there will also be a few extras such as fully paid holidays in Miami and a car allowance, as well as a company lunch every month at one of the best restaurants in town. If, like me, you're highly motivated, in this firm your career can really take off.

C **Arantxa**

I graduated last year and shortly afterwards I was taken on here as a Graduate Engineer. Unlike some of my colleagues I didn't have any work experience and the tasks I was given were quite varied, so there was a tremendous amount to take in all at once. And in those early days I had a little trouble meeting deadlines, though as I gained experience I quickly got over that. From next autumn I'll become a buyer for the firm, purchasing imported goods and equipment, which means I'll control a fairly large budget. That's going to be quite a challenge. At present I'm keen to remain here at this branch, though that may be affected if the rumours that a major corporation is considering taking the firm over turn out to be true.

D **Matthew**

I would like to have studied Law at university but I didn't have the grades, so I went straight from school into a law firm. I spent two years there, and then took up my current post in Local Government as a Trainee Legal Assistant. It's interesting work, with lots of variety within the field of planning law. I have particular responsibility for public transport, for instance giving legal advice on any new schemes or proposed changes in the bus, tram or suburban rail networks. That means doing a lot of research, so a basic requirement of the job is the ability to work on one's own, rather than as part of a group. The salary here is reasonable, although in the present economic climate, with such huge cuts to public spending, that may not be the case for much longer. Still, I feel it's a worthwhile job, and fairly secure, too.

5 Make sure you have put a letter in every space.

Phrasal verbs with *take*

6 Match these phrasal verbs in the text with meanings 1–8.

take out (A)	took to (B)	taking on (B)	take off (B)
taken on (C)	take in (C)	taking over (C)	took up (D)

1 started doing (a job)
2 getting control of (a company)
3 employed
4 started to like
5 understand completely
6 obtain, from a bank or insurance company, for example
7 suddenly start to be successful
8 accepting (a responsibility)

7 Complete the sentences with phrasal verbs. Use the correct form of *take* and a suitable adverb particle.

1 Now that exports have increased, the firm is going to .... 100 more staff.
2 At first I didn't really .... the new boss, but I quite like her now.
3 When our company was .... by a much bigger firm, some people lost their jobs.
4 Simon has .... far too much work. He looks exhausted all the time.
5 Sales of our new product have really .... since we began advertising it on TV.
6 We would like you to .... the position of Assistant Manager from next month.
7 If you drive a car, you must .... insurance in case you have an accident.
8 So much was new on my first day at work that it was hard to .... everything ....

5 SPEAKING

Countable and uncountable nouns

G Page 107

1 Look at these extracts from the text in Reading and Use of English on page 43 and complete the rules with the words *countable nouns* and *uncountable nouns*.

taking on a lot of added responsibilities
there will also be a few extras
a little trouble meeting deadlines
That's going to be quite a challenge.
It's interesting work
That means doing a lot of research

1 We can use *a* or *an* with singular .... We can use (*a*) *few, many* or *a lot of / lots of* with them in the plural.
2 We can't use *a* or *an* with .... and there is no plural. We can use (*a*) *little, much or a lot / lots of* with them.

2 Correct the mistakes in these sentences written by exam candidates.

1 I can go there by bike, on foot, or even use public transports.
2 I get many information from the Internet.
3 I have a big room with old furnitures, and pictures on the walls.
4 I do not have many news to tell you.
5 For my project I had to do a lot of practical works.
6 The problem is that I have only a few money.
7 My computer's memory is very big, so it has a lot of space to install other softwares.
8 I always paint when I have a spare time.
9 Now the recession is getting worse and unemployments are increasing.
10 I am very keen on music, but I have very few experience of singing in public.

3 Are these nouns usually countable or uncountable? Write phrases with six of them.

Example*: a little knowledge*

advertising advice commerce deal discovery duty earnings education homework institution knowledge leisure manufacturing opportunity position production profession qualification research responsibility technology

Part 1

S Page 97

4 1.12 You are going to hear two very strong students, Alisa and Francesco, doing Part 1. The first time you listen, tick the topics that the examiner asks them about.

a travel
b science and technology
c education and work
d the media
e family
f leisure activities

5 1.12 Listen again. How do Alisa and Francesco use these words and phrases? Which are countable, and which uncountable?

spare time pleasure overtime management engineering course research degree

Quick steps to Speaking Part 1
- Be confident and speak loudly enough for the examiners and your partner to hear you.
- Listen to the examiner and your partner speaking to each other. This will help you get used to their voices.

6 Work in pairs. Ask and answer these questions.

1 How well do you think you'll do in your next exams?
2 What are you going to do when you've finished your studies?
3 Do you think you'll use English a lot in your job? Why? / Why not?
4 What kind of studies or work do you think you'll be doing in three years' time?
5 What are you going to do when you next have some free time?

Exam tip

Don't try to make a speech that you prepared earlier! It may not answer the question asked, and it wouldn't sound natural.

7 Tell your partner how well you think they answered the questions in Exercise 6. Be polite and give helpful advice.

5 READING AND USE OF ENGLISH

Part 3

1 Complete the sentences with the correct form of the words in brackets. Use suffixes, and plural forms where necessary.

1 I've always been interested in nature and I'm going to become a .... (biology).
2 I'm in charge of the office, so I have a lot of .... (responsible).
3 We will increase .... (produce) as demand for what we manufacture grows.
4 We always ask the .... (interview) why he or she wants to join the company.
5 I had little .... (know) of other cultures before I worked abroad.
6 Some .... (employ) make their staff work longer hours than others.
7 On my first day at work, the boss gave me some .... (advise).
8 Some people say there is too much .... (advertise) on television.
9 Why do .... (politics) have such long holidays when the country has so many problems?

Quick steps to Reading and Use of English Part 3

- If the missing word is a noun, decide whether it's countable or uncountable. If it's countable, does it need to be plural?
- Make sure that the word you have written makes sense in the sentence as a whole.

2 Look at the exam task. Quickly read the title and the text, without filling in any gaps for now. Which graduates are most likely to find jobs, and which are least likely?

Exam tips ›

- Check your spelling. You will lose marks if it isn't correct.
- When you have finished, make sure you have changed all the words in capitals.

3 Look at the example (0). Answer the questions. Then do the exam task.

1 What kind of word (noun, adjective, etc.) is *employ*?
2 What kind of word is needed for the gap?
3 What suffix is required?
4 Is *employment* countable or uncountable? Does it need a final -s?

Exam task

For questions **1–8,** read the text below. Use the word given in capitals at the end of some of the lines to form a word that fits in the gap **in the same line**. There is an example at the beginning (**0**).

Example: 0 EMPLOYMENT

Jobs for graduates

Although most graduates find **(0)** .... within a year of leaving university, and their **(1)** .... tend to be substantially higher than those of non-graduates, the rates vary from subject to subject. **EMPLOY** **EARN**

Recently, **(2)** .... carried out a survey of over 200,000 graduates who stated their **(3)** .... for work, and found that nearly all those with degrees in medicine and dentistry had jobs twelve months after graduating. **RESEARCH** **AVAILABLE**

Education comes next in the list, showing that a teaching **(4)** .... usually leads pretty quickly to a job, followed by law. For those looking for work as **(5)** .... , the prospects aren't quite so bright, especially in the physical sciences. **QUALIFY** **SCIENCE**

It's a similar story for business and administrative studies, though many graduates find positions in junior **(6)** .... in large organisations, while others become trainee **(7)** .... in smaller firms. People with degrees in technology do less well, with quite a few **(8)** .... still unemployed. **MANAGE** **CONSULT** **ENGINE**

4 Make sure the completed text makes sense, and you have spelt all the words correctly.

5 WRITING

Part 2 formal letter of application

W Page 90

1 Look at the exam task and answer the questions.

1 Which organisation placed the advertisement?
2 What kind of job is advertised?
3 What does the work involve?
4 What three requirements are there?
5 Who must you write to, and in what style?
6 What must you aim to do in your letter?

Exam task

You have seen this advertisement in an English-language newspaper.

International Student Fair **Fair requires staff**

The International Student Fair helps people choose the right college or university, and we are looking for assistants for this year's Fair. Duties will include giving directions and offering advice.

- Do you like helping people?
- Do you have experience of choosing a place of study?
- Are you willing to work evenings?

If so, apply to the organiser, Ms Evie Ross, saying why you think you are suitable for the job.

Write your **letter of application** in **140–190** words in an appropriate style.

Quick steps to writing a Part 2 formal letter of application

- Say why you're writing and where you saw the advertisement.
- Make sure you deal with all the points in the advertisement.
- Vary the expressions you use. For example, instead of using *I can* all the time, say *I believe I am capable of*.
- Write in complete sentences, where possible using passive verb forms, formal linkers and longer words.
- Don't use conversational expressions, abbreviations or contracted forms, and try to avoid using phrasal verbs.

2 Read the model letter. Which phrases and sentences does the writer use to do these things?

1 begin and end the letter formally
Example: *Dear Ms Ross, Yours sincerely,*
2 give a reason for writing
3 say how he heard about the job
4 answer each of the questions in the advertisement
5 ask about pay and conditions
6 describe any relevant experience
7 say what he has sent with the letter
8 offer to give the reader more information
9 state availability for interview

Dear Ms Ross,

I would like to apply for the post of assistant at this year's International Student Fair, as advertised in the newspaper on 2 January.

I am aged 19 and in my second year of a Mechanical Engineering course. Before deciding on City College I looked at the advantages and disadvantages of many academic institutions, and I therefore feel capable of offering advice to young people who are at that stage now.

The work sounds extremely interesting. Could you please tell me how much I would be paid, and whether training would be necessary?

I would be available to work evenings as all my lectures are in the afternoons and consequently I can study in the mornings.

I have always enjoyed assisting others and last year I worked as a volunteer at a book fair.

Details of this, plus personal details including qualifications, are shown in my curriculum vitae, which I enclose.

If you need any further information, please do not hesitate to contact me. I would be able to attend an interview any morning.

Yours sincerely,

Jonas Meyer

3 Plan your own letter to Ms Ross. Make notes about how you will answer the three questions and how you will convince her of your suitability for the job. Then decide how many paragraphs you are going to use and which points will go in which.

4 Write your letter, following your plan. You can use some of the formal expressions from Jonas's letter, but you should give different details about yourself and ask different questions.

Exam tip

Never begin your letter *Dear Manager* or *Dear Organiser* – use *Dear Mr* or *Dear Ms (their surname).*

5 When you have finished, check your work as in Unit 1 Writing Exercise 5 on page 14.

5 REVISION

1 Decide which answer (A, B, C or D) best fits each gap.

1 My sister has a .... in Physics from Cambridge University.
A title B degree C grade D mark

2 At the last History seminar I attended, there were just five other students and our ....
A tutor B trainer C coach D consultant

3 There's a lot of unemployment, partly because firms aren't .... new workers.
A taking up B taking over C taking off D taking on

4 The .... at this unversity are given by experts in their subjects.
A classes B lectures C talks D speeches

5 As an 18-year-old .... , it was my first year in higher education.
A postgraduate B master C bachelor D undergraduate

6 I had to read the instructions twice before I could .... all the details.
A take on B take out C take in D take to

7 After Carlos left .... school, he started work in a car factory.
A higher B academic C secondary D superior

8 By this time next year, I will have .... from university.
A qualified B graduated C educated D succeeded

2 Complete the sentences with *(a) few* or *(a) little* and the correct form of the nouns in brackets.

1 We'll have very ....little homework.... (homework) to do once the exams are over.
2 Joe's from the city, so he has .... (experience) of working on a farm.
3 You will have .... (opportunity) as good as this one, so take the job now.
4 We need to do .... (research) into why so many businesses fail here.
5 Nowadays, ... (profession) pay as well as medicine or dentistry.
6 Sometimes I do .... (overtime) to increase my earnings.

3 Choose the correct option.

1 *I'm helping / I'll help / I'm going to help* you with your homework if you like.
2 Here are your tickets for 6 July. Your flight is *taking / takes / will have taken* off at 0745.
3 You can borrow my sister's books. She *won't mind / isn't going to mind / won't be minding.*
4 I can't come with you for lunch because *I'm seeing / I'll see / I see* the boss in a few minutes.
5 It's now 8 p.m., so by the time I go home at 8.30 I *will work / will have been working / will be working* for twelve hours non-stop.
6 This time next week *I'll surf / I'll be surfing / I'm surfing* on Bondi Beach!

4 Use the word given in capitals at the end of some of the lines to form a word that fits in the gap in the same line.

Checking out my old classmates

Last week I had a look at a website called Schoolfriends and I made some interesting (1) .... about the people who were in my class many years ago. **DISCOVER**

Many of them went to university, and since their (2) .... most of them have gone into well-paid professions. **GRADUATE** Lena Fischer, for instance, is now an (3) .... with a multinational company, **ECONOMY** and Jeff Haslam is also in finance, working as an (4) .... in a local firm. **ACCOUNT** Viktoria Petrov, who also loved reading, now works at a local college as a (5) .... **LIBRARY**

Of those who went straight into jobs on leaving school, Rajan Singh works in the town as an (6).................... , **ELECTRICITY** Sandra Ortiz – who I remember always liked travelling – is now a flight (7) .... with a big airline, **ATTEND** and Steve Richards is a supermarket (8) .... **EMPLOY** I think I saw him working at the checkout there recently.

See the CD-ROM for more practice.

Medical vocabulary

1 Put these words into the correct groups: a) people, b) injuries and illnesses, c) treatments.

ache bandage bruise disease fever fracture graze infection injection medicine nurse operation pain patient plaster porter prescription specialist sprain stitches surgeon tablets temperature thermometer wound

2 Use words from Exercise 1 to say what is happening in each of the pictures. Then talk about the treatment you received when you last had a minor illness or injury. How long did it take you to get better?

1
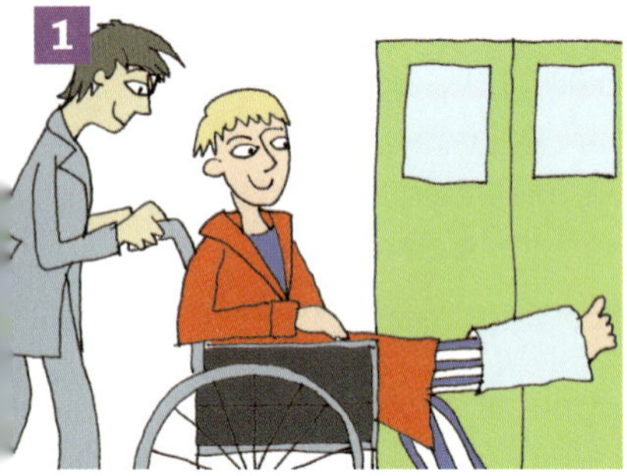

2

3

3 Put these senses in order of importance for you. Then say why you chose that order.

hearing sight smell taste touch

Part 5

Quick steps to Reading and Use of English Part 5

- Remember that questions 1–5 normally follow the order of information in the text.
- Look at options A–D after you've read what the text says. Otherwise the wrong answers might mislead you.
- You don't need to understand everything in the text to answer the questions, so don't spend a lot of time on words or phrases you don't know.

4 Quickly read the text and answer these questions.

1 Which of the five senses had Kathy lost?
2 Was her operation successful?

5 Look at each of questions 2–5 and find the relevant part of the text. Draw a line in pencil with the question number next to it, as in the example for question 1.

Exam tips›

- Question 6 in Part 5 may test your overall understanding of the text.
- Look for evidence that your answer is right, and that any references to the other three options are wrong.

6 Do the exam task on your own. Find the answer to each question by looking at the part of the text that you have marked.

7 Make sure you have answered every question. For any you aren't sure about, cross out the options you know are wrong and then choose from the rest.

8 Imagine you had never had one of the other senses: hearing, touch, taste or smell, and then experienced it for the first time. What would you enjoy most?

Exam task

You are going to read an extract from a novel. For questions **1–6**, choose the answer (**A**, **B**, **C** or **D**) which you think fits best according to the text.

The operation took place at the hospital in California. Dr Percival, the surgeon, thought it went well, but Kathy would need to rest in bed for three weeks with a bandage over her eyes.

In those weeks Kathy had plenty of time to think about what she had done. There were moments of doubt, almost panic, when she asked herself if she had done the right thing. She thought she had long since put away the foolish hopes for sight she had once held as a girl. Yet here she was, hoping like a girl again. She felt afraid, yes, but also excited at the thought of entering a world that would be totally unfamiliar to her, a world where she could see. It would be like being born a second time. Q1

She wondered what colour would be like. Although it was a word she had often used and heard before, she had never experienced colour. She just could not picture it in her mind, no matter how hard she tried. Kathy gave up trying and waited patiently for the day her bandages would be removed.

The day came. Dr Percival closed all the curtains in Kathy's room so that the light was low. He turned to her and spoke.

'Now, Kathy, we have to take things slowly. Even if things go well, you won't have full eyesight to begin with. First of all, let's see if your eyes are recognising light. We're going to take the bandage off and hold a light in front of your eyes. Are you ready?'

Kathy nodded.

Dr Percival held a small light in front of her eyes as a nurse slowly and carefully removed her bandage. Then Kathy sat up with her eyes still closed. Slowly she opened them and stared at the light. Quickly, she turned her face away.

'Ow! What was that? It felt strange – there's something there, trying to get into my head!'

Dr Percival told the nurse to replace the bandages and then turned to Kathy.

'Kathy,' he said with obvious delight, 'that "something" is light! You've seen light for the first time! Congratulations – you can see!'

Kathy felt confused.

'But ... I thought there would be more to it than this ... I mean ... I mean ... Oh, I don't know what I mean!'

'Don't worry, Kathy,' he said as he smiled. 'All you saw then was pure light. It will take time for your eyes to get used to seeing colours and shapes. Your brain has to do a lot of sorting out of new information that it has never had to deal with before. It's bound to take a little while. The main thing is that you can see!'

'I can see,' said Kathy softly. And underneath her bandages she was crying.

Over the next few weeks Kathy was progressively allowed to use her eyes more often. Soon she could tell dark from light, then she could recognise colours and shapes. But, for a while, she found it very difficult to deal with the huge amounts of extra information that her new sense was giving her every day. It was particularly hard to tell the difference between near and far objects. She would reach out for those across the room as if they were near to her, or she would walk into close objects without realising how close they were.

But Dr Percival was patient. Kathy was taken on walks around the hospital gardens, taken for drives in the car, and shown films and television programmes. Her eyes were gently exercised until they worked well.

'In fact, Kathy,' Dr Percival told her, 'your eyes are better than mine are. I need glasses and you don't!'

What Kathy liked most was seeing the pleasing effects shapes and colours produced. She would see ordinary things as objects of great beauty – the black and white squares on a chess board, the shape of a hand, the colours of a flower. Sounds, for the first time in her life, took second place. Colours and shapes now filled her mind with pleasure beyond her powers to describe.

1 How did Kathy feel during the three weeks after her operation?
- A She had the impression she had been born again.
- B She was looking forward to new experiences.
- C She wished that she had not had the operation.
- D She was glad that she was still a young girl.

2 What did Kathy do when the nurse took her bandage off?
- A She changed her position in bed.
- B She told the doctor she wasn't ready.
- C She looked at the light from the windows.
- D She immediately opened her eyes.

3 What was Kathy's first reaction to seeing the light?
- A She felt it was much as she had expected.
- B She was disappointed it went out so quickly.
- C She found it an uncomfortable experience.
- D She was delighted she could see so much.

4 What was Kathy's biggest problem once she could see?
- A She could not understand everything the doctor told her.
- B She found it difficult to judge the distance of things.
- C She quickly became tired as a result of looking at everything.
- D She was unable to distinguish between certain colours.

5 To help improve her eyesight,
- A the hospital staff filmed Kathy's progress.
- B Kathy had a second, smaller, operation.
- C Kathy went outside with the hospital staff.
- D the nurse put lighter bandages over Kathy's eyes.

6 How did Kathy's life change during the extract?
- A She felt that she was gradually becoming much more confident as a person.
- B She began to enjoy what she had previously not even been able to imagine.
- C She found that seeing and hearing were now equally important to her.
- D She came to realise that there would always be limits to what she could see.

6 LISTENING

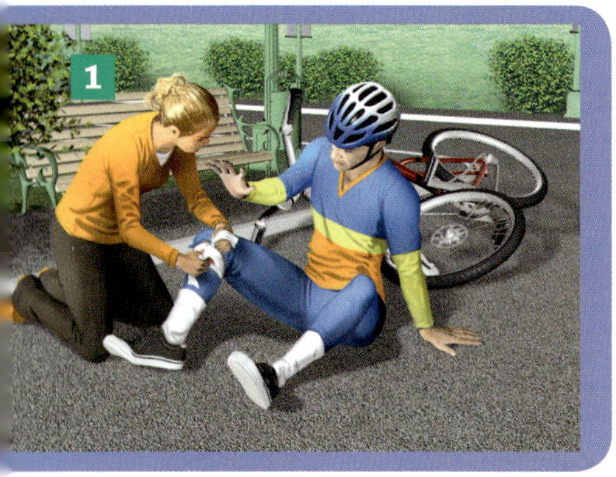

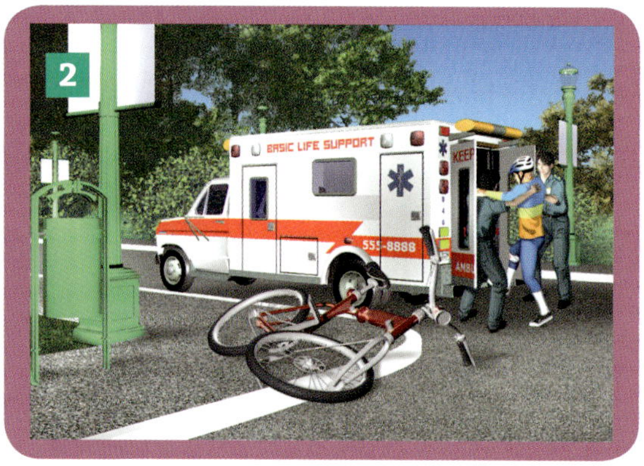

Part 1 L Page 94

1 Look at the introductory sentence and question in the example below. Underline the key words and answer these questions.

1 What's the focus, e.g. opinion, purpose?
2 Who's talking to whom?
3 Where?
4 Why?
5 When?

Example:
You hear a woman telling a neighbour in the street about a road accident she has just seen.
What happened?
A An ambulance took the cyclist to hospital.
B The cyclist was uninjured.
C Someone gave the cyclist first aid.

2 Match options A–C in the example with pictures 1–3. (Remember that there are no pictures in the exam.)

3 2.02 Listen and choose the best answer (A, B or C).

Quick steps to Listening Part 1
- Quickly read the first line of each question. Decide what the situation is and how many speakers you will hear.
- Before the recording is played, think of words connected with those in the question. For example: *Why … ? – because, so, as, reason, result.*
- You may hear words from all three options, but be careful: in two cases, the speaker is saying something else.

4 2.02 Listen again and identify the part that relates to each option. What is the correct answer?

5 Look at the first line of questions 1–6 in the exam task. In each case, underline the key words. Then answer as many of the questions from Exercise 1 as you can.

Example: Question 1 *1 man, work, Who; 1 someone's job; 2 man/ colleague; 3 restaurant; 4 to talk about work; 5 at a mealtime*

6 2.03 Now listen and do the exam task.

Exam tip ›

Once the recording finishes and you have chosen your answer, forget about that question and focus on the next one.

Exam task

You will hear people talking in six different situations. For questions **1–6**, choose the best answer (**A**, **B** or **C**).

1 You overhear a man in a restaurant talking to a colleague about his work.
Who is he?
A a police officer
B a doctor
C a sports coach

2 You hear a woman talking to a friend in the street.
Where is she going now?
A to the hospital
B to the cinema
C to the shops

3 You hear a patient talking on the phone.
What does he dislike about the hospital?
A the quality of the food
B the amount of noise
C the medical treatment

4 You overhear two people talking in a doctor's waiting room.
How does the man feel now?
A angry
B amused
C relieved

5 You hear a young woman talking to a friend about a cross-country race.
What do they agree about?
A He should take up swimming now.
B He should continue to run every day.
C He should withdraw from the race.

6 You overhear a woman on the phone.
Why is she calling?
A to complain about something
B to make an appointment
C to ask for information

7 Make sure you have answered all the questions. If you can't decide which of options A–C is right, cross out the one you are sure is wrong and guess.

6 GRAMMAR

Phrasal verbs with *up*

1 Look at these extracts from the recording in Listening. What do the phrasal verbs mean?

Many young men in Newtown, where he grew up, are involved in crime.
I've got that cross-country race coming up in two weeks.
It'll have cleared up in time for the race.

2 Complete the sentences with the correct form of these verbs. Then match the phrasal verbs you have made with meanings a–j.

dig	eat	heal	run	speak	speed	split
sum	tidy	use				

1 Green vegetables are very good for you, so .... up!
2 If we don't change our way of life, we'll .... up all the Earth's resources.
3 Whenever they play in this room, I have to .... up afterwards.
4 I can't hear. Will you .... up, please?
5 The champion had to .... up to win the race.
6 The band .... up after 20 years together.
7 Jo was hurt, but her injuries had .... up quickly.
8 Three players .... up to the referee to demand a penalty.
9 When they built the Athens Metro, they .... up many ancient objects.
10 To .... up, it was an exciting match, but it lacked quality play.

a separated completely
b talk more loudly
c go faster
d finish your food quickly
e end by restating the main points
f brought to the surface
g approached quickly
h got completely better
i put everything where it belongs
j completely finish

Relative clauses (G Page 108)

3 Look at these pairs of sentences and answer the questions.

1 a My sister who is a nurse works there. (defining relative clause)
b My sister, who is a nurse, works there. (non-defining relative clause)
Who has only one sister? Who has more than one sister?

2 a For the first time I saw a match which was exciting.
b For the first time I saw a match, which was exciting.
Who had never seen a match before? Who had only seen boring matches before?

3 a The race which I saw was very close.
b The race, which I saw, was very close.
In which sentence could we leave out *which*? Why?

4 Look again at the sentences in Exercise 3 and answer the questions.

1 Which kind of relative clause, defining or non-defining, gives essential information?
2 Which kind gives extra information?
3 Which kind uses commas? Where?

5 Join these pairs of sentences with non-defining relative clauses. Use *who*, *which*, *when*, *where* and *whose*, adding commas where necessary.

1 Rafael Nadal has won many championships. He is very popular.
Rafael Nadal, ...who is very popular, has won many... championships.
2 Emily's novel was successful. It was set in a school.
Emily's novel .... successful.
3 The World Cup was held in South Africa in 2010. Spain won.
In 2010 .... won.
4 The two cyclists were in an accident. They still finished the race.
The two cyclists .... still finished the race.
5 Laura won a medal. Her mother had also been a top swimmer.
Laura .... medal.
6 Everyone in the stadium was excited. The final was about to start.
In the stadium .... excited.

6 Correct the mistakes in these sentences written by exam candidates by either replacing the relative pronoun or adding commas where necessary. Then underline the word(s) in each sentence that the relative pronoun refers to, as in sentence 1.

1 I've chosen two activities, whose are sailing and climbing.
2 We went to Davos which is a famous ski resort.
3 You can come in June, where courses usually start.
4 I'd like to meet people which have the same interests as me.
5 The CD was dedicated to a man who name was Carl.
6 Mark who is keen on birds of prey saw some eagles and falcons.
7 I wonder if there is a gym which we can do some sports?

6 SPEAKING

Sports vocabulary

1 Match the sports in box A with the places in box B.

A

athletics baseball basketball boxing cycling diving football golf gymnastics hockey ice skating motorcycling rugby sailing skiing snowboarding squash surfing tennis

B

course court gym pitch ring rink sea slope track

2 What do we call people who take part in these sports? Use *do*, *play* or *go* and a defining relative clause.

Examples:

Someone who plays football is a footballer.

A person that does gymastics is a gymnast.

A skier is someone who goes skiing.

3 Say what sports people do with these objects. Which ones have you *worn*, *used* or *kicked*?

ball bat board club gloves helmet racket skates skis

Example:

A footballer kicks a (foot)ball.

Agreeing and politely disagreeing

4 2.04 Listen to these extracts from the recording in Listening question 5, and practise saying them with the same intonation.

I think you're probably right.
I don't think so. My own feeling is …

5 2.05 Complete expressions a–h with these words. Then listen to check your answers.

absolutely agree just keen know so sure what

Agreeing
a Yes, you're .... right.
b I think .... , too.
c Yes, I .... with that.
d That's .... what I was thinking.

Politely disagreeing
e Perhaps, but .... about … ?
f I'm not so .... Don't you think … ?
g I don't .... about that.
h I'm not really so .... on …

Part 3

S Page 99

6 2.06 Look at the exam task instructions and listen to students Tomasz and Eva doing the task. Answer these questions.

1 Which sport do they agree is not very dangerous?
2 Which sport do they agree is one of the most dangerous?
3 Which other sports does Tomasz suggest as the most dangerous?
4 Which other sport does Eva think is the most dangerous?

7 2.06 Listen again. Which expressions from Exercise 5 do Tomasz and Eva use? Number them in the order you hear them.

Exam task

You are going to talk about something together for about two minutes.

Here are some sports that can be dangerous. Look at the task and talk to each other about what can happen to people doing these sports if they are not careful.

rugby | motorcycle racing | underwater diving

What can happen to people doing these sports if they are not careful?

gymnastics | surfing | boxing

Now you have a minute to decide which two are the most dangerous sports.

Quick steps to Speaking Part 3
- Talk about each thing in turn, giving reasons for your opinions.
- Don't try to get through all the things too quickly.
- You should agree or disagree with what your partner says, but you must always be polite.

8 In pairs, do the same exam task as Tomasz and Eva. Use expressions from *Agreeing and politely disagreeing*.

Exam tip ›

Begin the discussion by saying something like *Would you like to start, or shall I?*

9 Compare your decision(s) with other pairs.

6 READING AND USE OF ENGLISH

Part 2

1 Imagine the Olympic Games are going to be held in your country next summer. Discuss these questions.

1. What jobs for volunteers might be available?
2. What could be the advantages and disadvantages of doing this kind of work?

2 Without filling in any gaps, quickly read *Working at the Olympics* to find out how the text answers the questions in Exercise 1.

3 Do the exam task.

Quick steps to Reading and Use of English Part 2

- For each question, look at the context and decide what kind of word, e.g. phrasal verb, relative pronoun, is needed.
- Look closely at the words either side of the gap for more clues.
- Remember that gaps may have more than one possible answer, but you must only give one.

4 Make sure the completed text all makes sense. Then check your answers.

Exam tip ›

Pencil in your answers on the question paper so that you can easily check the complete text when you have finished.

Exam task

For questions **1–8**, read the text below and think of the word which best fits each gap. Use only **one** word in each gap. There is an example at the beginning (**0**).

Example: 0 UP

Working at the Olympics

With the Olympic Games coming **(0)** .... fast, interviews for voluntary work will begin soon. The organisers will be looking for people **(1)** .... aim is to help make the Games a success for everyone, from athletes to members of the public, and **(2)** .... have excellent customer service skills.

The work, **(3)** .... may start several days before the Games actually begin, will be unpaid and staff will have to make their **(4)** .... arrangements for accommodation. In addition, they will have to pay their travel costs to the stadium or site **(5)** .... they will be working.

There will be many different kinds of jobs, ranging **(6)** .... checking tickets and handing out uniforms to showing spectators to their seats and tidying **(7)** .... after events have finished.

Volunteers will have to give up two weeks of their summer holidays, and there will also be a training course, **(8)** .... lasts three days.

6 WRITING

Purpose links

G Page 108

1 Look at Purpose links on page 108. Then choose the correct option in these sentences. Sometimes both may be possible.

1. I joined the sports club *so that / to* make new friends.
2. We've changed the rules *in order that / so as to* more goals are scored.
3. Jeff took off his sock *in order to / so that* the doctor could see his ankle.
4. *In order to / In order that* avoid injury, start with gentle exercise.
5. I left early *so as to / so that* avoid the traffic.
6. You should wear good walking shoes *in order not to / so that you don't* damage your feet.
7. *So as not to / So that I didn't* wake anyone up, I spoke quietly.
8. He hit the ball hard *so that / so as* the other player couldn't reach it.

2 In pairs, ask and answer the questions using purpose links.

Why do some people:

1. go to the gym?
   Example: *in order to get fit* or *so that they can get fit*
2. buy big TV screens?
3. go to a pharmacy?
4. want to eat less food?
5. take part in competitive sport?
6. send their children to summer camps?

Part 2 letter

W Page 90

3 Look at the exam task and answer the questions.

1. What kind of text have you received?
2. Who wrote it and what are they planning to do?
3. What do they want you to do?
4. Do they mainly use formal or informal language? Give examples.

Exam task

You have received a letter from an Irish penfriend, Linda. Read this part of the letter and then write your letter to Linda.

> I'm really looking forward to spending my summer holidays in your country – and to seeing you! As you know, I always try to keep quite fit. So can you give me some tips on the sports I could do in your town while I'm there? Write back soon,
> Linda

Write your **letter** in **140–190** words. Do not write any addresses.

Exam tip ›

The style of language in the text you have received can help you decide how formal or informal your reply should be.

Quick steps to writing a Part 2 letter

- Put the opening (e.g. *Dear Jenny*), the closing (e.g. *Best regards*) and your own name on separate lines.
- Don't use the same expression too often. For example, instead of repeating *please tell me*, say *I'd like to know* or *can you let me know*.

4 Read Sam's letter and answer the questions.

1. Which paragraph deals with: a) indoor sports, b) sports they can do together, c) outdoor sports?
2. What examples can you find of: a) informal language, b) relative clauses, c) purpose links?

> Hi Linda,
>
> Thanks very much for your last letter. I'm fine, and I'm glad to hear you're well, too.
>
> I'm sure you'll have a great time here. There are lots of sports you can do in the countryside, such as hill-walking or mountain-biking, as well as water sports like rowing and sailing on the lake. It will be too cold for swimming, though.
>
> If you'd rather go to a sports centre there's a really good one which has facilities for things like squash and basketball, and an Olympic-size pool where they play water-polo. Now that really is good exercise: I tried it once and I was exhausted after about ten minutes!
>
> Actually, it'd be nice if we could both do the same sports so that we have more time together. I sometimes go ice skating – would you like to try that? Or how about playing tennis? If so, I'll need to book ahead to make sure we get a court.
>
> Anyway, let me know what you'd like to do and I'll make some arrangements.
>
> Bye for now.
>
> Sam

5 Plan your letter. Think about the topic and your reader, and the number of paragraphs and writing style you will need.

6 Write your letter. When you have finished, check your work as in Unit 1 Writing Exercise 5 on page 14.

6 REVISION

1 Complete the crossword with words from Unit 6.

Across
1 place where football is played
3 place where people run
7 person who goes sailing
9 pain over an area of the body
11 person who cares for ill people
12 dark area on skin caused by injury
14 place where tennis is played
16 person being treated by a doctor
17 place where golf is played

Down
2 object worn by a rider
4 person who does athletics
5 broken bone
6 injury caused by twisting
7 the ability to see
8 person who rides a bicycle
10 injury, such as a cut
12 piece of a equipment used by a baseball player
13 place where people go skiing
15 place where people do boxing

2 Complete the sentences with relative pronouns, adding commas where necessary. In which of your answers could you leave out the relative pronoun?

1 This finger, ...which...... is a funny shape, is the one ......that/which...... I fractured.
2 In 1995 .... I was born very few people .... lived in my village did any sports.
3 Mark is the boy .... brother recently had an operation .... saved his life.
4 That's the hospital .... patients .... need specialist care normally go.
5 Jensen is the driver .... car was damaged in the accident .... I was telling you about.
6 The doctor .... I spoke to said there is no need to worry .... is a relief.

3 Read the text below and think of the word which best fits each gap. Use only one word in each gap.

Preventing sports injuries

No matter what sport you play, there is always a risk of injury. In (1) .... to avoid it happening to you, here are some simple rules.

Firstly, anyone (2) .... is thinking of taking up a sport should make sure they're already fit enough, (3) .... necessary by doing regular exercise before they start. People (4) .... only training is at the weekend have a high rate of injury.

It is also important, particularly in contact sports like rugby, to keep to the rules, (5) .... are there to protect players from serious harm. In the (6) .... way, it is essential to wear equipment like helmets in high-speed sports (7) .... keep your head safe.

Finally, remember that you need rest days (8) .... that your body can recover. And you should never, in any circumstances, carry on training when injured.

4 Complete the second sentence so that it has a similar meaning to the first sentence, using the word given. Do not change the word given. You must use between two and five words, including the word given.

1 The swimming pool will be closed tomorrow for cleaning.
ORDER
The swimming pool will be closed tomorrow .... can be cleaned.

2 Emilio spent his childhood in Milan and he still lives there.
GREW
Emilio, ... in Milan, still lives there.

3 Harry made up an excuse to avoid getting into trouble.
SO
Harry made up an excuse .... into trouble.

4 We began to collect the rubbish lying on the ground.
WAS
We began to pick .... lying on the ground.

5 Some people say they're ill so that they don't have to go to work.
IN
Some people say they're ill .... have to go to work.

6 At our local hospital there is a heart specialist called Dr Valentine.
WHOSE
At our local hospital there is a heart specialist .... Dr Valentine.

See the CD-ROM for more practice.

7 Green issues

LISTENING

Part 3 L Page 95

1 Match the words in box A with the words in box B to form expressions that describe environmental issues. Which of these are good for the environment, and which are harmful?

A

acid animal carbon climate global industrial melting oil renewable solar

B

change conservation emissions icecaps power rain resources spills warming waste

2 Which of these weather conditions are shown in the photos?

extreme rainfall freezing temperature frost hailstorm heatwave light breeze mild weather mist tornado tropical storm

1

2

3

4

3 Look at the exam task instructions and options A–H. What will the five people be talking about?

4 Underline the key words in each of options A–H. Note down some expressions with similar or opposite meanings to these words.

Example: *A injured – fractured, scratched, unhurt*

Quick steps to Listening Part 3

- Wait to hear everything the speaker has to say before you answer a question.
- Be careful if you hear words from an option, but with different grammar, e.g. a conditional.

5 Look at this sentence spoken by Speaker 1. Is F the correct option? Why? / Why not?

If there had been shelter around I would've used it, but there just wasn't any.

6 2.07 Now listen and do the exam task.

Exam task

You will hear five different people talking about extreme weather events that they have seen. For questions **1–5** choose from the list (**A–H**) what each speaker says about what happened. Use the letters only once. There are three extra letters which you do not need to use.

A I was injured while it was going on.

B I was glad I'd decided to go by train.

C I had to swim to reach safety.

D I stayed where I was all the time it was happening.

E I managed to help some people while it was going on.

F It was fortunate that I found a place to take shelter.

G It was more severe than in previous years.

H I wasn't sure what to do in the situation.

Speaker 1		**1**
Speaker 2		**2**
Speaker 3		**3**
Speaker 4		**4**
Speaker 5		**5**

Exam tip ›

Each time you choose an answer, cross it out lightly in pencil and then focus on the other options.

7 Have you chosen a letter for each of questions 1–5? Check your answers.

7 GRAMMAR

Review of conditionals 1–3

G *Page 108*

1 Look at these extracts from the recording in Listening. In each case, say which verb forms are used and answer the corresponding questions.

> a *If I have to travel next Christmas, I'll take the train.*
> b *If it happened again, I'd find somewhere safe much sooner.*
> c *If I'd stayed there I would've been in big trouble.*

a Will she definitely travel next Christmas? Is it likely or unlikely that she will take the train?
b Is it likely or unlikely to happen again? Will she probably need to find somewhere safe again?
c Did she stay there? Was she in big trouble?

2 Match the sentence halves.

1 If it doesn't rain soon,
2 If the river had risen any higher,
3 If the warm Atlantic current stopped,
4 Unless it stops snowing,
5 If the desert had a rainy season,

a the airport will be closed.
b Western Europe would get much colder.
c there won't be any water for the crops.
d it would be possible to live there.
e it might have flooded the city.

3 Correct the mistakes in these sentences written by exam candidates.

1 If I were you, I will try to have a rest.
2 If I had studied more, I would have write to you in Spanish.
3 If I would live near my work, I would prefer to go by bicycle.
4 If the climate keeps changing, we would have only two seasons.
5 Frankly, if I had a lot of money, I would have spend my entire life shopping.
6 If I would have known what was going to happen that night, I would never have gone there.

4 Use the given conditional form to complete the questions. Then work in pairs and ask your partner the questions.

1 If the weather .... (be) fine this weekend, where .... (you go)? (first conditional)
2 If the summers where you live .... (become) much hotter, what .... (you do)? (second conditional)
3 If .... (you be able) to control the weather, what .... (the seasons be) like? (second conditional)
4 What .... (you do) last week if bad weather .... (prevent) you going out? (third conditional)

Mixed conditionals

G *Page 109*

5 In these extracts from the recording in Listening, second and third conditional forms are mixed. Answer the questions.

> a *If it (the tornado) hadn't changed direction, I wouldn't be here now.*
> b *If I had a bigger car, I could have slept in it.*

1 Which part of a and b refers to the present or to a permanent situation? Which refers to the past?
2 In a, did the tornado change direction? Is the speaker still here?
3 In b, does she have a big car? Did she sleep in her car?

6 Use mixed conditionals to complete the second sentence so that it means the same as the first.

1 You're not cold now because you brought your coat.
You would be cold now if ....
2 I have to work this month, so I couldn't go skiing with my friends last week.
If I didn't have to work this month, I ....
3 Those drivers are stuck in the snow because they didn't check the weather forecast.
If those drivers had checked the weather forecast, they ....
4 We polluted the air for many years, so now the climate is changing.
The climate wouldn't be changing now if we ....
5 Your bill is so high because you wasted so much electricity.
If you hadn't wasted so much electricity, your bill ....
6 The summer heat in Italy didn't bother me because I'm from Australia.
The summer heat in Italy might have bothered me if ....

7 Work in pairs. Imagine these situations and tell your partner about them, using mixed conditionals.

1 You grew up in another country, with a different climate and way of life. How would your life be different now?
2 You're somebody of another nationality who lives in your country. What would you have had to get used to?

7 READING AND USE OF ENGLISH

Part 6

1 What do you do with possessions like mobile phones, computers, or iPods when you no longer need them? What do you think happens to things like these when people throw them out?

2 Look at the exam task instructions and read quickly through the text, ignoring sentences A–G for now. Which paragraphs mainly describe the problem, and which mainly describe possible solutions?

Quick steps to Reading and Use of English Part 6

- When you first skim through the main text, decide what each paragraph is about.
- Look for expressions that indicate examples, explanations, comparisons, and adding or ordering of points.

3 Look at sentences A–G. Reference words in A and a linking expression in B have been underlined. Underline similar words in sentences C–G.

Exam tip ›

Look for reference words such as *this* or *they* both in sentences A–G and in the main text.

4 Do the exam task, using the underlined words as clues. Look for similar words in the main text, as well as vocabulary linkers.

Exam task

You are going to read an article about the growing amount of waste created by electronic goods. Six sentences have been removed from the article. Choose from the sentences **A–G** the one which fits each gap (**1–6**). There is one extra sentence which you do not need to use.

The problem of electronic waste

Michael McCarthy

Modern electronic devices might look clean on the outside, but inside they contain a lot of materials used in manufacture which may be dangerous to human health. Most of these substances can be removed safely, but a lot of investment in waste-handling equipment is needed to do so. Many countries have refused to make the investment and instead taken the 'out of sight, out of mind' attitude, and simply shipped their e-waste abroad, usually to developing nations. **1** ____

The latest United Nations Environment Programme (UNEP) report estimates that, worldwide, electronic waste is increasing by about 40 million tons a year. Globally more than a billion mobile phones were sold last year, with most of them likely to be thrown away at the end of their lives. In many parts of Africa, telephone communications have skipped the landline stage and gone from no phones to mobile phones in one step. **2** ____ 'The issue is exploding,' says Ruediger Kuehr, of the United Nations University in Tokyo.

So what can we do about it? The first thing to do is recognise the problem. The electronics revolution of the past 30 years has seemed different in kind from the original industrial revolution, with its chimneys pouring out very obvious dirt. **3** ____ But we have gradually come to realise that in two ways in particular, modern hi-tech can be bad for the planet too.

The first is its energy use; the worldwide scale of information technology is so enormous that electronics now produce fully two per cent of global carbon emissions, which is about the same as the highly controversial emissions of aeroplanes. **4** ____ This, increasingly, is pretty short. We have hardly noticed this important stream of waste, so much so that a Greenpeace report on e-waste two years ago referred to it as 'the hidden flow'. We need to be aware of it.

The European Union has recognised the problem by adopting a key principle: producer responsibility. **5** ____ In practice, an EU regulation now means that electronics dealers must either take back the equipment they sold you, or help to finance a network of drop-off points, such as council recycling sites. Its main feature is quite ambitious: it aims to deal with 'everything with a plug'.

The new UN report suggests that all countries should start to establish proper e-waste management networks, which could both cut down on health problems and generate employment, reduce greenhouse gas emissions and recover a wide range of valuable substances from gold to copper. They could also do something about the problem with a change in design. Groups such as Greenpeace have led the way in putting pressure on major manufacturing companies to find substitutes for the toxic chemicals inside their products. **6** ____ This may be the real way forward.

- A Encouragingly, they have had some success in forcing them to develop non-poisonous alternatives to these.
- B In other words, making it the duty of manufacturers of electronic goods to ensure their safe disposal at the end of their lives.
- C Compared with that, it has seemed clean and green.
- D Much of this, such as the plastic covering on cables, is worth nothing at all.
- E There, instead of being properly processed, items are either dumped in unmanaged landfills or broken up in unofficial recycling facilities – often by children.
- F Add to that the vast amounts of e-waste that are still being imported from rich countries, and you have an enormous e-waste mountain in prospect, with its corresponding dangers for human health and the environment.
- G The other is the hardware, when it comes to the end of its natural life.

5 Read the complete text, including the sentences you have chosen for gaps 1–6. Does it all make sense? Make sure you have chosen one letter for every question. Then check your answers.

6 Match the expressions from the text or sentences A–G with the words and phrases on the right with similar meanings. The paragraph number (the same as the gap number) or sentence letter is in brackets to help you.

substances (1)	materials (1)
globally (2)	worldwide (2)
flow (4)	thrown away (2)
reduce (6)	stream (4)
forcing (A)	responsibility (5)
poisonous (A)	cut down on (6)
alternatives (A)	putting pressure on (6)
duty (B)	substitutes (6)
dumped (E)	toxic (6)
enormous (F)	vast (F)

7 Find words or phrases in the text that mean the following.

- a pieces of equipment (1)
- b tall, hollow structures that let smoke out of a building (3)
- c most recent and advanced equipment (3)
- d official rule that controls something (5)
- e using plastic, paper, etc. again (5)
- f create (6)
- g gas that traps heat in the atmosphere, e.g. carbon dioxide (6)
- h substances used in manufacturing (6)
- i getting rid of something (B)
- j dealt with (E)

7 SPEAKING

Comparative forms

G Page 109

1 Study these example sentences and complete the summary with the words given.

a *Mobile phone sales rose faster in June than in May, but less quickly than in April.*
b *The river isn't so dirty as in the 1990s, though the air is worse than it was then.*
c *This vehicle goes as fast as that one, and it uses fuel more efficiently than most.*

as less so than

When we make comparisons, we use (1) .... after the adjective or adverb. To say two things are the same we put (2) .... both before and after it. To say one thing is less than another we use *not as* or *not* (3) .... , or we can put (4) .... before the adjective or adverb.

2 Complete the second sentence so that it means the same as the first sentence.

1 In the first picture it's much windier than in the second one.
In the second picture it's
..much less windy than in the first one.. .
2 These people seem to be working harder than those.
Those people seem to be working ....
3 New kinds of pollution are no less harmful than old ones.
New kinds of pollution are just as ....
4 Big companies have more success dealing with the problem than smaller firms.
Smaller firms deal with the problem ....
5 Both these ideas for preventing accidents are sensible.
The first idea for preventing accidents is ....
6 Driving a car has a more negative effect on the environment than going by bus.
Going by bus doesn't affect the environment
....

Part 2

S Page 98

Quick steps to Speaking Part 2

- Compare the scenes by using adjectives and adverbs with *more/less ... than* and (*not*) *as/so ... as.*
- Speak at normal speed until the examiner tells you it's time to stop.

3 Look at photos 1 and 2 on page 101. Which of these features is in each photo?

factories gardens homes lake/river noise offices parks people pollution traffic

4 Look at the instructions for Exam tasks 1 and 2. What does each candidate have to do?

5 In pairs, do Exam tasks 1 and 2. Then change roles and repeat the task.

Exam tip ›

If you can't think of the word for something, explain it in English. Say, for example: *It's the place where ... .*

Exam task 1

Candidate A: Look at photographs 1 and 2 on page 101. They show two different towns. Compare the photographs, and say what you think could be good or bad about living there.
Candidate B: Which place would you prefer to live in?

Exam task 2

Candidate B: Look at photographs 3 and 4 on page 101. They show people who are concerned about the environment. Compare the photographs, and say why you think the people have chosen to take part in those activities.
Candidate A: Which of these activities do you think will do more to help the environment?

6 Did both of you do the two things you were asked to do during your long turn? Do you think you did them well? Why? / Why not?

7 READING AND USE OF ENGLISH

Phrases with *in*

1 Match the underlined phrases with meanings a–j.

1. In all, there were 20 volunteers working on the project.
2. Work is in progress on a new wind-power scheme.
3. I am in favour of banning cars from the town centre.
4. The results will be made known in due course.
5. In practice, the new regulations have done little to reduce waste.
6. When we decide what to do, we'll need to bear in mind the cost.
7. Rising sea levels will do damage in the long term.
8. Everyone should play a part in helping to conserve areas of natural beauty.
9. It's 9.15 and my appointment isn't until 10. In the meantime, I'll text my friends.
10. Spending cuts mean that the future of the park is now in doubt.

a the real situation is that
b over a period of time continuing far into the future
c at a suitable time in the future
d happening or being done now
e agree with an idea or plan
f be involved in
g uncertain
h in the time between two events
i the total number
j remember to consider something

2 Complete the text using phrases with *in* from Exercise 1.

A plan to set up a paper recycling scheme is (1) .... at our college, enabling everyone to (2) .... reducing the amount of paper thrown away. (3) .... , it means that special bins will be placed at various points in the school, and the paper collected will, (4) .... , be sent for recycling. The original plan was to have a bin outside every room, which would have meant over ninety (5) .... by the end of this term. That number, though, must now be (6) .... because of the cost, and there are unlikely to be that many until the end of next year. (7) .... , it will require just a short walk to the nearest collection point. Perhaps the move towards paperless offices will one day reach colleges like mine, so that (8) .... the bins may not be needed at all.

Part 4

3 Look at the exam task example. What kind of grammatical changes have been made? Which words get marks?

4 Look quickly at questions 1–6 and decide what main change you should make. Then do the exam task.

Quick steps to Reading and Use of English Part 4
- Decide whether you must change the grammar, the vocabulary, or both.
- Include all the information from the first sentence in your answer, without anything added.

Exam task

For questions **1–6**, complete the second sentence so that it has a similar meaning to the first sentence, using the word given. **Do not change the word given**. You must use between **two** and **five** words, including the word given. Here is an example (0):

Example:

0 My advice to you is to change your job.
IF
I'd change ....MY JOB IF I WERE....... you.

---

1 I didn't call because I forgot your phone number.
WOULD
I .... hadn't forgotten your phone number.

2 Carmen is a better driver than her boyfriend.
SO
Carmen's boyfriend doesn't .... she does.

3 Some people don't agree with the idea of building more power stations.
IN
Some people .... of building more power stations.

4 I missed the speech because my train was late.
ARRIVED
If my train hadn't been late, I .... time for the speech.

5 Burning rubbish is probably more harmful than burying it.
NOT
Burying rubbish is .... burning it.

6 These energy-saving measures don't work because we started them too late.
HAD
These energy-saving measures .... started them sooner.

5 Make sure your spelling and grammar are correct.

7 WRITING

Contrast links

G Page 109

1 Choose the correct option.

1. *Even though / Despite* it had stopped raining, the river was still rising.
2. These trees reach their full height quickly, *nevertheless, / whereas* those grow more slowly.
3. Coastal areas are becoming wetter. *In contrast, / While* the interior is getting drier every year.
4. *On the other hand, / Despite the fact that* it is a beautiful country, few people visit it.
5. *In contrast, / Despite* the strong wind, the ferry arrived on time.
6. On the one hand, cars are now designed to pollute less. *On the other hand, / Whereas* there are far more of them.

Part 1 essay

W Page 88

2 Look at the exam task instructions and answer these questions.

1. What is the situation?
2. Who will read your essay?
3. What is the topic?
4. Do you agree with the statement?

Exam task

Your English class has done a project on the subject of the environment. Now, your teacher has asked you to write an essay.

Write an essay using all the notes and give reasons for your point of view.

We are not doing enough to protect our world.

Notes

Write about:

1. the harm we are doing to the environment
2. what we are doing to save the environment
3. your own idea

Write your **essay** in **140–190** words. You must use grammatically correct sentences with accurate spelling and punctuation in an appropriate style.

Exam tip ›

Use a suitable expression such as *in my view …* to give your own opinion.

3 Read the model essay and answer these questions.

1. Is the answer about the right length, and in a suitable style?
2. Which paragraph contains the following?
   - a the writer's own opinion
   - b arguments against the statement
   - c a reference back to points already made
   - d a general comment on the topic
   - e arguments for the statement
3. Find examples of the following:
   - a contrast links
   - b addition links, e.g. *also*
   - c conditional forms
   - d comparative forms

Nowadays, everybody is talking about the need to save the planet. Despite this, the problems are getting worse all the time, so maybe we should do more than just talk about them if we really want to make a difference.

Firstly, we use more energy and create more waste than ever before. For instance, we drive to the supermarket to buy imported goods wrapped in plastic, and fly halfway round the world for our holidays. In addition, global warming is destroying rainforests, rivers and icecaps while we, in contrast, keep cool by using air conditioning.

On the other hand, we are now trying to lead a greener way of life. For example, we produce much of our energy from wind and solar power, we can take fast trains instead of planes, and people now recycle rubbish and unwanted household items.

Nevertheless, these measures alone are insufficient. I believe we should change our lifestyle completely, for instance by becoming vegetarian, buying far fewer manufactured products and travelling much less. And unless richer nations give up making constant economic growth their objective, our planet will in the long term face disaster.

4 Think about the following to get some ideas for your essay.

- environmental problems you have heard or read about
- what scientists are saying about the future of our planet
- what countries are doing to reduce the harm to the environment
- what ordinary people are doing to try to help

5 Look at the *Quick steps* and plan your essay. Remember to note down reasons and/or examples, plus some key vocabulary.

Quick steps to writing a Part 1 essay

- Decide how many paragraphs you will need and put your ideas under headings. Include one or two sentences about each of the notes you are given. In a short introductory paragraph, comment generally on the topic.
- Connect your points with contrast links such as *whereas*.
- Where possible, use your own words – not those in the notes.

6 Write your essay. When you have finished, check your work as in Unit 1 Writing Exercise 5 on page 14.

7 REVISION

1 Read the text below and think of the word which best fits each gap. Use only one word in each gap.

Shanghai seasons

The great Chinese city of Shanghai has a generally much warmer climate (1) .... the capital Beijing, which is much (2) .... north. If the summers are much hotter and (3) .... humid than visitors expect, this is hardly surprising given that Shanghai is next to the sea and it lies (4) .... far south (5) .... parts of Mexico, or the Sahara Desert in Africa. Spring and autumn, though, are (6) .... more pleasant, with warm temperatures and blue skies. Also, the violent thunderstorms that often occur in summer are, fortunately, much (7) .... common after September and before mid-June. Winter is perhaps not (8) .... warm (9) .... one might like, although it snows much (10) .... often than in the colder interior of the country.

2 Decide which word or phrase (A, B, C or D) best fits each gap.

1 Our train doesn't leave until 19.30. In .... , let's have a cup of coffee.
A the middle B the meantime C the end D the long run

2 In spring, the countryside here is quite green. .... , by July everything is dusty and dry.
A Even though B In contrast C While D Despite the fact that

3 We must use more .... resources such as wind, wave and solar power.
A recycled B renewable C rebuilt D replaced

4 In 1830, a terrible .... storm sank the pirates' ship near a Caribbean island.
A heat B extreme C tropical D tornado

5 Sarah has two dogs, three cats and a horse, so she has six pets in ....
A all B number C general D short

6 They still burn rubbish, ... they know it causes terrible pollution.
A even though B whereas C despite D on the other hand

7 Work on the new motorway is now in .... , in spite of protests by environmentalists.
A practice B fact C progress D advance

8 Please be patient. We will tell you the result of your test in ....
A the future B the short term C those days D due course

3 Make questions with the given conditional form of the verbs. Then answer the questions.

1 Where / you / go / next summer / if / be / very hot? (first conditional)
2 What / you / most / like / to see / if / you / go / to Antarctica? (second conditional)
3 If / it / snow / last month / you / go / ski / then? (third conditional)
4 What / happen / to the rainforests / if / we / not / protect / them? (first conditional)
5 If / you / not / have / any electronic items / you / miss / them? (second conditional)
6 Do you think / you / do / better / in your last exam / if / you / revise / more? (third conditional)
7 What / life / be / like / today / if / we / not / invent / the car? (mixed conditional)

4 Complete the second sentence so that it has a similar meaning to the first sentence, using the word given. Do not change the word given. You must use between two and five words, including the word given.

1 This river is rather less dirty than it used to be.
SO
This river isn't .... it used to be.

2 It's a good thing we ate before we set out or we'd be hungry by now.
EATEN
We'd be hungry by now .... before we set out.

3 Some scientists believe that the Arctic icecap will eventually melt completely.
TERM
Some scientists believe that .... the Arctic icecap will melt completely.

4 I got soaked because I forgot to take my umbrella with me.
REMEMBERED
If .... my umbrella with me, I wouldn't have got soaked.

5 In your situation, Neil, I'd move away from the coast.
YOU
I'd move away from the coast .... , Neil.

6 I couldn't have managed without their help.
THEY
I couldn't have managed .... me.

See the CD-ROM for more practice.

8 Sci & tech
READING AND USE OF ENGLISH

Communications vocabulary

1 Which of 1–6 show these forms of communication? Which of them are becoming more popular, and which less popular? Which do you use?

blogging	emailing	instant messaging
social networking	texting	video conferencing

1

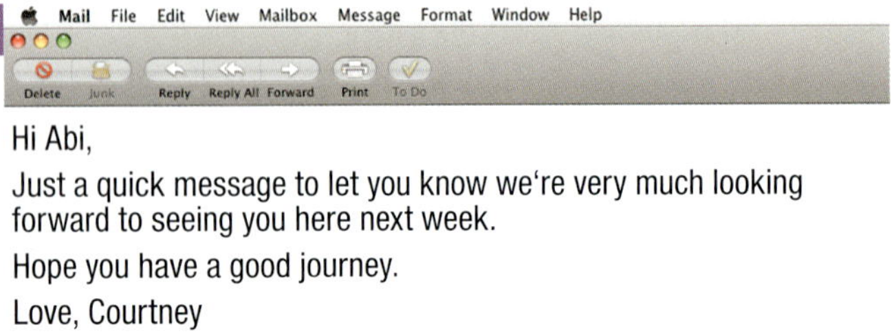

2

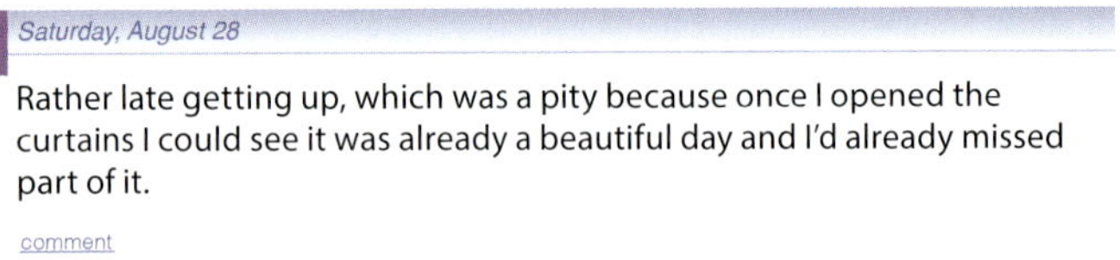

3

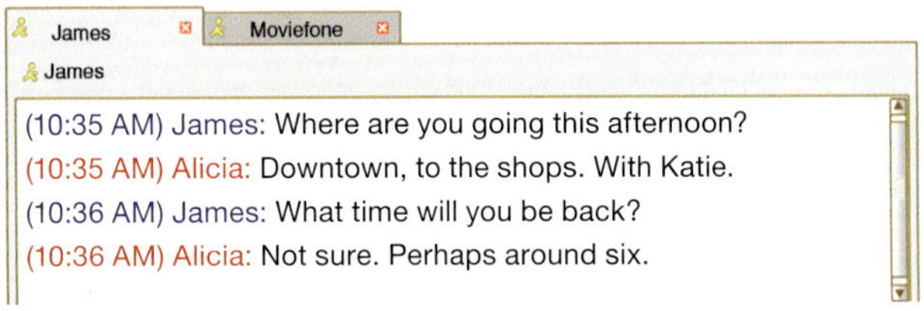

4

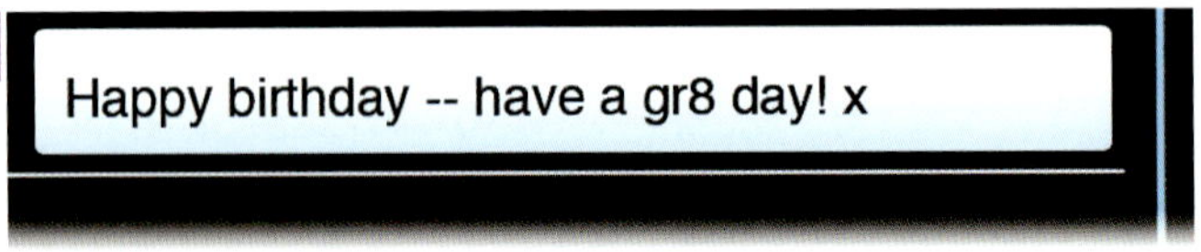

5

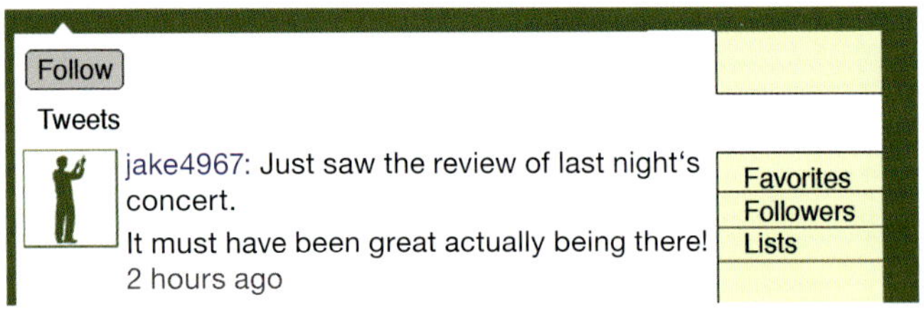

6

2 Compound nouns are formed from two words that function together as a noun, e.g. *backup*, *laptop*, *webcam*. Match the words in box A with the words in box B to form compound nouns. Which compound nouns do you associate with a computer, which with a mobile phone, and which with both?

A

book	broad	data	desk	hand	key	pass	ring
spread	web						

B

band	base	board	mark	set	sheet	site	tones
top	word						

3 What changes has the Internet made to people's lives? Do you think all of these changes have been positive? Why? / Why not?

Part 5

4 Quickly read the text. What is the writer's answer to the question in the title?

Quick steps to Reading and Use of English Part 5

- To answer a question about the meaning of a word or phrase, look for an explanation in the text, or for words with a similar or opposite meaning.
- For questions like *What does 'this' refer to?*, study everything before and after the reference word in that part of the text.
- If a question says the writer's purpose is to show something is true, look for an example.

5 Look quickly at the questions. Which focus on: a) the meaning of a particular phrase, b) a reference word, and c) an example?

6 Do the exam task on your own.

Exam tip ›

Use only the information in the text to choose your answers, not your own knowledge or opinions.

7 Make sure you have answered every question. For any you really aren't sure about, cross out options that are definitely wrong and choose from those that remain.

8 Discuss which of the writer's points you agree with, and which you don't. Say why.

Exam task

You are going to read part of an article about the Internet. For questions **1–6**, choose the answer (**A**, **B**, **C** or **D**) which you think fits best according to the text.

Has the Internet brought us together or driven us apart?

In recent years, the Internet has totally transformed the world. But as we welcome this new-found connectedness, asks Johann Hari, are we losing our culture?

The Internet has changed the way we think about ourselves – the groups we belong to, the information we know, even the people we date. The story of this century so far is the story of the World Wide Web.

It has transformed the way we interact with our friends. When I sent my first email, I was at university, and my main way of contacting my friends if their phone was off was to leave a written note – on a piece of paper! – on their door. When I told this to my 10-year-old nephew, he was astonished, as if I was describing how we had to hunt our own food and then cook it on an open fire built from damp branches.

The web also contains a huge amount of information, but there's a catch. We expect this information to be free – no matter what it costs to produce. This has virtually destroyed the newspaper and record industries, whose products are available online across the world for free. This is obviously good news for the consumer in the short term – but only while enough other people pick up the bill by buying the print copies and CDs. As their numbers decline, there will be a hole left. We will never know all the news stories that won't get written, or the songs that will never be recorded – and there will be many.

In the time I have been writing this article, I have received 36 emails, four texts, two phone calls, and seven instant messenger chat requests. We live in a state of 'permanent partial attention', where we are attempting to focus simultaneously on a whole range of things. But as human beings, we're not very good at it. We evolved to focus on one big task at a time. We can adjust to a degree: if you look at brain images of 'digital natives' – kids who were born in the Internet age – they look different to us 'digital migrants', who came to it as adults. They can focus on more varied distractions for longer. But we can only adjust so far.

There's another strange aspect to Internet communication: our manners haven't caught up. I find it much easier to get into arguments with people online than I ever would on the phone, or in person. It's partly because you can't hear their tone of voice: you can read unfriendliness where there is none. We write emails as casually as we make a phone call – but we read them with the seriousness with which we take a letter. Something written in a casual second can be reread and reread for hours.

As I was trying to think through all the complexities of the Internet, I had a thought. What if we logged on tomorrow and the Internet had vanished? Would we be relieved to be suddenly freed from the endless arrival of emails and updates? Would we find our concentration spans mysteriously widening again? Would we see the newspaper and record industries rise again, as people had to pay for their goods once more? Maybe. But I suspect we would feel oddly alone if the great global conversation with 3.2 billion other people – the conversation that has defined this century so far – went dead.

1 The writer mentions talking to his nephew to show how much
- A we have changed the way we do household tasks.
- B the Internet has changed human communication.
- C mobile phones have changed in the last ten years.
- D the importance of friendship has changed.

2 What is the writer's attitude to free online news and music?
- A The public will always continue to benefit from access to it.
- B It will mean higher prices for people who still buy newspapers and records.
- C It will eventually reduce the amount of both reporting and composing.
- D The only losers from it will be media organisations and record companies.

3 What does 'it' in line 29 refer to?
- A concentrating on different matters at the same time
- B behaving in the way a human being is expected to
- C giving all our attention to one subject for a short time
- D communicating with people in different ways

4 The writer uses the expression 'digital migrants' in lines 32–33 to mean people who
- A came from countries where Internet use was less common.
- B can adapt more easily to the nature of Internet communications.
- C think that children who use the Internet are not like them.
- D never had the opportunity in their childhood to go online.

5 Why, according to the writer, can an email anger people so easily?
- A The reader takes less care reading it than the writer has writing it.
- B People who send emails are often less polite than letter-writers.
- C It is more likely than a letter or phone call to be unfriendly.
- D The reader assumes the writer has given a lot of thought to it.

6 What point is the writer making in the final paragraph?
- A People are starting to wish the Internet had never been invented.
- B It is now impossible to undo any of the harm the Internet has caused.
- C People need the communication with others that the Internet provides.
- D One day we will have to learn to live in a world that has no Internet.

Science vocabulary

1 Test your knowledge of science by filling in the gaps with these words.

atom breakthrough carbon dioxide carbon monoxide cell discovery element energy experiments gas invention laboratories liquid living oxygen solid substances test tubes

SCIENCE QUIZ

1 Biology is the study of .... things.
2 Chemistry is the study of .... and how they react or combine with each other.
3 Physics is the study of matter and .... , and their effect on one another.
4 Oil is a .... , steam is a .... , and copper is a ....
5 People breathe in .... and breathe out .... Cars give off ....
6 Scientists working in .... often use glass .... to carry out ....
7 An .... is the smallest unit that an .... can be divided into, and a .... is the smallest unit of a plant or animal.
8 The .... of electricity, which led to the .... of the light bulb, was a huge .... in scientific knowledge.

2 2.08 Listen to check your answers to the quiz.

3 How important do you think it is for young people to be interested in science and technology? Why?

Part 2 L Page 95

Quick steps to Listening Part 2
- When the answer is a number, take care with other numbers you may hear that don't answer the question.
- After listening, make sure the completed sentences make sense, with no spelling or grammar mistakes.

4 It is easier to recognise numbers you hear if you are familiar with their pronunciation. How are these numbers pronounced?

31st 1989 (year) 463 3.55 12th 60% ⅓ 12,300 35° 22nd 2015 (year) ¾

5 Look at questions 1–10 in the exam task. Which focus on numbers? What kind of number is it in each case?

Exam tips›
- Use figures in your answers, for example *40* instead of *forty*.
- For each question, the speaker will say something that indicates the answer is coming soon.

6 2.09 Listen and do the exam task.

Exam task

You will hear a journalist reporting on a prize for young scientists and engineers. For questions **1–10**, complete the sentences.

Last year's winners of the National Science & Engineering Competition were both aged [**1**] .

The competition was first held in the year [**2**] .

The bicycle at the Big Bang Fair was used to produce [**3**] .

The main aim of the Fair is to create interest in [**4**] in certain branches of science and engineering.

About [**5**] of the people attending the Fair were young.

A total of [**6**] people took part in the competition.

One project involved using a fuel extracted from [**7**] to run a motor vehicle.

In the final of the competition, the judges listen to a fairly detailed [**8**] of each entry.

The judges assess the [**9**] of the team or individual, as well as their project.

The date of the announcement of this year's winners is [**10**] .

8 GRAMMAR

Review of passive forms

G Page 110

1 Underline the passive verbs in this extract from the recording in Listening and complete the rule below.

This is done in a wide range of ways, and a study into how this can be extended is currently being carried out by the Centre for Science Education.

The passive uses a form of the verb (1) .... followed by the (2) ....

2 Rewrite these sentences in the passive. Then match them with uses of the passive a–e.

1 Someone has broken the equipment.
2 Firstly, you heat up the liquid.
3 You must wear safety glasses in the laboratory.
4 A very young student won this year's Science Competition.
5 People say that Dr Liu is a brilliant scientist.

a describing a process
b when we don't know who did something
c what people in general believe, expect, etc.
d polite rules and requests
e if the object is more important than the subject

3 Which of these sentences written by exam candidates contain mistakes? Correct the mistakes.

1 Electric light has invented in the 19th century, I think.
2 The final decision is be made right now.
3 You will be ask some questions by the panel of judges.
4 The museum was closed because it was being painting
5 It is thought that cycling improves your health.
6 When I was a student at school, I used to be teaching science every day.
7 Democracy had born in my country many years before then.
8 Their hearing is said to have worsened considerably.

4 Replace the underlined active verbs with passive forms. Use *by* only where necessary.

When (1) you warm a meal up in a microwave oven, (2) the food absorbs radio waves and these are converted into heat. While (3) it is cooking the meal, only the food gets hot. So when (4) it has heated the food up, the dish, glass or plastic container will still be relatively cool, as (5) these materials will not have absorbed the radio waves. This means that (6) we can describe microwaving as quite an efficient use of electricity.

Although (7) we often think of the microwave as a fairly modern appliance, in fact (8) someone invented it back in 1945. The first microwaves were huge, nearly two metres high, but (9) restaurants were already using them in the 1950s. Within twenty years manufacturers were producing much smaller models, and by 1975 (10) they had sold over a million in the USA alone.

5 Which of these do you think is the most useful household appliance? Without saying which, use passive verbs to tell your partner about it and see if they can guess. Say where and when you think it was invented, how it is used, and how you think its job will be done in the future.

air conditioner   cooker   dishwasher   electric heater   electric iron
freezer   fridge   toaster   vacuum cleaner   washing machine

6 Use passive verbs to complete the second sentence so that it means the same as the first sentence. There's no need to use *by*.

1 We hope there will be an update soon.
It is hoped there will be an update soon .
2 Scientists believe there is water on that distant planet.
It ....
3 The public know those chemicals are dangerous.
Those chemicals ....
4 We think researchers have made a breakthrough.
Researchers ....
5 Nowadays, people consider it essential to have a mobile phone.
Nowadays, it ....
6 There are reports that doctors have found a cure.
It ....

7 Work in pairs. Think about recent news stories and tell your partner about three things that are said to have happened. Give more information, using *It is reported that* … .

8 SPEAKING

Articles

G Page 110

1 Complete the rules with *the, no article* and *a/an*.

1 We use .... with singular countable nouns mentioned for the first time, with people's jobs and some expressions with numbers.
2 We use .... when we mention something again or it is common knowledge, when there is only one of something, with superlatives, inventions, types of animal, musical instruments, and certain groups of people, e.g. *the young, the unemployed.*
3 We use .... when we talk in general and in the plural, with abstract nouns, or with sports, certain illnesses and some expressions following *to*, such as *work, bed* and *school.*

2 Correct the mistakes in these sentences written by exam candidates.

1 I have just recovered from a flu.
2 I think one of the most important inventions is telephone.
3 He was an officer in army.
4 I think cars are greatest danger of all.
5 There was 7.8 per cent increase in sales last year.
6 I enjoy riding more than playing piano.
7 I am engineer in Shanghai.
8 I must tell you: I've found the very interesting job.

3 2.10 Fill in the gaps with *a, an* or *the*, or leave the gap blank if no article can be used. Then listen to students Lena and Felix to check your answers.

Lena: I think (1) .... geology would be (2) .... most interesting science to study. It's (3) .... pity we don't do it at (4) .... school because I like (5) .... idea of becoming (6) .... geologist.

Felix: I think (7) .... one that appeals to me most is (8) .... zoology. It'd be fantastic to get (9) .... job in (10) .... countryside in (11) .... Africa studying (12) .... animals like (13) .... lion or leopard.

Part 4

S Page 100

Quick steps to Speaking Part 4
- Think of at least two points to make in reply to each of the examiner's questions.
- If you don't know any facts about the topic, give your opinion.
- Encourage the other candidate to say more. Ask questions like *What's your opinion?*

4 2.11 Listen to Lena and Felix practising Part 4. How many points do they each make? Then listen again. Which of these expressions do they use to add more points?

and also ...	apart from that, ...
and then there's ...	as well as that, ...
and what's more, ...	even better, ...
and not only that, ...	just as importantly, ...
and there's another thing, ...	worse still, ...

5 In pairs, ask and answer this Part 4 question: *Do/Did you enjoy studying science at school?* Add some of these points to your own ideas, and introduce them with expressions from Exercise 4.

harder than some other subjects	can lead to a good job
memorising facts and figures	developing thinking skills
not enough practical work	good science teachers
poorly equipped laboratories	interesting experiments
some lessons can be boring	learning practical skills

6 In groups of three, choose four of these questions and think of as many ideas as you can for each.

- How well is science taught at school in your country?
- Why are some students good at science, and others aren't?
- Which science subjects do/did you enjoy most at school, and which least? Why?
- Which other branches of science would you like to study? Why?
- What kinds of job in science sound interesting? Why?
- What is the most important scientific discovery of the last 20 years? Why?
- What breakthroughs would you like to see scientists make?
- How are scientists often shown in films and TV programmes? Is this fair?

7 Work as an 'examiner' and two 'candidates'. The examiner asks the candidates the questions chosen in Exercise 6. The candidates discuss the answers together as fully as they can. The examiner then comments on how well they have done.

Exam tip ›

Look at the examiner to answer his or her questions, but at your partner when you are talking together.

8 READING AND USE OF ENGLISH

Collocations

1 Match the verbs in box A with the nouns in box B to form collocations.

A

attach	browse	carry out	charge
prove	run	store	undo

B

a change (you have made)	a mobile phone
data (on a hard disk)	a program
an experiment	a theory
a file (to an email)	websites

2 Choose the correct word (A, B, C or D). Which word(s) in the sentence does each form a collocation with?

1 Zena's voice was very .... over the phone. I could hardly hear her.
A faint B pale C dull D faded

2 Close any .... like word processing before shutting down your computer.
A bookmarks B hardware C networks D applications

3 It's easy to .... the text on the screen, and then edit it.
A display B extend C present D spread

4 My PC .... and wouldn't start up at all.
A collapsed B crashed C scratched D folded

5 Thirteen .... seventeen is two hundred and twenty-one, I think.
A plus B for C times D from

6 The accident was caused by a .... of poor maintenance and human error.
A connection B composition C combination D conjunction

7 I've got a computer .... , so I'm going to run the anti-virus software.
A insect B worm C pest D bug

Part 1

Quick steps to Reading and Use of English Part 1

- Prepare by noting collocations, e.g. *scientific discovery*, in your vocabulary notebook.
- Look for collocations formed by words before or after the gap.

3 Think of uses for satellites. Then quickly read the text and check your answers.

Example: *helping ships navigate*

4 The example answer forms a collocation with *rocket*. Underline words that may collocate with gaps 1–8. Then do the exam task.

Exam tip ›

Writing in the example word can help you understand the text when you read it through.

Exam task

For questions **1–8**, read the text below and decide which answer (**A**, **B**, **C** or **D**) best fits each gap. There is an example at the beginning (**0**).

Example: 0 A fired **B** launched **C** flown **D** lifted

What on Earth would we do without satellites?

Since the first satellites were **(0)** ....B.... by rocket over 50 years ago, the number of communications satellites in space has increased enormously.

As part of **(1)** .... positioning systems they tell us where we are on the planet, and can help save lives by, for instance, directing the emergency **(2)** .... to the scene of an accident.

Satellites are essential for accurate weather forecasting, and also for space **(3)** .... Because they are above the Earth's atmosphere, right on the edge of **(4)** .... space, telescopes on satellites can see distant objects up to ten **(5)** .... more clearly than they could from the surface of the Earth.

We rely, too, on satellites to make **(6)** .... phone calls, and in some remote regions they make it possible for us to **(7)** .... the Internet. And of course many people watch TV programmes **(8)** .... from the other side of the world thanks to satellites, which enable us to watch hundreds of channels in a whole variety of languages.

	A	B	C	D
1	A global	B universal	C regional	D external
2	A brigades	B services	C agencies	D departments
3	A exploration	B appreciation	C examination	D investigation
4	A outer	B further	C broader	D fainter
5	A points	B times	C items	D numbers
6	A long-running	B long-range	C long-term	D long-distance
7	A connect	B link	C access	D log
8	A published	B browsed	C displayed	D broadcast

5 Read through the complete text, making sure that everything makes sense with the missing words added.

8 WRITING

Reason and result links

1 Complete the underlined expressions with these words. Which are quite formal?

account	because	consequently	owing	reason
result	since	therefore	view	why

1 As a .... of the extra tax, the price of electronic goods went up.
2 Ice occupies more space than water, and that is .... frozen pipes burst.
3 It would take years to reach even the nearest stars, ... to their huge distance from Earth.
4 Some programs may be running slowly on .... of a bug in the computer.
5 Metal is heavier than water. .... , if a ship fills with sea water it sinks.
6 Laptops are becoming very popular, and the .... is that you can take them anywhere.
7 .... the tunnel is so far underground, mobile phones don't work.
8 In .... of the fact that hot air is lighter than cold air, a hot-air balloon rises from the ground.
9 Sales of cameras are falling .... of the increasing use of phones to take photos.
10 Copper is a lot cheaper than gold and .... it is widely used for carrying electricity.

Part 2 article

W Page 91

2 Look at the exam task and answer these questions.

1 Who will read your article?
2 Why should you write it?
3 What two things do you have to do?

Exam task

You see this announcement in an international magazine.

> What is the most important piece of technology you have?
> Write us an article about it, saying why it is so important to you and how it could be improved. The writer of the best article will win a prize.

Write your **article** in **140–190** words.

3 Read the model article and answer these questions.

1 Is the style very formal or very informal – or somewhere in between? Give some examples.
2 Which paragraphs describe the good things? Which mention problems and suggest improvements?
3 How are readers encouraged to start and continue reading? What are they asked to think about at the end?

4 Find the following:

a reason or result links
b lively expressions
c passive verb forms

My laptop and me

I couldn't imagine a world without laptops. I use mine at home every day and it's also my main link to the outside world. And since it's so small it goes everywhere with me.

As an engineering student I need to do lots of research. As a result, I spend hours online searching for information, and later I key in my assignments. Although I stay in most evenings, I'm never lonely because of all the ways I can keep in touch with friends: email, instant messaging, Skype and Facebook. Without my lappy, my life would crash.

Wonderful though laptops are, technology moves on and that is why they could be even better. For instance, they can't always be connected to mains electricity, and for that reason more powerful batteries are needed.

Looking further ahead, perhaps one day we'll be interacting with our laptops just by thinking, rather than through a keyboard, touchpad or mouse. Then we could store our thoughts, analyse them or even send them to other people.

Quick steps to writing a Part 2 article

- Write in an entertaining way that will hold your readers' interest, using some lively expressions.
- Give reasons for your opinion, and possibly also examples.
- Use linking expressions, such as *on account of* and *in view of*.
- Get readers to think about what you have written by making the ending interesting.

5 Think about these questions to get some ideas for your article.

1 Which piece of technology do you know something about?
2 What will interest your readers about this topic?
3 Have you had any interesting experiences with this technology?
4 How might this technology change in the future?

Exam tip ›

Prepare for this task by reading articles in English in magazines or online.

6 Write your article. When you have finished, check your work as in Unit 1 Writing Exercise 5 on page 14.

8 REVISION

1 Complete the crossword with words from Unit 8.

Across

1 smallest living part of an animal or plant
3 extra copy of computer information
4 change back (something on a computer)
6 use a computer program
7 relating to the whole world
9 information stored in a computer
12 new information
14 look at information on the Internet
15 stop working suddenly (computer)

Down

1 put electricity into something
2 send into the sky
3 an online record of your thoughts
5 slight and difficult to see, hear or smell
8 '... space', i.e. beyond the Earth's atmosphere
10 see information using a computer
11 smallest possible unit of an element
13 show that something is true, e.g. a theory
14 problem in a computer program

2 Complete the sentences with these words to form collocations.

access   charge   exploration   outer   times   video

1 Spacecraft can fly over twenty .... faster than aeroplanes.
2 If I don't .... my mobile phone, the battery will be completely flat soon.
3 Scientists have discovered a planet in .... space that in some ways is like Earth.
4 It's usually impossible for aeroplane passengers to .... the Internet.
5 I'm abroad, but I can see and talk to my family in an Internet café by .... conferencing.
6 The first stage in space .... , over 40 years ago, was when Sputnik 1 went into space.

3 Fill in the gaps with *a/an* or *the*, or leave the gap blank if no article can be used.

Nowadays, I use **(1)** .... Internet for almost everything. I'm **(2)** .... student so I need it to do **(3)** .... homework, especially for science subjects like **(4)** .... biology. It's by far **(5)** .... quickest way to find **(6)** .... information I need, for instance if I have to write **(7)** .... essay about **(8)** .... particular kind of creature such as **(9)** .... salt-water crocodile. In fact, I probably use it **(10)** .... hundred times every week to look up things ranging from who invented **(11)** .... telephone and what **(12)** .... capital of **(13)** .... Canada is, to what's **(14)** .... best way to avoid catching **(15)** .... flu and how to learn to play **(16)** .... guitar, or **(17)** .... table-tennis. I really missed it when I went on **(18)** .... holiday last summer, so I'm going to buy **(19)** .... laptop and take it with me to **(20)** .... seaside this year.

4 Complete the second sentence so that it has a similar meaning to the first sentence, using the word given. Do not change the word given. You must use between two and five words, including the word given.

1 It's possible that nobody warned them of the danger.
MIGHT
They .... warned of the danger.

2 People expect there will be a sudden fall in prices next year.
EXPECTED
Prices .... next year.

3 Now they even suggest there could be life on Mars.
IT
Now .... there really could be life on Mars.

4 Experts believe that carelessness caused the accident.
BELIEVED
It .... the cause of the accident.

5 Many people say that Charles Babbage invented the computer.
BEEN
Charles Babbage .... the inventor of the computer.

6 They are making constant changes to the rules to prevent another accident.
CHANGED
The rules .... to prevent another accident.

See the CD-ROM for more practice.

9 Fame and the media
LISTENING

Media vocabulary

1 Which of these words and phrases do you associate with television and radio? Which do you associate with newspapers and magazines? And which two expressions are used in both?

broadcasting	circulation	commercials	episode
gossip column	illustrations	network	news items
print version	publication	remote control	
satellite dish	tabloids	the headlines	the press

2 How many kinds of TV programme can you name? Which of these do you often watch? Which do you never watch? Why?

***Examples**: chat shows, reality TV shows*

3 What do these TV people do? Which job would you most like to do? Why?

camera operator	editor	interviewer
investigative journalist	newsreader	news reporter
presenter	producer	scriptwriter	set designer

Part 4

L Page 96

4 Look at the exam task instructions. Answer the questions.

1 What kind of extract will you hear?
2 Who will you hear?
3 What is the likely topic?

5 2.12 Look at the stem of questions 1–7 and for each one note down the kind of information you need to listen for, e.g. opinion, activity. Then listen and do the exam task.

Quick steps to Listening Part 4
- Study the instructions, and think about who and what you will hear.
- Quickly read the stem of each question, and decide what kind of information you will need to listen for.

Exam task

You will hear part of a radio interview with Kirsty Ross, who works as a television presenter. For questions **1–7**, choose the best answer (**A**, **B** or **C**).

1 Before Kirsty became a television presenter, she was
A an actor.
B a university student.
C a musician.

2 How did Kirsty learn about presenting before she first applied for work as a presenter?
A She went on a training course for presenters.
B She spent a lot of time watching presenters on TV.
C She did an unpaid job for a television company.

3 What does Kirsty believe is her best skill?
A interviewing people
B speaking directly to the camera
C interacting with an audience

4 Kirsty delivered the film of herself to the company
A by hand.
B by email.
C by post.

5 How did Kirsty feel when the company invited her to do a test?
A She lost her self-confidence.
B She became rather nervous.
C She was extremely pleased.

6 What did Kirsty find most difficult to learn to do?
A always remember everything in the script
B look into the right camera all the time
C know exactly what the producer wanted her to do

7 What, according to Kirsty, is the most important quality a presenter should have?
A the capacity to remain calm under pressure
B the ability to do their own research
C a willingness to work as part of a team

6 Make sure you have answered every question. Then check your answers.

Review of reported speech and reporting verbs

G Page 111

1 2.12 Rewrite these sentences in the actual words used in the recording in Listening. Then listen again to check your answers.

a He said he had a guest whose voice would be familiar.
b She said that sitting there being asked all those questions was making her nervous.
c She said it had happened recently, and that the week before her guest had suddenly walked out.

2 Look at the verbs in the sentences in Exercise 1. How do these tenses change in reported speech?

present simple	*will* future	present continuous
present perfect	past simple	

3 How have these words changed in the reported speech in Exercise 1? Think of other words that change in the same ways.

I here these me last week my

4 Change the sentences to reported speech. In which sentence does the tense stay the same?

1 'I don't want to watch this programme now,' said Jaime.
2 'I'm going out when my boyfriend gets here,' Louise told me over the phone.
3 'I saw the match at my friend's house last night,' Joey said on Monday.
4 'Later this evening I'll be talking to my favourite TV star,' my sister said.
5 'I'd been working in entertainment ever since I left school,' Anna told the presenter.
6 'I've always wanted to be on TV, and tomorrow I will be,' said Julia.

5 Change these questions from the recording in Listening into reported speech. Then answer the questions.

a *Did you do that?*
b *How did they respond?*

a The interviewer asked Julia ....
b He asked her ....

How do we form reported questions? What do we add to reported *yes/no* questions? Check your answers in the Grammar reference on page 111.

6 Complete the sentences with these reporting verbs.

admit apologise offer suggest tell

1 Paul ...offered... to lend me his copy of the DVD.
2 Leena .... that we should watch TV.
3 A police officer .... the man not to move.
4 I .... for losing the TV remote control.
5 Two youths .... stealing the satellite dish.

7 Put the reporting verbs from Exercise 6 into the correct group, a, b, c, d or e. Some verbs can go into more than one group. Then do the same with these verbs.

advise decide deny explain insist invite order persuade promise recommend refuse remind threaten warn

Verbs followed by
a *to*: ...offer...
b object + *to go*: ....
c *-ing*: ....
d (*that*) + clause: ....
e preposition + *-ing*: ....

8 Complete the second sentence so that it has a similar meaning to the first sentence, using the word given. Do not change the word given. You must use between two and five words, including the word given.

1 'I won't listen to you ever again,' my sister said to me.
REFUSED
My sister .... ever again.

2 'Don't forget to bring your pens,' the teacher said to us.
REMINDED
The teacher .... pens.

3 'Would you like to meet my parents, Jo?' said Rosa.
INVITED
Rosa .... parents.

4 'I've done nothing wrong,' the man said when he was arrested.
DENIED
The man .... when he was arrested.

5 'I don't think you should go there on your own,' Abigail's mother said.
AGAINST
Abigail's mother .... there on her own.

6 'Let's go this way home,' said Jay as we left the club.
SUGGESTED
Jay .... home as we left the club.

9 READING AND USE OF ENGLISH

Part 7

1 Discuss these questions.

1 Who are currently the biggest celebrities in your country?
2 What is your opinion of them?
3 What do you think are the advantages and disadvantages of being famous?
4 Would you like to be a celebrity? Why? / Why not?

2 Read the exam task instructions, and look at the title and layout of the text. Answer these questions.

1 What is the topic?
2 How many people are there?
3 Who are they?

Quick steps to Reading and Use of English Part 7

- Look for the parts of the text that express the same idea as the questions, not the same words.
- As you go through the questions, cross out those you have already answered so that you don't keep looking at all of them.

3 Underline the key words in questions 1–10. Then do the exam task, looking for parts of the text that express the same ideas as those words.

4 Make sure you have answered all the questions, and that any alterations you have made are clear. Remember that in the exam you will need to rub out any answers you want to change.

Exam task

You are going to read a magazine article about four people who have become famous in their country. For questions **1–10**, choose from the people (**A–D**). The people may be chosen more than once.

Which person

sometimes finds that being a celebrity can be expensive?	**1**	
regrets becoming famous?	**2**	
suggests the media can be too aggressive with celebrities?	**3**	
at first found it hard to accept they should set an example for young people?	**4**	
is pleased that their experience enables them to advise other people?	**5**	
says that most people would enjoy being celebrities?	**6**	
believes it is impossible for celebrities to keep anything secret from the media?	**7**	
accuses some celebrities of thinking they are more important than other people?	**8**	
says that some famous people are suspicious of other celebrities?	**9**	
wishes they hadn't said some things in public?	**10**	

A **Jake Mackenzie** hit the headlines as a teenager when he disappeared while sailing a small boat in the Pacific. He was eventually found safe and well, and instant fame followed. He became a regular guest on TV chat shows and his agent sold the film rights to his story for a considerable sum. 'It'd always been my dream to be famous,' said Jake, 'though I never imagined it'd happen this way.' Whatever the reason for it, he's certainly enjoying it: 'I'm meeting some big stars, and I'm doing worthwhile things, too. Such as giving survival tips on TV, which one day might help someone in the situation I was in.' The only disadvantage, he says, is when he's in hotels or taxis: 'I have to leave extra-large tips in case they recognise me. If not, the next thing I know is that some tabloid will be calling me "mean", or worse.'

B Soap actor **Rachita Patel** began her career in theatre. 'Becoming quite well known happened gradually as the series grew in popularity, and I must admit I'd miss being in the public eye if it all suddenly came to an end. I've made good friends on this show, though one or two of those I work with clearly believe they're in a world where nobody can be trusted, that everyone's talking behind their back. Maybe it's understandable if they've been given a bad time by the press, with reporters pushing cameras and microphones in their face and shouting really nasty personal questions at them. But they're big stars, and I'm happy as I am. People sometimes recognise me and if they do they might smile, but other times nobody gives me a second glance, and that suits me fine, too.'

C Winning that gold medal,' says ice-skater **Elka Kaminski**, 'changed my life. Being invited onto TV shows and interviewed by the press was a dream come true, though back then I was totally inexperienced and I now regret one or two of the comments I made to them. I've met a lot of big stars and actually most of them are quite pleasant people, though there are one or two who show off and look down on everyone else. Funnily enough, they tend to be the ones who've achieved nothing in particular, they're just "famous for being famous". I'd like to think my success in skating might inspire other kids from poor backgrounds like mine, though I was initially uncomfortable with the idea of being a role model. But in the end I got used to the idea and I quite like it now.'

D Singer **Marcos Carvalho** still enjoys performing, though he's convinced he should have remained an unknown in a small town. 'It's a pity I didn't realise sooner that I'm not the sort of person who's comfortable with publicity. I mean, the press will always find out every personal detail about you. I know they're only doing their job, but the reality is there's no privacy at all. Having said that, I wouldn't want to put anyone off the idea of making a name for themselves, because I'm sure for the vast majority it'd be tremendously exciting. It also usually means not having to worry about where your next pay cheque is coming from any more.'

Exam tip ›

Be careful with questions that say the same as the text, but are about a different person, e.g. about a friend or relative of one of A–D.

5 Rewrite the following from the text in reported speech.

1. 'I never imagined it'd happen this way.'
   Jake said he'd never imagined it would happen that way.
2. 'I'm meeting some big stars, and I'm doing worthwhile things, too.'
3. 'I have to leave extra-large tips in case they recognise me.'
4. 'I've made good friends on this show.'
5. 'I'm happy as I am.'
6. 'Winning that gold medal changed my life.'
7. 'It's a pity I didn't realise sooner.'
8. 'The press will always find out every personal detail.'

6 Find words or phrases in the text that mean the following:

1. person invited to appear on a TV or radio programme (A)
2. person whose job is to deal with business for someone else (A)
3. legal permission to make a film of a book (A)
4. being written and talked about in the media (B)
5. devices used to record a voice, or make it louder (B)
6. try to make people admire them, in an annoying way (C)
7. think that someone is less important than them (C)
8. make people feel they want to do something and can do it (C)
9. person who others admire and try to copy (C)
10. information about someone or something in the media (D)
11. right to do things without other people seeing or hearing (D)
12. becoming well known by doing something special (D)

7 Would you like to be famous for any of the things that A–D have done? Say why or why not.

Keeping going

1 2.13 Listen to student Maruja comparing photos A and B and saying how the people might feel. Which of points 1–8 does she mention?

A

B

1 what's happening
2 where it's happening
3 how the people feel
4 why they feel like that
5 their ages
6 their clothes
7 their hairstyles
8 people in the background

2 2.13 Listen again. Which expressions does Maruja use to add points?

3 Work in groups. Look at photos C and D, and note down as many similarities and differences as you can.

C

D

4 Work in pairs. Take it in turns to discuss photos C and D. Compare the photos and say how the people might feel. When your partner has finished, tell them how long they were speaking.

Part 2

S Page 98

5 Look at the instructions for Exam tasks 1 and 2. What does each candidate have to do? Make a list of points you can include when you speak.

6 In pairs, do the exam tasks. Add as many points as you can to make sure you keep talking for a full minute.

Quick steps to Speaking Part 2

- At home, practise speaking for a minute about pairs of photos, for example in a magazine or on the Internet. Time yourself, or ask a friend to!
- Don't talk for less than a minute. You can't get good marks if you don't say enough.
- Remember that in the exam you will see the question written above the pictures.

Exam tip ›

Imagine you are describing the pictures to somebody who can't see them.

Exam task 1

Candidate A: Look at photographs 1 and 2 on page 102. They show television programmes. Compare the photographs, and say what you think people find interesting about each type of programme.
Candidate B: Which of these kinds of programme would you prefer to watch?

Exam task 2

Candidate B: Look at photographs 3 and 4 on page 102. They show media people and celebrities. Compare the photographs, and say which situation you think celebrities may like or dislike more.
Candidate A: Would you like to work as a reporter or a press photographer?

7 Change roles and repeat Exam tasks 1 and 2.

8 Did you both talk for a full minute? Discuss this with your partner.

9 READING AND USE OF ENGLISH

Noun suffixes

1 Look at the underlined nouns in these extracts from the recording in Speaking. Answer these questions.

1 What verb is the noun formed from?
2 What suffix does each noun have?
3 Are there any other spelling changes?

a Their appearance is different.
b The woman gives an explanation of what happened.
c That interview is for entertainment.
d She has a sad expression on her face.
e Another difference is that the TV presenter has some notes.

2 Form nouns from these verbs and write them in groups a–e. Which require extra spelling changes?

arrange contribute disappear exist expect identify intend introduce maintain prefer recommend require vary

3 Use suffixes to correct the mistakes in these sentences written by exam candidates.

1 My father did not believe my explication.
2 I saw your advertise in yesterday's *TV Gazette*.
3 I hope you will find my suggests useful.
4 This TV set meets my requires, such as a big screen.
5 As a student I was hoping to get a reduce in the price.
6 I believe that this problem has many possible solves.

Part 3

4 Complete the sentences with these nouns. Say which verb or adjective each noun is formed from.

choice depth ~~heat~~ height proof

1 With all the studio lights on, the ......heat...... makes air conditioning necessary. (adjective: ......hot......)
2 Viewers have a .... between satellite television and cable TV. (verb: ....)
3 A TV crew used a helicopter to film from a .... of 100 metres. (adjective: ....)
4 The media have accused ministers of lying, but there is no .... that they did. (verb: ....)
5 A nature programme filmed fish at a .... of 6,000 metres. (adjective: ....)

Quick steps to Reading and Use of English Part 3
- Note words with prefixes and/or suffixes you see when you are reading in English.
- When you look up a new word, note any prefixes and/or suffixes you can add and how these affect its meaning.

5 Quickly read the text. Decide how the writer answers the question in the title. Then do the exam task.

Exam tip ›
Look out for internal spelling changes when forming a word, e.g. *long – length*.

Exam task

For questions **1–8**, read the text below. Use the word given in capitals at the end of some of the lines to form a word that fits in the gap **in the same line**. There is an example at the beginning (**0**).

Example: 0 GROWTH

Has TV viewing reached its peak?

For over half a century, the **(0)** .... in television audiences continued steadily. Now, though, following **(1)** .... of a report into the nation's viewing habits, a TV marketing **(2)** .... claims this may no longer be the case. — **GROW**, **PUBLISH**, **ORGANISE**

The report found that last year the average **(3)** .... of time spent watching live TV was four hours and two minutes a day, including an average of 46 **(4)** .... , and although these figures were up on the previous year, the authors of the report believe the rate of increase is now slowing. — **LONG**, **ADVERTISE**

They point to a **(5)** .... of factors, including the economic crisis, to explain the rise in the number of TV **(6)** .... since last year, and insist that the long-term trend is downwards. — **VARIOUS**, **VIEW**

This report, however, ignores the increasingly wide **(7)** .... that people now have in the ways they can watch TV, ranging from home computers to mobile phones, and it is my **(8)** .... that total viewing figures will keep going up. — **CHOOSE**, **BELIEVE**

6 When you have finished, make sure the text makes sense and that you have made all the necessary changes to the words.

9 WRITING

Part 2 report

W Page 92

1 Complete the underlined expressions with these words and phrases.

carried out   challenge   conclusion
purpose   recommendation   step   sum

1 This report makes the .... that work should start on a new theatre immediately.
2 In .... , I believe that this town definitely needs an improved bus service.
3 The next .... will be to ask residents what their preference would be.
4 To .... up, it is clear that there are more advantages than disadvantages.
5 A key .... is the limited amount of money available for this project.
6 A survey was .... which showed that most people approved of the plan.
7 The .... of this report is to describe the measures being taken to reduce pollution.

2 Look at the exam task and answer these questions.

1 Who is your report for?
2 Why do you need to write it?
3 What information should you give?
4 What question do you have to answer?

Exam task

A group of English-speaking people are planning to visit your town next winter. You have been asked to write a report about the television and radio there, and say which kinds of programme you think the group might enjoy watching and listening to.

Write your **report** in **140–190** words.

3 Read the model report and answer these questions.

1 How many paragraphs does the writer use?
2 Do the title and the headings tell the reader what to expect?
3 Is the report written in a formal, a neutral or an informal style?
4 What recommendation(s) does the writer make?
5 Find examples of the following:
   a expressions similar to those in Exercise 1
   b linking expressions
   c reported speech

The media for visitors

Introduction
The aim of this report is to inform visitors about the media here, and to suggest which types of programme may appeal to them.

What's on television
There are five national channels, all of which show a huge variety of programmes ranging from sports and soaps to quiz shows and chat shows. In addition, channels such as CNN and the BBC are available in buildings with a satellite dish.

What's on the radio
There is a wide range of radio stations, both national and local, offering music, drama, comedies, sports commentaries, news bulletins and weather forecasts. There is also a station for tourists, broadcasting in three languages.

Programmes of interest
Many tourists have said they were able to enjoy the sports, nature and arts programmes on TV, while most films and drama series are in English with subtitles. Radio, too, has a lot to offer, and I strongly recommend the wonderful 24-hour music stations.

Conclusion
To sum up, there is plenty to enjoy on TV and radio here, even if you do not understand our language. And listening to it is an excellent way to learn it.

Quick steps to writing a Part 2 report
- Decide what the readers of your report will want to know.
- Make notes on any facts you know about the subject and any personal experience you may have.
- Think of a good title that tells readers about the content.
- Plan your report, including recommendations and suggestions at or near the end.
- In your first paragraph, say what the aim of your report is.
- Write in an appropriate style for your readers.

4 Get ideas for your report by thinking about these questions.

1 What do you know about your national and local TV and radio?
2 Which programmes do you like watching and listening to?
3 Which kinds of programme might your visitors enjoy? Why?
4 What would be a good title for your report?
5 Which of the expressions in Exercise 1 will you use?

Exam tip
Use paragraph headings if you think they will make your report clearer.

5 Write your report. When you have finished, check your work as in Unit 1 Writing Exercise 5 on page 14.

9 REVISION

1 Match the words in box A with the words in box B. Complete the sentences with six of the compound nouns.

A

camera current drama gossipt investigative remote satellite set soap talent

B

affairs column control designer dish journalist opera operator series show

1 Hana deserved to win the .... because she was by far the best singer.
2 We can pick up more TV channels now that we have a .... on the roof.
3 I never read the .... in the paper as I'm not interested in celebrities' lives.
4 A suspicious .... found out that the politician had been telling lies.
5 They've started showing an excellent .... set in the 19th century on TV.
6 The .... took a close-up shot of the champion as the interview began.

2 Read the extract from a soap opera script. Then complete the reported speech version.

Lyn: You look fed up, Joe.
Joe: Yes, I am.
Lyn: What's wrong?
Joe: I lost my job yesterday.
Lyn: Have you told your parents?
Joe: I can't.
Lyn: Why not?
Joe: My dad's in prison.
Lyn: Where's your mum?
Joe: She disappeared last week.
Lyn: What will you do?
Joe: I don't know. I'm thinking about it.

Lyn told Joe that (1) .... fed up, and he said (2) .... When she asked him what (3) .... , he explained (4) .... day. Lyn then asked him (5) .... parents, but Joe replied that (6) .... When Lyn asked him why not, he told (7) .... , so she asked him where (8) .... but he said (9) .... before. Finally she asked (10) .... , to which he replied (11) .... , though he added (12) .... about it.

3 Complete the second sentence so that it has a similar meaning to the first sentence, using the word given. Do not change the word given. You must use between two and five words, including the word given.

1 'I'll talk to my producer about it,' said Carol.
PROMISED
Carol .... producer about it.

2 'Don't touch this cable,' the electrician told us.
WARNED
The electrician .... that cable.

3 'What's the depth of the river?' the reporter asked.
DEEP
The reporter wanted to know ....

4 'I'm sorry I interrupted your TV programme,' my brother said.
APOLOGISED
My brother .... TV programme.

5 'Do you know who I am?' a celebrity said to her, but she ignored him.
ASKED
A celebrity .... who he was, but she ignored him.

6 'Put your hands where I can see them,' Taylor said to the suspects.
HE
Taylor told the suspects to put .... see them.

4 Read the text below. Use the word given in capitals at the end of some of the lines to form a word that fits in the gap in the same line.

THE ROLE OF NEWSPAPERS

The most obvious role of newspapers is to inform, by providing (1) .... with a	READ
wide range of facts and figures supported by photos, charts and (2) .... They also	ILLUSTRATE
aim to educate, by going into news stories in far greater (3) .... than is possible on television.	DEEP
A good newspaper also provides (4)	ENTERTAIN
in the forms, for example, of political cartoons, crossword puzzles and (5) .... columns,	HUMOUR
as well as making (6) .... on its review pages for what to read, watch and listen to.	RECOMMEND
Some say the press has become too (7) .... in present-day society, but	POWER
newspaper (8) .... reply that politicians have always said that, and that it is no more true today than it was a hundred years ago.	EDIT

See the CD-ROM for more practice.

10 Clothing and shopping
READING AND USE OF ENGLISH

Clothing and shopping vocabulary

1 Find pairs of adjectives with opposite meanings used to describe clothes.

***Example**: bright – dark*

~~bright~~	casual	clashing	cool	~~dark~~	formal	loose	matching
patterned	plain	simple	smart	sophisticated	tight		
unfashionable	untidy						

2 Which of the adjectives in Exercise 1 form adverbs that can be used with *dressed* in phrases such as *smartly dressed* or *a smartly dressed woman*?

3 Describe the people and clothes in the photos.

4 Make sure you understand the words in *italics*. Then discuss these questions.

1 Which celebrities do you think wear the most *stylish outfits*?
2 How far do you think people's clothes *reflect* their personalities?
3 Do you prefer comfortable *items of clothing*, or fashionable ones?
4 How important to you is it that clothes have *designer labels*?
5 What styles and colours of clothes *suit* you best?
6 What do you like to buy in the *sales*?

5 For each sentence, explain the difference between the expressions in *italics*. Some are opposites, others are not.

1 Size 38 is currently *out of stock*, but I think we have a size 40 *in stock*.
2 If it's *a bargain* I'll buy it, but if it's *poor value for money* I won't.
3 No, I don't want to *exchange* the item. Please give me *a refund*.
4 A week after their new style of shirt was *launched*, it was *sold out*.
5 Unfortunately, this country *imports* more clothes than it *exports*.
6 Our online store sells *false* eyelashes made from *genuine* hair.
7 *Budget* airlines offering cheap fares have made traditional airlines *uncompetitive*.
8 *Consumers* need to be careful if they buy from *dealers* in second-hand goods.
9 The new line in jeans was so popular that *shopkeepers* soon ran out and asked their *suppliers* for more.
10 Customers are making fewer clothes *purchases*, so the store must increase *sales* of other items.

6 What kinds of job are there in the fashion industry? Which would you like to do? Why?

Part 6

Quick steps to Reading and Use of English Part 6
- Look for ideas, opinions or events that develop through the main text.
- Look for language clues before you decide on each answer.

7 Quickly read the exam task instructions and the main text. In which order does the writer mention these aspects of the work?

a negative aspects of the job
b pay and career development
c the kind of person suited to the job
d how to do well in the industry
e positive aspects of the job
f what the job consists of

8 Underline the words and phrases in A–G that may provide clues.

***Example: A** them, one*

9 Do the exam task, using the words you underlined to help you.

Exam tip ›

Don't choose an option just because it contains the same word, number or name as a particular paragraph.

10 Make sure that the completed text makes sense, and that you've chosen a letter for all the answers.

Exam task

You are going to read an article about a woman who works for a department store. Six sentences have been removed from the article. Choose from the sentences **A–G** the one which fits each gap (**1–6**). There is one extra sentence which you do not need to use.

My job: fashion buyer

Lindsey Friedman, 27, is a product development manager at a major department store in the capital. She is in charge of buying men's branded casualwear.

What do I actually do? Well, I work with clothing suppliers to select and build the perfect range of clothes for our target customer. **1** ___ Much of the job involves building relationships with our suppliers, negotiating prices and making sure that deliveries of new stock arrive on time. I also work with department managers and a marketing team within the store to build my vision.

The most satisfying thing for me about the job has been building my department into a credible fashion destination, as people often think of a department store as just a place to buy their cushions. **2** ___ When you've spent months planning a new collection, seeing it launched is so exciting. It's amazing when we take a gamble and include an unconventional look and it quickly takes off and sells really well.

On the other hand, it's my job to stay on top of the trends and create newness, so if I want to try out a new brand I have to drop an existing one, even if we've always had a long working relationship. **3** ___ The other side of the coin is that we're playing catch-up in fashion terms, and sometimes we get rejected too. There are cool brands of clothing that we'd like to sell that don't want to have too many accounts, so they won't let us stock them, unfortunately.

People sometimes ask me what skills you need to be a successful buyer, and I reply that any type of fashion degree is a good way to start – mine was in textiles and clothing management. **4** ___ Obviously, you need to be really enthusiastic and motivated. You also have to be strategic, analytical and very well-organised, and you need to have a creative vision of what the perfect collection should look like. And you have to be good with figures, too, because you need to balance your budget.

The advice I would give to someone starting out in buying is to join an executive training programme. **5** ___ For instance, you can go from being a buyer's administrative assistant to an assistant buyer to a junior buyer in just a few years. You also need to stay on top of the fashion industry and keep reading fashion magazines. Learn as much as you can about the product you are buying, and think carefully about the target customer you are selling to.

In general, the salaries are competitive and the career path is quite well defined. At the lower end, a buyer's administrative assistant might earn a little over the average national wage, but an experienced buyer might earn more than double that. You can move into the supply side, or work your way up to become a buying manager for a department store. **6** ___ Most of them, sadly, fail in their first year.

A Many department stores run them, and if you can get a place on one it will move you up the ladder very quickly.

B But whether or not you're a graduate in something like that the main thing is to get retail experience by working on the shop floor.

C This has led to an overall drop in sales, a trend that isn't likely to be reversed for quite a while.

D This means I need to find the right balance between choosing some unusual, on-trend fashion pieces, as well as other clothes, such as classic white T-shirts, which I know will sell really well.

E That can be unpleasant, but you have to take the emotion out of it and remember that it's business.

F Of course, not everyone can or wants to be promoted in that way, and lots of people dream of opening boutiques, but it's very risky.

G Consequently, we've had to shout about the fact that we do stylish items of clothing, not just household goods like those.

Position of adverbs of manner and opinion G Page 112

11 Find the adverbs *quickly*, *well*, *unfortunately*, *obviously*, *carefully* and *sadly* in the text. Notice their position in the sentence.

12 Correct the mistakes with adverb position in these sentences written by exam candidates. There is only one mistake in each sentence, but in some cases more than one answer is possible.

1 Most local people do not speak well English.
2 I am a member of that club because I like very much doing sports.
3 I had read carefully the store's catalogue.
4 I swore that I would never do that again and they thankfully believed me.
5 The sightseeing tour gave us the opportunity to get to know better the city.
6 You can send very quickly an email to the seller.
7 I don't like cars, so I have naturally a bicycle.
8 After a week, I learned that I hadn't unfortunately passed the examination.

10 LISTENING

Part 3

L Page 95

1 2.14 Complete the text with these words. Then listen to check your answers.

brand	catalogue	checkout	debit	debt
guarantee	mall	off	on offer	trolley

I always try to get everything I need for the week down at the shops and supermarket at the big shopping (1) .... on the outskirts of town. At the supermarket, I fill up my (2) .... with my favourite items of food, sometimes choosing a different (3) .... from the one I usually buy if it happens to be (4) .... , for instance 'Buy 2 and get 1 free', or '20% (5) ....'. At the (6) .... I normally pay cash or by (7) .... card rather than by credit card, as I don't want to get into (8) .... by spending more than I can afford. Sometimes I call in at one of the other shops to buy something for the house, though for a big item I usually look it up in the (9) .... first. I always check it has a good (10) .... in case anything goes wrong after I've bought it.

2 Say what you think is happening in the picture, using words from Exercise 1.

3 Look at the exam task. What will all the people be talking about?

Quick steps to Listening Part 3

- Listen for ideas similar to those in sentences A–H, not just words or phrases.
- Remember it isn't necessary to understand every word that all five speakers say.
- Don't forget that three of sentences A–H aren't needed.

4 2.15 Underline the key words in sentences A–H and think of expressions with similar or opposite meanings. Then listen and do the exam task.

Exam tip ›

If you think you may have answered one question incorrectly, make sure that it hasn't led to other mistakes.

Exam task

You will hear five different people talking about shopping experiences. For questions **1–5** choose from the list (**A–H**) what each speaker says. Use the letters only once. There are three extra letters which you do not need to use.

A I bought more things than I had intended to.

B I bought an item that was good value for money.

C I did something that made someone else angry.

D I asked the shop to make something specially for me.

E I was shopping over the Internet for the first time.

F I tried to get them to give me my money back.

G I realised that the advertisement had not been truthful.

H I was glad I had an alternative way of paying.

Speaker 1		**1**
Speaker 2		**2**
Speaker 3		**3**
Speaker 4		**4**
Speaker 5		**5**

5 Make sure you have answered all the questions.

10 GRAMMAR

Review of *wish* and *if only*
G Page 112

1 Look at these extracts from the recording in Listening and answer the questions.

> a *I wish I still had those 150 euros.*
> b *I wish I'd been more careful measuring the wall.*
> c *I wish people would check they have enough money before they go shopping.*

1 Which sentence expresses regret about the past?
2 Which sentence expresses a desire for change in the future, in this case something annoying that other people do?
3 Which sentence refers to a present situation we would like to be different?
4 In which sentence(s) could you use *If only* instead of *I wish?*

2 Correct the mistakes in these sentences written by exam candidates.

1 I wish you were there with us last Friday.
2 We all wish scientists can find a new form of energy.
3 I wish I bought a red coat, not a grey one.
4 As soon as I heard his voice, I wished I didn't answer the telephone.
5 If only I would have known what was going to happen that night.
6 I wish you came to my house this evening and keep me company.
7 I wish I will have more time to spend with you.
8 Her first thought was: 'I wish I haven't decided to wear these shoes.'

3 What would you say in these situations? Write two sentences for each, using *wish* or *if only.*

1 You bought a jacket in a shop, but then saw the same jacket on sale for less in the market.
I wish I hadn't bought it at the shop. If only I'd bought it at the market.
2 You saw a shirt on offer on Friday, but when you went to buy it on Monday it had gone.
3 You're in a shop on a Saturday morning, but it's crowded and people are pushing.
4 The sales start tomorrow, but you have to go to work so you won't be able to go.
5 Your sister keeps borrowing your things without asking you first.

Review of causative *have* and *get*
G Page 113

4 Study these example sentences and answer the questions.

> a *He had his suit made to measure.*
> b *We're going to get the house decorated.*
> c *Yesterday I had my phone stolen.*

1 When we use *have* or *get* like this, do we do something ourselves?
2 Do we use *have* or *get* when something unpleasant is done to us?
3 What form of the verb do we use after *have* or *get* + noun (or pronoun)?

5 Complete the sentences with the correct form of *have* or *get* and these verbs.

clean	cut	deliver	repair	test	waste

1 It would have cost too much to .... my shoes .... so I bought a new pair.
2 I'm tired of .... my time .... by people phoning to try to sell me things.
3 If I have enough time, I .... my hair .... later today.
4 I must .... my suit ....before the interview next week.
5 Some sports fans believe that referees should .... their eyes .... more often.
6 Nowadays I order food over the Internet and .... it .... to my house.

6 Imagine you have won millions on the lottery. Say what you would have done for you.

Example*: I would have my hair done by my own hairdresser.*

10 SPEAKING

Parts 3 and 4

S Pages 99–100

1 2.16 Complete the summary with these expressions. Then listen to check your answers.

Right, we're agreed.
Well, are we both in favour of this one?
Which do you think would be best?
Let's leave it at that.
OK, those are the ones we'll go for.
So which shall we choose?
Let's just agree to disagree.
Shall we go for those two, then?

To bring the conversation towards a conclusion, you can say (1) .... or (2) .... , and to try to reach a decision you can use expressions such as (3) .... or (4) .... If you both decide on the same one or ones, say something like (5) .... or (6) .... , but if you can't reach a decision, just say to your partner (7) .... or (8) ....

Quick steps to Speaking Part 3

- To keep the conversation going, say *What about this one?* or *Let's go on to the next one* to your partner.
- Remember that you have a full minute to make a decision together.

2 Read the exam task instructions. How many things do you have to look at? What two things do you have to do?

3 Work in groups of three: one 'examiner' and two 'candidates'. The examiner reads the instructions to the candidates, then lets them talk for two minutes. The candidates listen to the examiner's instructions, then have one minute to do the task together. Include some expressions from Exercise 1 at the end of your conversation.

Exam tip

Don't talk too long without letting your partner speak, or you may lose marks.

Exam task

You're going to talk about something together for about two minutes.

Here are some different kinds of shop.

Look at the task and talk to each other about what might be good or bad about buying things in each of these shops.

clothes shop | supermarket | furniture shop

What might be good or bad about buying things in each of these shops?

bookshop | sports shop | electrical shop

Now you have a minute to decide which two are the best places to go shopping.

Quick steps to Speaking Part 4

- You can ask the examiner to repeat a question by saying, for example: *Sorry, I didn't catch that*, or *Could you repeat that, please*?
- Show interest in what the other candidate is saying. For example, nod, or say *Yes* or *Right*.

4 Stay in your groups for Speaking Part 4 and do the exam task below.

Exam task

Examiner: Ask both candidates three or four questions from this list.
Candidates: Discuss the examiner's questions with your partner, thinking of as many ideas as you can for each and giving full answers.

- How might the increase in the number of big supermarkets affect small shops?
- Why is it important to compare prices before buying something?
- Is it better to go shopping alone, or with someone else? Why?
- What do you think might be good, or not so good, about working in a shop?
- In what ways have people's shopping habits changed in recent years?
- What do you think are the main disadvantages of shopping online?
- What do most people of your age wish they could afford to buy? Why?
- How do you think people will do their shopping in the future?
- Do you think people should spend less and save more? Why? / Why not?

5 In your group, discuss how well the candidates did Parts 3 and 4.

Exam tip

Remember that in the actual exam the examiners can't answer questions about how well you have done in the test.

6 Change roles so that the examiner becomes a candidate, and repeat Exercises 3–5.

Phrasal verbs with *out*

1 Use the context to work out the meaning of each of the underlined phrasal verbs.

1 Those scarves are very popular with customers and we've <u>run out</u> of them completely.
2 Those old socks have got holes in! When are you going to <u>throw</u> them <u>out</u>?
3 We'll <u>be out of</u> petrol if we don't find a garage soon.
4 My brother's got a new bike and I want to <u>try</u> it <u>out</u>.
5 I'm going to the bank to <u>take out</u> some money.
6 Our cat <u>stays out</u> at night, unless it's very cold.
7 Goods advertised as 'on offer' sometimes <u>turn out</u> to be poor value.
8 The prices are so low that everything will <u>sell out</u> in a few hours.

2 Complete the sentences with the correct form of these verbs + *out*.

back	breathe	cross	rush	shut	wear

1 The doctor asked me to .... while she examined me.
2 Someone shouted 'Fire!' and people .... of the shop, but it was a false alarm.
3 If you make a mistake, ... it .... and then write the correct word.
4 We have an agreement, so I hope they aren't going to .... at the last minute.
5 The stadium was full for the big match and many people without tickets were ....
6 I've been on my feet shopping all day and I'm feeling .... now.

Part 4

Quick steps to Reading and Use of English Part 4
- If you can't give the whole answer to a question, write as much as you can. You might get one mark.
- Write only the missing words and the key word on your answer sheet, not the whole sentence.

3 Look at the exam task example and note down the grammatical changes that have been made in the answer.

4 Look quickly at questions 1–6 and decide what the focus of each question is. Then do the exam task.

Exam tip

Part 4 carries more marks than Parts 1–3 of Paper 1, so you may want to spend a little more time on key word transformations than those other three parts.

Exam task

For questions **1–6**, complete the second sentence so that it has a similar meaning to the first sentence, using the word given. **Do not change the word given**. You must use between **two** and **five** words, including the word given. Here is an example (**0**):

Example:
0 Before I bought that bike, I should've gone for a ride on it.
OUT
I wish .....I'D TRIED OUT..... that bike before I bought it.

1 I think Sarah regrets spending all that money.
WISHES
I think Sarah .... all that money.

2 They may search your luggage at the airport.
HAVE
You .... at the airport.

3 I should have come home earlier last night.
STAYED
I wish .... so late last night.

4 It's a pity there were no tickets left by the time we got there!
OUT
If only the tickets .... by the time we got there!

5 If I buy one of those T-shirts, I'll ask them to send it by post.
GET
If I buy one of those T-shirts, ... by post.

6 The driver regrets not asking the garage to check his tyres.
HAD
The driver wishes he .... by the garage.

5 Make sure all your completed sentences make sense, and that you haven't made any spelling mistakes or used too many words.

10 WRITING

Extreme adjectives

1 You can make your writing more lively by using extreme adjectives. For example, instead of *interesting*, we might say *fascinating*. Match the adjectives in box A with the more extreme adjectives in box B.

A

angry   big   bright   pleasant   silly strange   suitable   surprising

B

absurd   bizarre   breathtaking   delightful furious   ideal   massive   vivid

2 Which of these extreme adjectives mean 'very good', and which mean 'very bad'?

disgraceful   dreadful   exceptional fine   outstanding   severe   stunning superb   tremendous

3 Complete the sentences with extreme adjectives from Exercises 1 and 2. In some cases more than one answer is possible.

1 I was .... when I realised my credit card had been used by someone else.
2 Alicia loves clothes with .... colours, though I prefer plain ones.
3 I find it quite .... that two kilos of apples cost less than one.
4 I'm fascinated by clothes, so being a fashion buyer is my .... job.
5 There are some .... views from the top of the mountain.
6 The firm made a .... mistake by producing goods that nobody wanted.
7 There is a .... water shortage following the very hot weather.
8 They sell some .... clothes in that shop, and I wish I could afford them.

Part 1 essay

W Page 88

4 Look at the exam task instructions and answer the questions.

1 What is the situation?
2 What do you have to do?
3 Which points must you include?
4 Do you agree with the statement?

Exam task

In your English class you have been talking about the advantages and disadvantages of buying things on the Internet rather than getting them in the shops. Now, your English teacher has asked you write an essay.

Write an essay using all the notes and give reasons for your point of view.

Shopping online is better than going to the shops. Do you agree?

Notes
Write about:
1 which is cheaper
2 which is easier
3 your own idea

Write your **essay** in **140–190** words. You must use grammatically correct sentences with accurate spelling and punctuation in an appropriate style.

5 Read the model essay and answer these questions.

1 Does the writer agree or disagree with the statement? In which paragraph?
2 Which paragraph discusses each of notes 1, 2 and 3? What reason is given in each case?
3 Which of the following does the writer use?
   a addition links
   b contrast links
   c adverbs of opinion or manner
   d extreme adjectives
   e causative *have*

Nowadays, more and more people are buying items on the Internet rather than in the high street, supermarket or shopping mall. Increasingly, websites are replacing department stores as places to shop. Not everyone, however, welcomes this change.

Certainly, being able to select from a massive range of products while sitting comfortably at home is an enormous advantage, as is having your purchases delivered. On the other hand, they may arrive late, or even not at all, and any faulty or unsuitable items have to be returned by post.

With so many sellers to choose from, it is possible to find some tremendous bargains online. Payment, though, is by a debit or credit card, which a young person may not have. Worse still, there is the risk of having your card details stolen.

On the high street, in contrast, you can pay in cash, avoid postal charges and easily return unwanted goods. Going to the shops, especially with friends, is also fun, and you can always try on clothes before you buy.

In conclusion, traditional shopping can be safer, more enjoyable and sometimes less expensive than buying online.

6 Plan and write your essay. When you have finished, check your work as in Unit 1 Writing Exercise 5 on page 14.

1 Choose the correct option.

1 This sweater doesn't fit me. I wish I *bought / 'd bought* a bigger one.
2 My weight is fine, but I wish I *am / were* a little bit taller.
3 If only I *waited / 'd waited* another week. I could have got those shoes more cheaply.
4 I wish I *didn't / don't* have to wear this stupid uniform.
5 I love going shopping, so I wish we *would live / lived* nearer the city centre.
6 It was my favourite hat. I wish I *didn't / hadn't* lost it.
7 If only someone *will / would* give me some money to spend!
8 I wish my parents *didn't / wouldn't* criticise the way I dress. It's so annoying.

2 Complete the second sentence so that it has a similar meaning to the first sentence, using the word given. Do not change the word given. You must use between two and five words, including the word given.

1 It's a pity I got rid of those old shoes of mine.
THROWN
I wish .... those old shoes of mine.

2 I'm fed up with them trying to sell me things I don't want.
WISH
I .... to sell me things I don't want.

3 The dressmaker is going to alter this skirt completely, I think.
HAVE
I'm going to .... , I think.

4 I'm sorry I didn't have enough time while I was shopping.
OUT
I wish I .... time while I was shopping.

5 I wish someone would iron my clothes for me this weekend.
HAVE
I wish I .... this weekend.

6 It's very sad that we couldn't meet last week.
ONLY
If .... to meet last week.

See the CD-ROM for more practice.

3 Write replies to the comments. Use *should*, *how about* or *why don't you* + causative *have* or *get* to give advice.

1 'This is a lovely painting.'
You should have it framed. or How about putting it on the wall? or Why don't you sell it?
2 'My printer's not working.'
3 'I've broken a tooth.'
4 'There's a stain on my coat.'
5 'My hair's a mess.'
6 'I need photos for my passport.'

4 Complete the crossword with words from Unit 10.

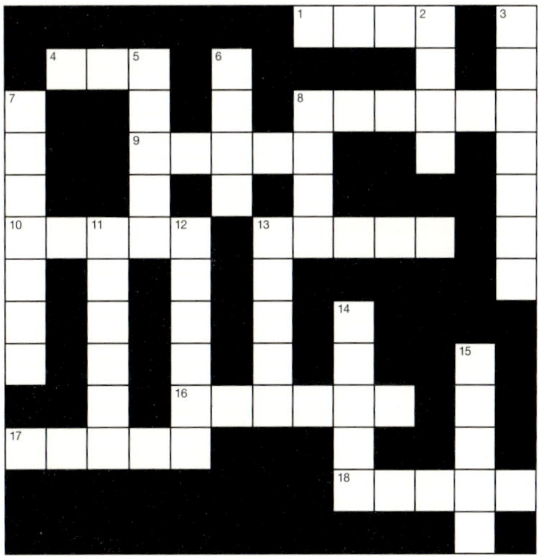

Across
1 one sock is an ... of clothing
4 50% ... means it's half the usual price
8 person who trades in something such as art
9 the opposite of *tight*
10 a designer ... is a make of expensive clothes
13 something that is in ... is available in a shop
16 clothes that are ... are not for formal wear
17 be exactly the same colour or type as something else
18 you can use a ... card to buy things

Down
2 large, covered shopping area for pedestrians
3 something on sale for less than its real value
5 not real
6 trendy
7 you push this round a supermarket
8 money that you owe somebody
11 strong in colour
12 make a product available for the first time
13 number of things sold
14 type of product made by a particular company
15 simple, opposite of *patterned*

WRITING GUIDE W

This guide will help you prepare for Writing, Paper 2 of *Cambridge English: First*. The two checklists give you suggestions of how to prepare for the Writing Paper, and key things to remember during the exam. You can use the second checklist as you work through the Practice tasks and model answers in the guide.

Before the exam

- Make sure you know what all the possible task types consist of so that in the exam you can choose the tasks and topics that best suit your experience and interests.
- Practise writing within the word limits. If you write too little you may not be able to complete the task properly; if you write too much there's a risk of repetition and irrelevance.
- Practise writing without dictionaries or computer spelling checks, as you can't use them in the exam.
- Get an idea of how many words you write in, say, ten lines, so that in the exam you don't waste time counting words to stay within the limits.

During the exam

- Plan the amount of time you're going to spend on each task, remembering to allow a few minutes at the end to check your work.
- Read the question very carefully, underlining the key words and then making a plan.
- Think about your reader in each task, and write in a suitably formal or informal style.
- Use linking expressions to connect ideas and help your readers follow your writing more easily.
- Make sure your handwriting is clear and that any corrections can be understood by the examiners.
- To get good marks your text must have a positive effect on the reader, be well-organised and cohesive, with a clear layout, and use a wide range of language.
- Try out new language. Correct grammar is always important, but if you make mistakes with more complicated structures the examiners will give you credit as long as they can understand what you have written.
- Remember that spelling and punctuation mistakes can cost you marks if they make it difficult to understand what you mean.
- If you use the blank pages for notes or to finish your work, make it clear to the examiners which writing is part of your answer.

Part 1

What to expect in Part 1

- Part 1 tests your ability to write an 'opinion' essay, usually for a teacher of English, in 140–190 words.
- You are given a question or statement to write about.
- You are also given some notes to guide your writing.
- You will need to develop an argument and/or discuss issues, giving reasons for your opinions.
- You need to organise your text into paragraphs.
- You have about 40 minutes to complete the task, including time to plan and check your work.
- You need to organise your text into paragraphs, with an appropriate beginning and ending.

How to do Part 1

- Look carefully at the instructions, the essay title and the notes with it.
- Note down as many ideas as you can and decide how many paragraphs you'll need.
- Group your best ideas together and organise your text to include an introduction, development of arguments and a clear conclusion. Make sure you cover all the points in the notes.
- If you decide to write arguments on both sides, use two headings in your plan so that your essay is balanced.
- If you can't think of arguments that you disagree with, imagine what someone who disagrees might say.
- Make a note of some useful expressions for each paragraph, but don't try to write a full draft – there isn't time in the exam.
- Write your essay, following your plan. Try to include one or two sentences about each of the notes.
- You can state your own opinion about the topic in general at the beginning of the essay, or leave it until the concluding paragraph.
- When you have finished, check your text for errors, and make sure it's the right length.

Practice task and model answer

1 Read the Part 1 task and answer the questions.

1 What is the background situation?
2 What is the topic of the essay?
3 Who will read it?
4 Look at the question. What is your point of view?
5 What notes are you given?

2 Read the sample essay and answer the questions.

1 What style is the essay written in? Give three examples.
2 How has the writer organised the essay?
3 Where does he cover each of the three notes?
4 What is his point of view?

Your English class has been discussing studying and jobs. Now, your teacher has asked you to write an essay.

Write an essay using all the notes and give reasons for your point of view.

Is it better to go into higher education rather than get a job straight from school?

Notes

Write about:

1 which has immediate advantages
2 which is better for your career
3 your own idea

Write your **essay** in **140–190** words. You must use grammatically correct sentences with accurate spelling and punctuation in an appropriate style.

For school leavers, the decision whether to look for work or go to university is particularly difficult in the current economic situation.

> Short introduction makes a general comment on the issue.

On the one hand, for many young people it is tempting to start earning as soon as possible, rather than have to wait years for their first salary. As well as that, they can avoid the increasingly high fees charged by universities, especially in English-speaking countries. Moreover, a degree no longer guarantees a job, as many recent graduates have discovered.

> Points on one side.

> Good linking expressions (*on the one hand, as well as, moreover, however, furthermore, also, to conclude*).

However, those who go to university are likely to benefit for the rest of their lives, as the average graduate earns considerably more than someone without a degree. Furthermore, higher education is not just about improving your career prospects. It is also, among other things, about developing your mind, studying a subject that interests you in depth, learning new skills and meeting new people.

> Points on the other side.

> Reasons.

To conclude, although there are economic arguments on both sides, my own view is that there are so many other good reasons for continuing your studies that going into higher education is by far the better option.

> Summing up main points.

Part 2

What to expect in Part 2

- Part 2 tests your ability to write one of the following texts in 140–190 words: an article, a letter, a report, a review.
- You choose one task from three possible questions.
- Questions are based on a variety of topics such as health, the environment, education and travel.
- For all Part 2 tasks you are given a context, a purpose for writing and an intended reader. The task may include a short text, plus instructions.
- You must deal with every element of the question in order to complete the task.
- You have about 40 minutes to complete the task, including time to plan your work and check for mistakes at the end.

How to do Part 2

- Look quickly through questions 2–4 and decide which of them you think you can do best.
- Study the instructions and any input text, highlighting the points you must deal with.
- Think about the kind of text you need to write and who will read it. Then decide whether a formal, neutral or informal style is appropriate.
- Think of as many ideas as you can and note them down. Then decide how many paragraphs you need.
- Make a plan, putting your best ideas under paragraph headings.
- Note down some useful words and phrases for each paragraph, but don't try to write a draft of your text.
- Write your text, following your plan. Use as wide a range of grammar, vocabulary and linking expressions as you can.
- Make sure your completed text is the right length and check it for errors.

Letter

What to expect in Part 2 letter

- The letter task in Part 2 tests your ability to write in response to a situation described in the question.
- You must use an appropriate style and tone.
- In an informal letter, you will need to give information, express your opinion and describe.
- In a formal letter, you may need to express enthusiasm, describe your skills and experience, and persuade.

How to do Part 2 letter

- Organise your letter into paragraphs, with a suitable beginning and ending.
- Make sure you cover all the points in the instructions.
- If you begin your letter *Dear Madam* or *Dear Sir*, end with *Yours faithfully*, but end your letter *Yours sincerely* if you use their surname, e.g. *Dear Mr Taylor*.
- Don't begin a letter *Dear friend* or *Dear Course Director*. Use the person's name.
- Use a variety of expressions. For instance, instead of repeating *I think*, say *it seems to me*, *my own feeling is* or other phrases for giving your opinion.
- Try to include some colourful language, e.g. extreme adjectives, to make your letter more lively.

Practice tasks and model answers

1 Read the Part 2 tasks A and B and answer these questions about each.

1 What do you have to read? In what style is it written?
2 What must you write? Which points must you deal with?
3 Who must you write to?

2 Read the model answers A and B and answer these questions about each.

1 Has she written in an appropriate style? Find three examples.
2 Is the layout of her letter correct?
3 In which paragraph does she deal with each point in the example task?

Exam task A

This is part of an email from your penfriend, Lena.

> When you visit my town next weekend, I'd like to invite you out for dinner. What's your favourite kind of food? Would you prefer a quiet little restaurant or somewhere with loads of people and good music? Where would you like to go afterwards?
>
> Best wishes,
>
> Lena

Write your **email** to Lena in **140–190** words. Do not write any addresses.

Model answer A

> Hi Lena,
>
> Many thanks for your email, and the kind invitation. Yes, I'd be delighted to join you for dinner!
>
> I particularly like Indian food, as long as it's not too spicy, so would you like to go for a curry? Alternatively, perhaps we could have an Italian meal? I really like pizza, but also meat or fish with pasta and lots of lovely salad.
>
> I don't really mind where we go, though as we've haven't seen each other for so long it might be nice to have a good chat together somewhere that's not too noisy, then head for somewhere a bit more exciting later on. What do you think?
>
> If we do that, I'd suggest having a coffee at one of the little cafés in the main square, then going dancing at one of those new clubs you mentioned that have recently opened near there. Or maybe we could go the cinema if there's a good film on later in the evening.
>
> But whatever we do, I'm sure we'll have a fantastic evening out!
>
> See you soon!
>
> Alexia

Opening on a separate line.

Thanks the other person for writing.

Short paragraph for each main point.

Gives a reason.

Friendly closing sentence (*But whatever we do …*).

Ending and name on separate lines.

Exam task B

You have seen this advertisement in an English-language newspaper.

Staff for summer sales

We are looking for Sales Assistants to work in our clothes store.

- Are you interested in clothes and fashion?
- Do you have a good level of English?
- Do you have any experience of selling in shops?

If so, apply to the manager, Mr James O'Neill, saying why you are suitable for the job.

Write your **letter of application** in **140–190** words in an appropriate style.

Model answer B

Dear Mr O'Neill,

I am writing to apply for the position of Sales Assistant at your store this summer, as advertised in today's newspaper.

I have always taken a keen interest in all kinds of clothing, including the latest fashions. I keep up to date with these by reading the top fashion magazines and following the main fashion shows in Paris, Milan and elsewhere, either on television or online.

Although I have not actually worked in clothing sales before, for the last three summers I have been employed as an assistant at a local bookshop. I very much enjoy working with the public, and I can provide excellent references from the shopkeeper.

In addition to studying English at school for many years, I have travelled frequently to English-speaking countries. I also often read articles about the fashion industry in English.

I have enclosed a full curriculum vitae, and would be happy to answer any further questions about my application that you may have.

I look forward to hearing from you.

Yours sincerely,

Anusia Krol

Gives a reason for writing.

Says where she heard about the job.

Sounds enthusiastic and confident.

Suitable linking expressions.

Says what she has sent with the letter.

Offers to give more information.

Polite final sentence.

Article

What to expect in Part 2 article

- The article task tests your ability to write an interesting article for an English-language newspaper or magazine.
- You may need to describe, give your opinion, make comments or give examples.
- You are writing for readers who are already interested in the topic.
- You can write in a neutral or fairly informal style.

How to do Part 2 article

- You can prepare for this task by reading articles in magazines and newspapers, or on the Internet.
- Only choose this task if you're sure you know enough about the topic to write a complete article.
- Think about what your readers would like to know.
- Think of a good title to attract the readers' attention.
- Write in a lively way that will hold their attention.

Practice task and model answer

1 Read the Part 2 task and answer the questions.

1 What is the topic of the article?
2 Where will it be published and who will read it?
3 What two things do you have to do?

2 Read the sample article and answer the questions.

1 What style is the article written in? Give two examples of this.
2 Which parts of the text deal with the two elements in the instructions?
3 What kinds of thing do we learn about this place?
4 How did the writer seem to feel about his visit there?

You have seen this announcement in a travel magazine.

A PLACE WORTH VISITING

Tell us about a place that you think is particularly interesting, and say what you most remember about your visit there. We will publish the best articles next month.

Write your **article** in **140–190** words.

Australian rock

It's a series of enormous chunks of spectacular red rock right in the middle of the Australian desert, and it's 200 metres taller than nearby Ayer's Rock. So what is it?

It's known as The Olgas, which consist of 36 rounded peaks separated by deep valleys, while underground the rock extends to the astonishing depth of five kilometres. The area has been inhabited for 22,000 years and, perhaps unsurprisingly, there are many legends associated with it, including the existence of a giant snake at the top of Mount Olga.

My walk there took five hours, first along a steep path through the hot, dry, apparently lifeless desert, and then up into the relative cool of the Valley of the Winds. There, in the partial shade, were pools of sparkling water, an unbelievable variety of vegetation and some truly amazing tropical birds.

It was then a short, steep climb to the top, where the views were so stunning that I hardly noticed something large moving quietly through the bushes. It was only later, on my way down from Mount Olga, that I recalled the story of the snake.

- Title to catch readers' attention.
- Introduction intended to get people reading.
- Direct question encourages readers to continue to the next paragraph.
- Interesting facts.
- Personal experiences.
- Range of colourful adjectives.
- Variety of grammatical structures.
- Ending makes readers think about what they have read.

Report

What to expect in Part 2 report

- The report task tests your ability to give factual information and to make recommendations or suggestions.
- The instructions include a description of a situation.
- You may be asked to write for a teacher or manager, or for a group such as classmates or club members.

How to do Part 2 report

- Before choosing a report question, be sure you know enough facts about the topic to write about it.
- Decide what style to use, depending on your readers.
- Note any knowledge or personal experience you may have, and include this in your plan.
- Organise your text well, possibly using headings.

Practice task and model answer

1 Read the Part 2 task and answer the questions.

1 What is the topic of the report?
2 Who will read your report?
3 What three things do you have to do?

2 Read the sample report and answer the questions.

1 What style is the report written in? Give three examples of this.
2 Which headings correspond to which parts of the instructions?
3 What two recommendations are made?

> Your teacher has asked you to write a report on a public park near your home. Give a brief description of the park, saying what people can do there and recommending some improvements.
>
> Write your **report** in **140–190** words.

Report on West Park

Title.

Introduction

Paragraph headings.

The aim of this report is to describe West Park, outline its leisure facilities and suggest what could be improved there.

States the purpose of the report, in different words from the instructions (*The aim …*).

Main features

This is by far the largest park in town and it is also the oldest, having originally formed part of the estate of a wealthy local family. This accounts for the magnificent trees, the gorgeous flowerbeds and the delightful lake there. There are also some lovely wide open spaces, although in places the grass is in poor condition and the footpaths are in need of repair.

Little-known fact (*having originally formed part of …*).

Extreme adjectives (*magnificent, gorgeous, delightful*).

Leisure facilities

Additionally, the park contains children's swings, a football pitch and tennis courts. On one side of the lake rowing boats can be hired, while at the main entrance it is possible to rent bicycles for use on the well-designed cycle tracks. Other sports are not catered for at this time.

Conclusion

West Park could become one of the most attractive in the country if it were looked after a little better. I would also recommend that more sporting activities should be made available, as not everyone wants to play football or tennis.

Clear conclusion, with reasons for recommendations.

Review

What to expect in Part 2 Review

- The review task tests your ability to describe and give your opinion of something you have experienced.
- You normally also have to make a recommendation, or advise people against it.
- The instructions describe a situation. Possible topics include a film, a book, a restaurant, a holiday, etc.
- You are told where the review will be published: usually an English-language newspaper, magazine or website.

How to do Part 2 review

- Read as many different kinds of review as you can.
- Practise writing positive and negative opinions.
- Before you write about an experience, e.g. a meal or a film, ask yourself whether you enjoyed it.
- Think of what you saw, heard or read. Or simply use your imagination.
- Think about your readers and what they will want to know.
- Decide on the appropriate style, depending on where your review will be published, and your readers.

Practice task and model answer

1 Read the Part 2 task and answer the questions.

1 What is the topic of the review?
2 Where will your review be published and who will read it?
3 What three things do you have to do?

2 Read the sample review. Which paragraph:

a says what the negative points of the pool are?
b describes the pool?
c makes a recommendation?
d says what the positive points of the pool are?

> An English-language website for visitors to your country has asked for reviews of swimming pools in your area. You decide to write a review of a pool you have visited. Describe the pool and say what you think of it. Would you recommend the pool to other people?
>
> Write your **review** in **140–190** words.

The Hillside Pool

Title.

The swimming pool at the Hillside Leisure Centre measures 25 metres by 15 metres, with a smaller pool for children accompanied by their parents. Access to the main pool is by four ladders, one at each corner, and there are lifeguards on duty at all times.

Contrast links (*while, on the other hand*).

While the pool itself is well maintained and the water appears clean, the same cannot be said for the changing areas and the showers, where the lighting is poor and the floors were rather dirty when I was last there. Furthermore, there are not nearly enough lockers to leave clothes and valuables in, especially at weekends when the pool can become horribly crowded.

Good use of grammar (*the same cannot be said for, not nearly enough lockers to leave, once the promised improvements have been made*).

Addition links (*furthermore, in addition*).

On the other hand, the staff there are extremely helpful, and they assured me that the facilities and standards of cleanliness will soon improve dramatically. In addition, the entrance fee is considerably lower than for other local pools, and there is also a reasonably priced café.

Variety of adverbs (*extremely, dramatically, considerably*).

For these reasons, I would recommend going for a swim at the Hillside Pool once the promised improvements have been made, preferably during the week.

Recommendation, but with conditions.

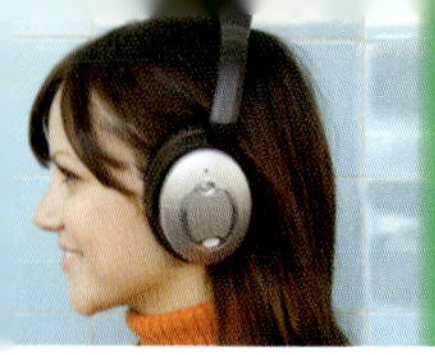

LISTENING GUIDE L

This guide will help you prepare for Listening, Paper 3 of *Cambridge English: First*. The two checklists give you suggestions for how to prepare for the Listening Paper, and key things to remember during the exam.

Before the exam

- Make sure you know what each part of the Listening test consists of and what you have to do.
- Listen to as much English as you can: on the radio and TV, and also online – for instance on international news websites.
- Listen to different accents: not just from the UK and USA, also from English speakers around the world.
- Listen to male and female voices of different age groups and backgrounds.
- Listen to other students during classroom discussions and in group work.
- Get into the habit of quickly reading questions before you hear the recording.
- Practise listening and writing simple answers to questions at the same time. Make sure that the words you write can be read!
- Get used to moving on to the next question rather than getting stuck on a question you find difficult.

During the exam

- You record your answers as you listen, either by choosing a letter or writing down a word or short phrase, depending on the task type.
- You will have five minutes at the end of the test to transfer your answers onto the separate answer sheet.
- Make sure you've given an answer to every question.

Part 1

What to expect in Part 1

- You hear eight short extracts, usually involving one or two speakers.
- There's no connection between the extracts, so you hear each one twice before the recording moves on.
- For each extract there is one multiple-choice question with three options: A, B, C.
- The introduction to each question contains information about the situation, e.g. *a conversation in the street*, and a direct question, e.g. *Who is she talking to?*

How to prepare for Part 1

- Listen to as wide a variety as possible of different text types, from theatre plays to weather forecasts, from radio phone-ins to people out shopping.
- Whenever you hear English on the radio, quickly try to identify the topic and the type of speaking.
- Practise listening for non-factual information such as how a speaker is feeling, or what their purpose in speaking might be.

How to do Part 1

- For each question, read the first line and ask yourself questions like *What's the situation? How many people will I hear? Male or female?*
- Underline the direct question, e.g. *Why is he phoning?*
- Think of words with similar meaning to this question, e.g. *phoning: ringing, call, mobile*. Then listen for these words.
- The first time you listen, try to answer the question in your mind. Then choose the option (A, B or C) most like your own answer.
- Check your answer when you listen again.
- Don't choose an answer until you've heard the complete text at least once.
- Always be sure you know which number text you are listening to.
- Be careful with the 'distractors' – the incorrect options that may contain words similar to those you hear, but are in fact about something else.
- If you really can't decide which is the right answer, cross out the one you're sure is wrong and then guess.
- After the recording has finished for the second time and you have noted down your answer, forget about that question and focus entirely on the next one.

Part 2

What to expect in Part 2

- You hear one text lasting about three minutes, played twice.
- There will be one speaker.
- You can both read and hear the instructions at the beginning. These will tell you who the speaker is.
- You read the questions while the recording is played, listening for particular words, numbers or phrases to complete the sentences.
- You write down the missing parts of the sentences exactly as you hear them.
- You won't need to write down more than three words, and none of these will be above First level.
- The questions are in the same order as the information you hear, so that each part of the recording relates to a particular question.
- If a missing word is spelt out on the recording, you must spell it correctly in your answer.

How to prepare for Part 2

- Practise listening to recordings and making brief notes about the key points. Then play the recording back to check how accurate your answers are.
- Make sure you know how figures, including dates and fractions, are pronounced, and practise writing them down when you hear them on TV, or on recordings.
- Get into the habit of always reading the words after each gap, not just the words that come before it.

How to do Part 2

- After you hear the instructions there is a 45-second pause. Use this time to look quickly through the task.
- Read the introduction and decide what kind of recording it is, what it's about, and who you will hear.
- Look quickly at the whole of each incomplete sentence and decide what kind of word(s) or number you need to listen for, e.g. a noun, a date.
- Underline the key words in the sentences to help you focus on the information you need.
- Listen for 'cues': words that express the same idea as a particular question and tell you the answer is coming soon.
- Write down the missing words as you hear them: you don't need to rephrase them.
- Take care with words or numbers you hear which might seem to fit a gap, but are not correct.
- Write your answers in pencil the first time you listen, in case you want to change them later.
- Only write one answer, even if you think more than one is possible.
- After the recording has finished, check that all completed sentences make sense and that you haven't made any spelling mistakes.

Part 3

What to expect in Part 3

- You hear five short texts involving one speaker each, played twice.
- The texts are related in some way, e.g. they are all about journeys, or all the speakers are complaining.
- The questions are not usually in the same order as the information you hear.
- You can both read and hear the instructions at the beginning of the task. These may tell you what the connection between the five texts is.
- The questions are not on the recording.
- You listen for the speakers to express the same ideas as five of options A–H.
- There are three options that don't exactly match what any of the speakers say.

How to prepare for Part 3

- Practise listening to a number of people talking individually about the same topic or speaking with the same purpose, e.g. in radio phone-in programmes.
- Get into the habit of studying the options carefully so that you know what you need to listen for.

How to do Part 3

- After you hear the instructions there is a 30-second pause before the recording begins. Look at the task during this time.
- Quickly read the introduction and decide what the link is between the five texts.
- Underline the key words in options A–H to get a clear idea of what you have to listen for.
- Listen to everything a speaker has to say before you note down your answer.
- Don't choose an answer just because you hear a similar word or phrase. Listen for the same idea as in the option.
- Remember that the speakers may say something linked to more than one option, but there can only be one correct answer.
- Each time you choose an option, cross it out lightly in pencil so you can focus on the remaining options.
- Wait until you've heard a speaker twice before you make a final decision on the answer.
- Remember that one wrong answer may have led to others.

Part 4

What to expect in Part 4

- You hear one text lasting about three minutes, played twice.
- There will be interacting speakers.
- The instructions you read and hear at the beginning of the task may tell you who the main speaker is and what kind of text it is, e.g. an interview.
- You read the seven multiple-choice questions while you are listening.
- The questions follow the order of the information you hear, so that each part of the recording corresponds to a particular question.
- The correct answers either report, rephrase or summarise the ideas of the speaker(s).

How to prepare for Part 4

- Listen to interviews, talks and discussions.
- Practise listening to understand people's opinions, feelings and attitudes, as well as factual content.
- Practise answering questions about recordings in your own words before looking at multiple-choice options.

How to do Part 4

- After you hear the instructions there is a one-minute pause. Use this time before the recording begins to look quickly through the task.
- Start by focusing on the introduction and deciding what kind of recording it is, what it's about, and who you will hear.
- Quickly read the first line of each question and decide what kind of information you need to listen for, e.g. *how somebody feels*.
- For each question, underline the key words. This will help you concentrate on the information you need.
- When you hear the recording, listen for the 'cue' for each question that tells you that the answer is coming soon.
- Listen for words or phrases that have similar or opposite meanings to those you underlined.
- Wait until the speaker has finished talking about that particular point before you choose your answer.
- Try to answer the question in your mind, then choose the option (A, B or C) that is most like your own answer.
- If you're not sure which option is right, mark the two most likely ones and choose from those on the second listening.

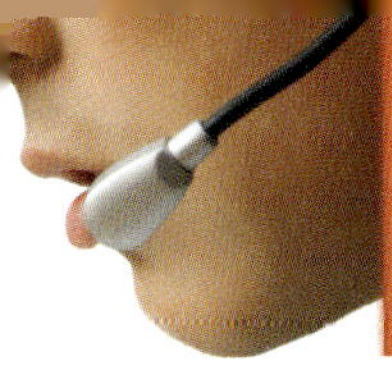

SPEAKING GUIDE S

This guide will help you prepare for Speaking, Paper 4 of *Cambridge English: First*. The checklist gives you suggestions of how to prepare for the Speaking Paper.

Before the exam

- Make sure you know what each part of the Speaking test consists of and what you have to do.
- Get used to listening carefully to instructions for speaking tasks so that you always know exactly what you have to do.
- Learn how to ask people politely to repeat questions and instructions if you don't completely understand what they say.
- Practise talking in pairs and small groups, using some of the *Useful language* in this guide.
- Develop your communicative skills, particularly the ability to start discussions and reply to what other students say.
- If people sometimes have difficulty hearing what you say, practise speaking more clearly and possibly also a little louder.
- Practise using different words to say things when you don't know or can't remember a particular word.

Part 1

What to expect in Part 1

- It lasts about two minutes.
- It tests your ability to give information about yourself and talk about your everyday life, your experiences in the past or your plans for the future.
- When you go into the room, one of the examiners tells you their names and asks you for yours. You give her or him your mark sheet.
- You don't usually speak to the other candidate.
- One examiner asks you some questions about yourself.
- You may then be asked, for example, about your work or studies, your interests, or your likes and dislikes.

How to prepare for Part 1

- Make sure you know the words you'll need in case you're asked about your home and family, your town, your work or studies, your hobbies, and so on. But don't prepare speeches or detailed answers to possible questions.
- If possible, practise talking to English speakers outside the class.
- Do role-plays with other students in situations where you need to introduce yourself, such as going to a new school or university, starting a new job, joining a club, or attending a conference.
- In groups, think of as many questions as you can for those situations, then ask students in different groups to answer those questions.
- Practise replying quickly to questions about yourself, giving complete answers.

How to do Part 1

- Be polite and friendly when you meet the examiners and the other candidate.
- Listen carefully to the examiner when he or she asks you questions.
- When you reply, look at the examiner who's asking you the questions, not the other candidate.
- If you don't understand a question, politely ask the examiner to repeat it. See *Useful language*.
- Say more than just 'yes' or 'no' in your answers.
- Use as wide a range of grammatical structures and vocabulary as possible.
- Where appropriate, give reasons, explanations and/or examples. See *Useful language*.
- Don't worry if you can't think of factual details, e.g. the exact month you started learning English. Remember it's a test of speaking, not a job interview!
- Listen to the examiner and the other candidate talking in order to get used to their voices.
- Don't worry if the other candidate seems to know more English than you. Look and sound confident!
- Remember that one aim of Part 1 is to help you relax by encouraging you to talk about a familiar topic: yourself!

Useful language for Part 1

Asking for repetition

Could you say that again, please?
I'm sorry, could you repeat that?
I'm afraid I didn't catch that.
Sorry, what did you say after ... ?
Pardon?
Sorry?

Giving reasons and explanations

the reason is ...
(that's) because ...
... so ...
what I mean is ...
that's to say ...
in other words ...
the point I'm making is ...

Giving examples

for example ...
for instance ...
such as ...
like ...
... say ...
a case in point is ...
a good example of this is ...

Part 2

What to expect in Part 2

- It lasts about four minutes.
- It tests your ability to organise your speaking, to compare, contrast, describe and give your opinion.
- You have a one-minute 'long turn' speaking, during which nobody will interrupt you.
- The examiner gives you two colour photos, and asks you to compare them and then answer a question.
- You can also read the question, as it is printed on the page above the photos.
- When you have finished, the other candidate will be asked a question about your photos.
- The other candidate speaks about their photos for a minute. You then speak for 30 seconds about their photos.

How to prepare for Part 2

- Time yourself speaking in English on particular topics for 60 seconds. This will give you an idea of what you'll need to do in the exam.
- If you can, listen to recordings of more advanced students or to your teacher doing a Part 2 task.
- Choose pairs of photos in magazines or on the Internet that have both similarities and differences, and practise speaking about them for a minute.
- Before you begin speaking, think quickly about how you will organise what you are going to say.
- Record yourself doing Part 2, and play it back to assess your stronger and weaker points. After you have done this a few times you may sound a lot more fluent!

How to do Part 2

- Listen carefully to the instructions, study the pictures and read the question at the top.
- Think quickly about what you're going to say. Remember that you have to do two things, so leave some time to answer the written question.
- As you speak, imagine you're talking about the pictures to somebody who can't see them, for instance someone on the phone.
- You don't need to describe the pictures in detail. Just compare them and then give your reaction to them.
- Begin by saying which picture you are talking about. See *Useful language*.
- Say what's similar and different about the pictures, and compare them. See *Useful language*.
- If you're not sure what's happening in the pictures, say something like *it looks like* ... or *it might be* ... .
- Use different words if you can't name something you see, e.g. *the thing that* ... .
- If you make a mistake you can correct yourself, but don't keep stopping or you won't finish the task.
- Keep talking by adding more points. See *Useful language*.
- When you answer the written question, give a reason and/or an example. See *Useful language for Part 1*.
- Don't worry about the time or keep looking at your watch. The examiner will tell you when time's up.
- Don't speak too quickly or stop before the minute ends.
- Listen to the other candidate without interrupting, and be ready to answer the examiner's question.

Useful language for Part 2

Saying which picture you're talking about

The top picture shows ...
In the other photo there are ...
In the one below it looks as if ...
Both pictures show ...
In both photos there are ...

Describing similarities and differences

This picture shows ... , but that one ...
In both pictures there's ... , though in this one ...
One difference between the pictures is that ...
In one respect the pictures are quite similar because ...
The two situations are completely different because ...
They are similar in that they both show ...
The biggest difference between them is that this one shows ... but the other one ...

Comparing

This looks far more ... than that.
The ... in this picture look much more ... than those.
What's happening in this picture is just as ... as what's going on there.
Doing ... like that isn't so ... as ...
These people are ... a lot more ... than those are.

Giving your opinion

In my opinion, ...
I'd say that ...
Well I think ...
It seems to me ...
Well, my own feeling is that ...
I'm convinced that ...
My own view is that ...

Adding points of similarity and difference

Another similarity/difference is ...
And something else that's different is ...
Another thing that's not quite the same is ...
They also differ in that ...
They're alike in another way in that ...

Part 3

What to expect in Part 3

- It lasts about four minutes.
- You work with the other candidate.
- It tests your ability to discuss different possibilities, to make suggestions, to give opinions and reasons for them, to agree or disagree, and to attempt to reach a decision with your partner.
- The examiner gives you and your partner written prompts which show different ideas or possibilities.
- The examiner will ask you to talk about these prompts together for two minutes, and will then ask you to reach a decision.
- You take turns with your partner so that you spend about the same amount of time speaking overall.
- There is no right or wrong answer to the task and it doesn't matter if you don't actually reach a decision.

How to prepare for Part 3

- Get lots of practice talking in pairs and small groups.
- Practise discussing a range of possibilities in different situations, e.g. which items to take with you on holiday, which pets are best to have.
- Get into the habit of turn taking so that your partner(s) and you speak for about the same length of time.
- Contribute to the conversation in a variety of ways, e.g. asking questions, agreeing, disagreeing.
- Time your discussions to get an idea of what two minutes is like without looking at your watch. That will help you manage your time in the exam.

How to do Part 3

- Listen to the examiner's instructions carefully and look at the prompts with the other candidate.
- Start the discussion by saying something like *Shall we begin with this one? or Would you like to start,* or *shall I?*
- Give your opinion about the first prompt, perhaps making a suggestion. Ask your partner what he or she thinks, and why.
- Talk briefly about each prompt, replying to your partner's comments with reasons.
- Take turns throughout. You may lose marks if you don't.
- Where you disagree with your partner's suggestions, be polite and give reasons. See *Useful language*.
- Use modal verbs to speculate, e.g. *They might be* … .
- Avoid pauses – or spending too long on one prompt – by suggesting you move on. See *Useful language*.
- Listen carefully to what the examiner says after two minutes, and move the conversation towards a decision. See *Useful language*.
- Say whether you have reached agreement or not by using an expression from *Useful language*.

Useful language for Part 3

Agreeing
Right. Yes, I agree with that.
I think so, too.
That's a great idea.
Yes, you're absolutely right.
That's just what I was thinking.

Politely disagreeing
Perhaps, but what about … ?
I'm not so sure. Don't you think … ?
I think I'd rather …
It might be better to …
I'm not really that keen on …
I don't really agree …

Giving reasons for disagreeing
That's because …
Well, the thing is …
The problem with that one is …
The main reason is that …
For one thing, … And for another, …

Keeping going
Shall we move on to the next one?
What about this one?
Let's go on to the next one.
What do you think of this idea?
How do you feel about that one?
Right, those are the ones we'll choose.
I don't think we agree, so let's leave it at that.
Let's just agree to disagree.

Reaching a decision
Which do you think would be best?
So which shall we choose?
Are we both in favour of that one?
Shall we have these two, then?
OK, we're agreed.
Right, those are the ones we'll choose.
I don't think we agree, so let's leave it at that.
Let's just agree to disagree.

Part 4

What to expect in Part 4

- It lasts about four minutes.
- You answer questions from the examiner and discuss them with your partner.
- It tests your ability to talk about issues in more depth than in other parts of the Speaking test.
- Questions are based on the topic introduced in Part 3.
- You are asked to give your opinions and reasons for them, and to express agreement or disagreement with different opinions.
- You may be asked to respond to your partner's opinions.
- At the end of Part 4, the examiner thanks you and says the Speaking test has finished.

How to prepare for Part 4

- Practise talking in groups of three, and in pairs, for about four minutes.
- Ask each other's opinion of stories currently in the news and about events in everyday life.
- When you're discussing news stories and events, ask yourself questions like *Who?*, *Where?*, *When?*, *How?* and *Why?* so that you can give fuller answers.
- In pairs or small groups, think of some interesting topics and note down some discussion questions. Then form new pairs or groups, asking them your questions and answering theirs.
- Practise turn taking, making sure that everyone speaks for about the same length of time.

How to do Part 4

- The questions in Part 4 are not written down, so listen very carefully. If necessary, ask for repetition as in *Useful language for Part 1*.
- Look at the examiner to answer their questions, but at your partner when you are speaking together.
- For each question, think of two or three things to say.
- Give reasons, explanations and examples to support your opinions. See *Useful language for Part 1*.
- Never just say *I don't know*. If you don't know any facts about the topic, say so and then give your opinion, e.g. *I don't know much about it, but I think ...* .
- Keep talking by adding more points. See *Useful language*.
- Listen when your partner is speaking. Show interest and, where appropriate, add to their ideas.
- If you disagree with what your partner says, say so politely and explain why. You can also try to change their opinion. See *Useful language*.
- If necessary, encourage your partner to say more by asking for their opinions and reasons for them. See *Useful language*.
- If your partner is talking a lot and you feel it's your turn, you can interrupt very politely. See *Useful language*.
- Remember there are no right or wrong answers. What matters is that you say what you think.
- Say goodbye to the examiners when they say the Speaking test is over. Don't ask them to comment on how well you did because they're not allowed to say.

Useful language for Part 4

Asking for opinions
What do you think?
Do you agree with that?
What's your opinion?
What are your feelings about this?
How do you feel about ... ?
What do you reckon?

Asking for reasons
Any particular reason?
Could you tell me why?
Is that because ... ?
Why do you think so?

Trying to change someone's opinion
But don't you think that ... ?
Yes, but isn't it true that ... ?
Though wouldn't you agree that ... ?
Yes, but on the other hand ...
But isn't it possible that ... ?
Perhaps another way of looking at it would be ...

Interrupting politely
Could I say something here?
Do you mind if add to that?
If I could just make a point here.
I'd just like to say something about that.
Yes, I'd like to comment on that.

Adding points
And another thing is ...
Apart from that, ...
As well as that, ...
Even better, ...
Just as importantly, ...
Not only that, ...
Then there's ...
Worse still, ...
There's also the fact that ...

VISUAL MATERIALS

Unit 7

Exam task 1

1

2

Exam task 2

3

4

Unit 9

Exam task 1

1

2

Exam task 2

3

4

GRAMMAR REFERENCE G

Unit 1

Present tenses

Present simple

The present simple is used

1 for describing routine actions or habits:
*Before breakfast, I **go** online to check my emails.* (It's my daily routine.)
*In this business, we **don't take** holidays in summer.* (Refers to every summer, not just this one.)

2 to show that a situation is permanent:
*His girlfriend **teaches** at a local primary school.* (It's a permanent job.)
*My grandparents **live** just around the corner from here.* (It's their permanent home.)

3 when something is always true, or a definite fact:
*In autumn, the trees in my garden **lose** their leaves.* (This always happens.)
*Water **freezes** at zero degrees Celsius.* (It's a scientific fact.)

Present continuous

The present continuous is used

1 to describe an action which is happening right at this moment:
*The children **are sleeping**, so we can't talk too loudly.* (They are sleeping right now.)
*Where **are** you **calling** from?* (We are on the phone right now.)

2 for a situation which is temporary, and will not last permanently:
***I'm doing** a training course at work at the moment.* (For a fixed period, not forever.)
***We're staying** with Jo while we look for a flat to rent.* (We'll leave Jo's home when we find a flat.)

3 when talking about changes or developing situations:
*The number of road accidents **is increasing** year by year.* (The situation is getting worse.)
Shopping online ***is becoming*** the most popular way to buy books. (It's developing.)

4 with *always*, when we want to show that we are annoyed or surprised by an action:
*My brother **is always borrowing** my laptop without asking me.* (This irritates me!)
*That new student **is always asking** the strangest questions in class!* (It's surprising.)

5 for **future arrangements** (see Grammar reference Unit 5):
***I'm having** dinner with Amy tomorrow night.*

The present continuous cannot normally be used with **stative verbs**, which describe a state (such as existing or feeling), as opposed to an action (such as walking or eating).

Some common stative verbs are: *agree, believe, belong, consider, consist, cost, disagree, exist, hate, have, know, like, love, matter, mean, need, own, prefer, realise, remain, remember, seem, suppose, think, understand, want.* For example:

*This car **belongs** to my uncle.* ✓ (state of possession)
~~*This car **is belonging** to my uncle.*~~
*That sound **doesn't exist** in my language.* ✓ (state of existence)
~~*That sound **isn't existing** in my language.*~~

However, some stative verbs can be used in the present continuous when they describe actions:

*John can't answer the phone because he**'s having** a shower.* ✓ (action, not state)
~~*John can't answer the phone because he **has** a shower.*~~
***Does** Claire's new apartment **have** a shower?* ✓ (state, not action)
~~***Is** Claire's new apartment **having** a shower?*~~

Present simple in time clauses

When we are talking about the future, the present simple must be used after time expressions like *when*:

*I'll send her an email when I **get** home.* ✓ (time clause after *when*)
~~*I'll send her an email when **I will** get home.*~~

Other expressions which are followed by the present simple are: *after, as soon as, before, by the time, next time, once, until.*

Unit 2

Past tenses

Past simple

The past simple is used for past events or actions:

*He **closed** the front door, **locked** it, and **set** off to work.*
*In the end, we **decided** not to move house.*

The past simple is often used with a specific time:

*The previous director **retired** in November.*
*She **wrote** her first novel in 2001.*

Past continuous

The past continuous is used for a continued action which was happening when another action took place:

*We arrived at the theatre just as the show **was starting**.*

In many cases, the continued action is interrupted:

*When he **called, I was watching** my favourite soap opera.* (His call interrupted me.)

The past continuous is also often used to set the scene at the beginning of a story:

*It **was raining** hard and an icy wind **was blowing**. Alex knew the journey would be impossible.*

The past continuous cannot normally be used with stative verbs:

*My grandparents rarely **disagreed** with each other.* ✓

~~*My grandparents **were** rarely **disagreeing** with each other.*~~

For a list of common stative verbs, see Grammar reference Unit 1: present tenses.

Past perfect

The past perfect is used to show that an action happened earlier than another past action:

*The police were unaware that the attacker **had** already **escaped**.* (The attacker escaped before the police realised.)

Sometimes it is not necessary to use the past perfect if it is very clear which action happened first:

*After we **finished** eating, we played cards.*

Past perfect continuous

The past perfect continuous is used for a continued action which happened before another past action:

*We**'d been working** so hard that we decided to take a break.* (We took a break after a continued period of work.)

The past perfect continuous can be used to show how long an action continued up to a certain point in the past:

*When the search began, the girl **had** already **been missing** for two days.* (She was missing for two days before the search began.)

used to / didn't use to

The structure *used to* + infinitive is used for repeated actions, habits or states in the past:

*Before the Internet, people **used to write** letters a lot more.*

The negative form of this structure is *didn't use to*:

*We **didn't use to have** a dishwasher in our old house.*

Used to is not normally used with time expressions which specify the duration of the action:

*I **smoked** for ten years, but then I gave up.* ✓

~~*I **used to smoke** for ten years, but then I gave up.*~~

Would + infinitive can also be used for actions and habits in the past:

*When I was a child, my dad **would** always **tell** me a story at bedtime.*

However, *would* cannot be used to talk about past states:

*This collection of paintings **used to belong** to a rich family.* ✓

~~*This collection of paintings **would belong** to a rich family.*~~

(*Belong* is a stative verb.)

Unit 3

Modal verbs

ability

To express ability in the present, we use *can* or *be able to*:

*On a clear day, you **can see** the mountains from my balcony.*

*I'**m not able to read** without my glasses.*

For general ability in the past, we use *could* or *be able to*:

*The sea was warm, so we **were able to swim** all year round.*

*In the old days you **could buy** everything at the local market.*

However, when we are talking about ability on one specific occasion in the past, we only use *be able to*, not *could*:

*Luckily we didn't get lost because Alice **was able to get** directions from someone.* ✓ (specific occasion)

~~*Luckily we didn't get lost because Alice **could get** directions from someone.*~~

possibility

To say that something is possible, we use *could*, *may* or *might*:

*Without treatment, your health **could be** at risk.*

*Let's have dinner indoors because it **might rain** later.*

*I **may be able** to join you later, but I can't say for sure.*

We use *could have*, *may have* or *might have* to talk about possibility in the past:

*She **could have let** us know about the change, but she forgot.*

*They **may have missed** the ferry because the traffic was bad.*

*This place **might have been** important in ancient times, but experts are not sure.*

impossibility

To say that something is impossible in the present, we use *can't*:

*You **can't cross** the river here because the bridge is closed.*

We use *can't have* or *couldn't have* to talk about impossibility in the past:

*You **can't have seen** James in town today because he was at home all day.*

*She **couldn't have won** the competition without her family's support.*

certainty

When we are certain about something, we use *must*:

*You **must be** exhausted after walking such a long way.*

To talk about certainty in the past, we use *must have*:

*They **must have been** terribly worried when their children didn't come home.*

obligation

To say that something is obligatory in the present, we often use *must* when the obligation is by the speaker:

Everyone ***must report*** *to me before they go home.*

When the obligation comes from outside, we often use *have to*:

The new law means that we ***have to pay*** *more for public transport.*

For both kinds of obligation in the past, we use *had to*:

We ***had to come*** *home by train because the airport was closed.*

no obligation / unnecessary

When there is no obligation to do something, or when something is unnecessary, we use *don't have to, don't need to* or *needn't*:

You ***don't have to bring*** *your own towel because everything is provided.*

You ***don't need to tell*** *me what happened. I saw it all for myself.*

We're going to eat out tonight, so you ***needn't cook*** *for us.*

We use *didn't need to* when something was unnecessary in the past, and did not happen:

We ***didn't need to pay*** *because the concert was free.* (We didn't pay because this was unnecessary.)

However, when we want to say that something unnecessary has happened, we use *needn't have*:

We ***needn't have hurried*** *because the train left late anyway.* (We hurried, but this was unnecessary.)

permission

To say that something is allowed, we use *can*:

You ***can park*** *outside the shop on weekdays.*

May is also used, but it is more formal:

May *I* ***ask*** *where you bought that beautiful dress?*

To talk about something that was allowed in the past, we use *could*:

When I was a child, we ***could play*** *outside as much as we wanted.*

When something is not allowed, we use *can't* or *mustn't*:

I'm sorry, but you ***can't sit*** *at this table because it's reserved.*

You ***mustn't start*** *writing until the teacher says so.*

For things that were not allowed in the past, we use *couldn't*:

In the old days, people ***couldn't travel*** *abroad without a visa.*

the right thing to do

When we want to say that something is the right or the wrong thing to do, we use *should / shouldn't* or *ought / ought not to*:

You ***shouldn't eat*** *too many sweets when you are on a diet.*

People ***ought to be*** *more careful about saving energy in the home.*

The past forms are *should have* and *ought to have*:

You ***should have asked*** *me before borrowing my bike.*

Adverbs of degree

These adverbs can be used with verbs, adjectives and other adverbs.

When we want to say 'a little', we can use *slightly* or *a bit* (less formal):

I'm feeling ***a bit*** *tired, so I'm going to bed now.*

When we want to say 'a lot' or 'very', we can use *absolutely, completely, extremely, really* or *totally*:

He drove ***extremely*** *fast all the way home.*

When we mean 'more than a little, but less than a lot', we can use *fairly, pretty, rather* or *quite*:

We were ***quite*** *surprised when she told us the news, even though we knew something was wrong.*

However, we normally only use *rather* with negative or surprising ideas:

I must say I was ***rather*** *disappointed with your exam results.*

With adjectives such as *right, sure* and *different*, ***quite*** means 'completely':

Are you ***quite*** *sure that you want me to tell Alex about this?*

With gradable adjectives and adverbs such as *good, happy* or *hard*, we use *extremely, fairly, quite, rather, really, slightly* or *very*:

She was ***very*** *angry when she heard what he had done.* ✓

(*Angry* is a gradable adjective, which means that it can be used to describe different levels of anger.)

~~*She was* ***absolutely*** *angry when she heard what he had done.*~~

With stronger (ungradable) adjectives and adverbs such as *wonderful, impossible* or *delighted*, we use *absolutely, completely, really* or *totally*:

She was ***absolutely*** *furious when she heard what he had done.* ✓

~~*She was* ***very*** *furious when she heard what she had done.*~~

(*Furious* is an ungradable adjective, which means that it describes an extreme state of anger which cannot have different levels.)

Unit 4

Verbs followed by *to* + infinitive or *-ing*

The following verbs are followed by *to* + infinitive: *agree*; *appear*; *choose*; *decide*; *expect*; *hope*; *learn*; *manage*; *offer*; *promise*; *refuse*; *seem*; *tend*; *threaten*; *want*:

*We **managed to finish** the report by the end of the day.*

The following verbs are followed by the *-ing* form: *admit*; *avoid*; *bother*; *deny*; *dislike*; *enjoy*; *finish*; *get round to*; *imagine*; *insist on*; *keep (on)*; *mind*; *miss*; *suggest*:

*I don't know anyone who **enjoys doing** housework.*

Some verbs can be followed by either *to* + infinitive or the *-ing* form, with no change in meaning. These verbs include *begin*, *continue* and *start*:

*You may **begin writing** as soon as I say so.*

*You may **begin to write** as soon as I say so.* (The meaning is the same in both examples.)

Other verbs can be followed by either *to* + infinitive or the *-ing* form, but with a change in meaning. These verbs include *forget*, *go on*, *remember*, *stop*, and *try*:

*I **forgot to talk** to her about it.* (I didn't talk to her because I forgot.)

*I'll never **forget talking** to her about it.* (I talked to her and now I won't forget.)

*He **went on to read** a book.* (He was doing something else and then started reading a book.)

*He **went on reading** a book.* (He continued to read the same book as before.)

I ***regret to tell*** you that nobody survived the fire. (I am sorry that I am giving you this bad news.)

*I **regret telling** you that nobody survived the fire.* (I told you, and now I wish I had not told you.)

*Please **remember to switch** the lights off.* (You shouldn't forget to do this.)

*I **remember switching** the lights off.* (I switched the lights off and I remember this fact.)

*I **stopped asking** him about his son.* (I didn't ask any more questions about his son.)

*I **stopped to ask** him about his son.* (I stopped what I was doing because I wanted to ask him about his son.)

*Have you **tried changing** your diet?* (Have you experimented with eating different foods?)

*Have you **tried to change** your diet?* (Have you made an effort to change what you eat?)

too and *enough*

When *too* is used before an adjective or adverb, it means 'more than we want or need':

I could tell by her smile that she was very happy. ✓

~~*I could tell by her smile that she was **too** happy.*~~ (This would mean 'happier than she wanted to be'.)

*I can't walk in these shoes because they're **too** small.* ✓

The structure *too* + adjective or adverb is often followed by *to* + infinitive:

*When we got home, we were **too tired to cook** dinner.*

Enough usually goes before a noun, but after an adjective. It usually means 'as much/many as we need':

*That plant isn't getting **enough sunlight**.*

*You will succeed if you work **hard enough**.*

Both structures are often followed by *to* + infinitive:

*We don't have **enough money to buy** a bigger house.*

Present perfect forms (with *for*, *since*, *already*, *yet* and *just*)

The present perfect can be used for an action or event that started in the past and is permanent:

*I**'ve known** Stephen since our university days.*

It is also used for a past action or event which has a result now:

*We**'ve** finally **finished** redecorating our house.*

However, it is not used when a past event is finished and has no connection with the present:

*When I was at school, my favourite subject **was** geography.* ✓

~~*When I was at school, my favourite subject **has been** geography.*~~ (My school days are finished and no connection is made with the present.)

For actions and events which began in the past and are still happening now, the present perfect continuous can be used:

*How long **have** you **been working** on this project?*

The present perfect continuous can be used to emphasise an action, while using the present perfect simple puts the emphasis on the result of the action:

*I**'ve been sending** emails all morning.* (emphasis on the action)

*I**'ve sent** twelve emails this morning.* (emphasis on the result)

We do not normally use the present perfect continuous with stative verbs:

*Animals **have existed** here for thousands of years.* ✓

~~*Animals **have been existing** here for thousands of years.*~~

(*Exist* is a stative verb.)

For a list of common stative verbs, see Grammar reference, Unit 1: present tenses.

We often use *for* and *since* with the present perfect simple and present perfect continuous. *For* is used to show the period of time during which an action or event took place, while *since* is used to show when an action or event started. They cannot be interchanged:

We've been sitting here ***for*** *over two hours.* ✓ (period of the action)

~~*We've been sitting here* ***since*** *over two hours.*~~

We've been sitting here ***since*** *lunchtime.* ✓ (time when the action started)

~~*We've been sitting here* ***for*** *lunchtime.*~~

Already is used when an event or action occurs sooner than expected:

I can't believe we've ***already*** *come to the end of our holiday.*

Yet is normally used with question forms and negatives. It shows that an action or event is expected, and often occurs at the end of a clause or sentence:

I know you need the report now, but I'm afraid I haven't finished it ***yet****.*

We use *just* to show that an action or event has occurred very recently:

Tania has ***just*** *called to say she won't be joining us tonight.*

Unit 5

Future forms

will

Will (the future simple) is used

1. for predictions about the future:
   *You**'ll feel** a lot better when you finish your exams.*
   Letters sent today ***will not arrive*** *until next week.*
2. for predictions which are uncertain:
   *I imagine they**'ll phone** you fairly soon.*
   Will *he* ***help*** *us find somewhere to stay?*
3. for sudden or spontaneous decisions:
   Is that the doorbell? ***I'll answer*** *it.*
   Who could help with this? I know! ***I'll give*** *Pete a call.*

going to

The *going to* future is used

1. for decisions or intentions about the future:
   *We**'re going to take** a longer holiday next year.*
   I'm *definitely* ***not going to call*** *him again.*
2. for predictions about the future based on evidence:
   *She looks awful. I think she**'s going to be** sick.*
   *You drive far too fast. You**'re going to have** an accident one of these days.*

Present continuous

The present continuous can be used for future arrangements:

I'm playing golf *with my brother later.*

*They**'re leaving** the country next week.*

The present simple can be used for future events which are fixed by a timetable or schedule:

The last bus ***leaves*** *at midnight.*

The show ***begins*** *at eight o'clock this evening.*

(For other uses of the present simple and continuous, see Grammar reference Unit 1.)

The future perfect is used for actions which will be completed before a particular point in the future:

Elena ***will have finished*** *her course by the end of July.*

Will *you* ***have decided*** *what to do by next week's meeting?*

Future continuous

The future continuous is used

1. for actions in progress in the future:
   *This time next week we**'ll be sunbathing** by the pool.*
   In many cases, the continued action may be interrupted:
   *Don't make too much noise when you come home tonight because I**'ll be sleeping**.*
2. for expected future events:
   I'll be seeing *John at work tomorrow so I'll ask him then.*
3. for polite questions:
   Will you be using *the car tomorrow?*

Countable and uncountable nouns

The indefinite article (*a/an*) can be used with singular countable nouns:

There seems to be ***a problem*** *with my laptop.*

With plural countable nouns, *(a) few*, *many* or *a lot / lots of* can be used:

She doesn't have ***many friends*** *apart from me.*

The indefinite article cannot be used with uncountable nouns:

Let me give you ***some advice****.* ✓

Let me give you ***a piece of advice****.* ✓

~~*Let me give you* ***an advice****.*~~ (*Advice* is an uncountable noun.)

Uncountable nouns do not have a plural form:

You can find more ***information*** *on our website.* ✓

~~*You can find more* ***informations*** *on our website.*~~

With uncountable nouns, *(a) little*, *much* or *a lot / lots of* can be used:

Anything is possible if you have ***a little patience****.*

Unit 6

Relative clauses

Defining relative clauses

Defining relative clauses are used to give essential information about a noun:

I've lost the book ***which you lent me***. (Gives essential information, defining which book we mean.)

How can I contact those men ***who helped you to move house***? (Gives essential information, defining which men we are talking about.)

The following relative pronouns can be used in defining relative clauses: *which* or *that* (for things); *who* or *that* (for people); *where* (for places); *when* (for times); *whose* (to indicate possession):

There are times ***when I feel like quitting my job***.

I've always admired people ***that know how to cook***.

Sometimes, *which* can refer to the whole clause or sentence which comes before it:

They've decided to move house, ***which I think is a good idea***. (Refers to their decision to move, not to the noun *house*.)

If the relative pronoun in a defining relative clause is the object, it can be omitted:

That isn't the woman ***I was talking about***. (The pronoun *who/that* is omitted.)

What's the most beautiful place ***you've ever been***? (The pronoun *where* is omitted.)

Non-defining relative clauses

Non-defining relative clauses are used to give extra information. They are usually separated from the main clause with commas:

The Prime Minister, ***who has visited the city on three previous occasions***, *will arrive here tomorrow.* (The meaning of the main part of the sentence does not change if the extra information is removed.)

The documents are kept in the Director's office, ***where they should remain at all times***.

That cannot be used as a relative pronoun in non-defining relative clauses. However, all the other relative pronouns mentioned above can be used:

The boy's parents, ***who were very concerned***, *contacted the police.* ✓

~~*The boy's parents,* ***that were very concerned***, *contacted the police.*~~

The relative pronoun cannot be omitted from non-defining relative clauses:

The city library, ***which many residents use on a regular basis***, *is expected to close next month.* ✓

~~*The city library,* ***many residents use on a regular basis***, *is expected to close next month.*~~

Purpose links

To express purpose, we use the structures *so that* and *in order that*, followed by a subject and a verb, either positive or negative:

I lent him some money ***so that he could*** *get a taxi home.*

Put your jacket on ***so that you don't get*** *cold.*

After *so*, it is possible to omit *that*:

I lent him some money ***so he*** *could get a taxi home.*

Put your jacket on ***so you*** *don't get cold.*

In order that is more formal:

The trial will be postponed until next month ***in order that*** *all the evidence can be collected.*

We can also use the structures *so as to* and *in order to*, followed by a verb in the infinitive:

They moved to Wales ***in order to*** *be closer to their family.*

The negative forms are *so as not to* and *in order not to*:

I walked upstairs very quietly, ***so as not to*** *wake the children.*

Unit 7

Conditional forms

Conditional sentences usually consist of a main clause and a conditional clause which begins with *if* or *unless*:

If I don't hear from her by tomorrow, *I'll call the police.*

It is possible to reverse the order of the clauses:

I'll call the police ***if I don't hear from her by tomorrow***.

The **first conditional** is used when we are talking about a possible future event. The present simple appears in the conditional clause. In the other clause, we use *will*, *may*, *might* or *could*:

If you ***call*** *me tomorrow,* ***I'll give*** *you all the information.*

The situation ***could*** *become dangerous unless immediate action* ***is taken***.

The **second conditional** is used when we are talking about a present or future event which is unlikely, imaginary or impossible. The past simple appears in the conditional clause. In the other clause, *would*, *might* or *could* is used:

If she ***found*** *out where he was, she* ***might try*** *to find him.*

They ***wouldn't behave*** *like that unless something* ***was*** *wrong.*

If I ***were*** *you, I* ***would wait*** *for a while before contacting them.*

We use the **third conditional** when we are talking about the imaginary result of a situation in the past. The past perfect is used in the conditional clause. In the other clause, we use *would*, *might* or *could* with *have* and the past participle:

*I **wouldn't have come** if I **had known** that you were ill.* (I didn't know you were ill, so I came.)

*If Mike **hadn't spent** so much time playing computer games, he **could have passed** his exams.* (He didn't pass his exams because he spent so much time playing computer games.)

Sometimes we use **mixed conditionals**, which include parts of both second and third conditional sentences. For example, when we imagine the present result of a situation in the past, we use the past perfect in the conditional clause, but complete the sentence with a second conditional form:

*If Jim **hadn't been** such a careless driver, he **would** still **be** with us today.* (Jim was a careless driver and as a result, he is not with us today.)

When we are talking about the imaginary result of a present or permanent situation, we use the past simple in the conditional clause, but complete the sentence with a third conditional form:

*He **wouldn't have been able** to help you if he **wasn't** a doctor.* (He was able to help you because he's a doctor.)

Comparison of adjectives and adverbs; superlative forms

We use the suffix *-er* to form the comparative of most one-syllable adjectives:

*They felt a lot **calmer** once they knew their children were safe.*

*The weather is **hotter** in the south of the country.*

The superlative form of these adjectives ends in *-est*:

*That's the **kindest** thing she's ever said to me.*

Some short adjectives and adverbs have irregular comparative and superlative forms. *Better* and *best* are the comparative and superlative forms of *good* and *well; worse* and *worst* are the comparative and superlative forms of *bad* and *badly*; *further* and *furthest* are the usual comparative and superlative of *far*.

One- and two-syllable adjectives which end in *-y* have comparative forms ending in *-ier*:

*She looks much **prettier** now that she's had her hair cut.*

The superlative form of these adjectives ends in *-iest*:

*July tends to be the **driest** month of the year in my country.*

More is normally used to form the comparative of adjectives and adverbs with two or more syllables:

*There's nothing **more irritating** than losing your keys.*

The superlative of these adjectives and adverbs is formed with *most*:

*Of all the presentations we heard today, yours was the **most carefully** prepared.*

When we want to say that two things are the same, we often use the structure *as ... as* with either an adjective or an adverb:

*The new traffic system is just **as slow as** the old one.*

The structure *not as / not so ... as* can be used with either an adjective or an adverb to compare two things which are not the same:

*Her new novel is **not as complicated as** the previous one.*

Less can also be used, with the same meaning:

*Her new novel is **less complicated** than the previous one.*

The superlative form of *less* is *least*:

*Henry is the **least successful** of the three brothers.*

Contrast links

However, *nevertheless* and *on the other hand* can be used to express contrast. They often come at the beginning of the sentence and are usually separated from the rest of the sentence with a comma:

*This problem is clearly getting worse. **However**, nobody seems to want to do anything about it.*

When *on the other hand* is used, the first sentence or paragraph often begins with *on the one hand*:

***On the one hand**, the problem is clearly getting worse. **On the other hand**, nobody seems to be doing anything about it.*

In contrast and *by contrast* indicate contrast between two things. They are also usually separated from the rest of the sentence with a comma:

*Traditional fuels can harm the environment. **In contrast**, solar power is far less damaging.*

Although and *even though* also express contrast, but they introduce a clause which contains a subject and a verb. They cannot be followed by a comma and they cannot be used when the sentence only has one clause:

*Some governments are refusing to take action **although** the situation is urgent.* ✓

~~*Some governments are refusing to take action. **Although**, the situation is urgent.*~~

While and *whereas* are followed by a subject and verb, and can be used to express a contrast between two things:

*A letter can take days to arrive, **whereas** an email can be sent in a few seconds.*

Despite and *in spite of* have a similar meaning to *although*, but they must be followed by an *-ing* form or a noun / noun phrase:

*Despite **having some advantages**, solar power is not widely used in my country.* ✓

*Despite **its advantages**, solar power is not widely used in my country.* ✓

~~*Despite **it has advantages**, solar power is not widely used in my country.*~~

If we add *the fact (that)* after *despite* or *in spite of*, we can finish the clause in the same way as with *although*:

*Recycling is essential, **although it takes time**.*

*Recycling is essential, **in spite of the fact that it takes time**.*

Unit 8

Passive forms

The passive is formed using the correct form of the auxiliary verb *be* and a past participle:

*Several parts of the city **were damaged** in the storm.*

The auxiliary and the past participle may be separated, for example by an adverb:

*Several parts of the city **were badly damaged** in the storm.*

The passive is often used in formal written English, for example in news reports, academic texts, or scientific or technical writing:

*Water **is pumped** through the system by a high-performance electric motor.*

The passive is sometimes formed using the auxiliary *get*, but this is informal and is most common in spoken English:

*There wasn't enough room in the car, so Janet **got left** behind.*

If we want to say who or what did the action, we use the preposition *by*:

*A new medical treatment is being developed **by scientists**.* (Scientists are developing a new medical treatment.)

The passive is often used when we don't know who did something:

*The woman **was attacked** on her way home from work.* (Her attacker is unknown.)

It can also be used to show that an event itself is more important than the person or thing which caused it:

*He will not be playing because he **was injured** during last week's match.* (The injury and its consequences are more important than the cause.)

We also use the passive when we don't need or don't want to say who did something:

*A 20-year-old man **was arrested** yesterday.* (It is obvious that the police arrested him.)

In more formal English, an impersonal passive can be formed using *it* and a verb such as *believe*, *consider*, *expect*, *know*, *report*, *say* or *think*:

***It is thought** that the President will arrive tomorrow.* (People think the President will arrive tomorrow.)

An impersonal passive can also be formed with verbs such as *believe*, *consider*, *feel*, *know* or *think*. However, in this type of passive structure, the passive verb is followed by *to* + infinitive, not *that* + clause:

*People **believe that he is** guilty.* ✓ (active)

*He **is believed to be** guilty.* ✓ (impersonal passive)

~~*He **is believed that** he is guilty.*~~

When we use this structure to report something which happened in the past, the passive verb is followed by *to* + perfect infinitive (*have* + past participle):

*People **think that he took part** in the robbery.* ✓ (active verb reporting a past event)

*He **is thought to have taken part** in the robbery.* ✓ (impersonal passive with perfect infinitive)

~~*He **is thought that he took part** in the robbery.*~~

Articles

We use the **indefinite article** *(a/an)* when we mention a singular countable noun for the first time:

*Just as I turned the corner, I saw **a car** coming towards me.*

We also use *a/an* when talking about people's jobs:

*She has been working as **a doctor** for more than twenty years.*

The indefinite article also appears in some expressions with numbers:

*We have seen **a 20 per cent** drop in sales this year.*

We use the **definite article** *(the)* when we have already mentioned something, or when it is common knowledge:

*At the zoo, we saw lions, tigers and elephants. **The tigers** were my favourite.* (They have been mentioned previously.)

*Do you mind if I open **the window**?* (We both know which window.)

We also use *the* when there is only one of something:

*I think you should tell **the manager** about this.*

The definite article is used with superlatives:

*That's **the most ridiculous** thing I've ever heard.*

The is also used with inventions, types of animal, and musical instruments:

__The computer__ was an important invention of the 20th century.

__The wild goat__ can be found in mountain areas.

My mother forced me to learn __the violin__.

When used with an adjective, *the* can indicate a certain group of people:

This problem does not affect __the rich__. (rich people)

No article is used when we are talking in general and in the plural, or with abstract nouns:

My city has never been popular with __tourists__.

To be a good parent, you need to have __patience__.

When we talk about sports or certain illnesses, no article is used:

She's absolutely brilliant at __tennis__.

Scientists have not yet found a cure for __cancer.__

However, some common illnesses are exceptions to this rule:

If you go out without a jacket you might catch __a cold__.

No article is needed before certain nouns in expressions with *to*, including *to bed*, *to work*, *to prison* and *to school*.

Unit 9

Reported speech and reporting verbs

Tenses in reported speech

When direct speech is reported in the past, verb tenses often change. Verbs in the present simple often change to the past simple:

'The boss __is__ really disappointed with your work.'

She explained that the boss __was__ really disappointed with my work.

Verbs in the present continuous change to the past continuous:

'We__'re watching__ TV at Dave's house.'

They said they __were watching__ TV at Dave's house.

Verbs in the present perfect change to the past perfect:

'__I've finished my__ essay.'

She said she __had finished__ her essay.

Verbs in the past simple often change to the past perfect:

'I __tried__ to call you three times.'

He said he __had tried__ to call me three times.

Many modal verbs do not change when they are reported, but *can* changes to *could*, and *may* changes to *might*. When we are talking about obligation, *must* often changes to *had to*:

'You __must tidy__ your room before going out.'

She said I __had to tidy__ my room before going out.

In the future simple, *will* changes to *would*:

'__I'll let__ you know as soon as possible.'

He said he __would let__ us know as soon as possible.

However, a change in verb tense does not always occur, especially when the situation is still the same when the verb is reported:

'I __don't eat__ meat.'

He told us that he __doesn't eat__ meat. (This is still true now.)

It isn't always necessary to change verbs from the past simple to the past perfect:

'As a boy, I __played__ tennis every day.'

He told me he __played__ tennis every day as a boy. ✓

He told me he __had played__ tennis every day as a boy. ✓

Other changes

Some other words may change when direct speech is reported. For example, pronouns and expressions of time and place may be different:

'I'll meet __you here tomorrow__.'

He promised to meet __me there the following day__.

Reported questions

In reported questions, the subject comes before the main verb (not after the main verb, as in direct questions). This means that reported questions have the same order as statements:

__I'm__ from Brazil. (statement)

Where __are you__ from? (direct question)

I asked her where __she was__ from. ✓ (reported question)

~~*I asked her where __was she__ from.*~~

The auxiliary verbs *do, does* and *did* are not used in reported questions:

What time did you get up?

They asked me what time __I had got up__. ✓

~~*They asked me what time __did I get up__.*~~

When 'yes/no' questions are reported, we add either *if* or *whether*:

'Did you enjoy your meal?'

He asked us __if__ we had enjoyed our meal. ✓

He asked us __whether__ we had enjoyed our meal. ✓

~~*He asked us had we enjoyed our meal.*~~

Reporting verbs

Reporting verbs can be divided into categories according to the grammatical patterns which come after them.

Some verbs, including *agree*, *claim*, *decide*, *offer*, *promise*, *refuse* and *threaten*, are followed by *to* + infinitive:

'I do not wish to comment on what happened.'

*He **refused to comment** on what happened.*

Other verbs, including *advise*, *ask*, *beg*, *forbid*, *invite*, *order*, *persuade*, *remind*, *tell* and *warn*, are followed by an object + *to* + infinitive:

'Don't forget to bring an umbrella.'

*She **reminded me to bring** an umbrella.*

Some verbs, including *admit*, *deny*, *recall*, *recommend* and *suggest*, are followed by the *-ing* form:

'It wasn't me who stole the money.'

*He **denied stealing** the money.*

Verbs such as *claim*, *complain*, *confess*, *decide*, *deny*, *explain*, *insist*, *mention*, *promise*, *recommend*, *reply*, *suggest* and *threaten* can be followed by (*that* +) a clause:

'I'll call you back by the end of the day.'

*She **promised that she would call** me back by the end of the day.*

Some other verbs are followed by a verb + preposition + *-ing*. These include *apologise for*, *insist on* and *advise against*:

'I'm really sorry I was so horrible to you.'

*She **apologised for being** so horrible to me.*

Accuse is slightly different, because it is followed by an object + preposition + *-ing*:

'We think you lied about your experience.'

*They **accused me of lying** about my experience.*

Unit 10

Position of adverbs of manner and opinion

When adverbs are used to describe how something happens, they are called **adverbs of manner**:

*They didn't like each other at first but after a while they got on **brilliantly**.*

*He spoke **calmly**, without showing how nervous he was.*

Adverbs such as *obviously* or *sadly* can be used to show our opinion of what is being said:

***Obviously**, parents are responsible for looking after their children.*

***Sadly,** they had to come home early because Martin got ill.*

Other adverbs which can be used in this way are: *actually*, *clearly*, *hopefully*, *interestingly*, *personally*, *strangely*, *surprisingly* and *unfortunately*.

As shown in the examples above, adverbs of manner and opinion may occur at the beginning, middle or end of a sentence or clause. However, they almost never appear between a verb and its object:

*He **slowly** took his phone out of his pocket.* ✓

***Slowly**, he took his phone out of his pocket.* ✓

*He took his phone out of his pocket **slowly**.* ✓

~~*He took **slowly** his phone out of his pocket.*~~ (*His phone* is the object of *took*.)

Adverbs of opinion are sometimes used between commas to show that the speaker is commenting on the whole clause or sentence:

*We have found that a number of drivers, **unfortunately**, fail to respect the speed limit.*

wish and *if only*

To express regret about a past situation, we can use *wish* or *if only* + past perfect:

***He** now **wishes he hadn't bought** a second car.* (He bought a second car, but now he regrets it.)

To talk about a present situation which we would like to change, we use *wish* or *if only* + past simple. *If only* is used when we feel very strongly:

***If only I lived** closer to my office.* (I don't live close to my office, but I would like to.)

To talk about something which we would like to happen in the future, we use *wish* or *if only* + subject + *could* + infinitive:

***I wish I could see** her again.* (I would like to see her again in the future.)

***If only I could see** her again.* (I feel very strongly that I would like to see her again in the future.)

When we use *wish* or *if only* + *would* instead of *could*, there is a sense that we are annoyed or frustrated:

***If only they would stop** making so much noise when I'm trying to sleep.* (It is annoying that I can't sleep because of the noise they are making.)

We cannot use *wish* + *would* + infinitive if the subject of *wish* is the same as the subject of *would*:

***She wishes she could get** better marks at school.* ✓

~~***She wishes she would get** better marks at school.*~~ (*She* is the subject of both *wish* and *would*.)

Causative *have* and *get*

We can use causative *have* when we ask or pay someone to do something for us:

My parents ***had their living room redecorated*** *last year.* (They paid someone to redecorate their living room.)

Causative *have* is formed with:

subject + *have* + object + past participle

My parents are going to have their living room redecorated.

In informal or spoken English, we sometimes use *get* instead of *have*:

*I can't meet you this afternoon because I'****m getting my hair cut****.* (I'm paying someone to cut my hair.)

We can also use this structure when we want to say that something unpleasant has been done to us:

Our neighbours ***had their car stolen*** *when they were on holiday.*

Irregular verbs

infinitive	**past simple**	**past participle**
break	broke	broken
bring	brought	brought
broadcast	broadcast	broadcast
build	built	built
choose	chose	chosen
cost	cost	cost
cut	cut	cut
deal	dealt	dealt
draw	drew	drawn
fly	flew	flown
forget	forgot	forgotten
grow	grew	grown
hear	heard	heard
hit	hit	hit
hold	held	held
mean	meant	meant
pay	paid	paid
rise	rose	risen
shake	shook	shook
sing	sang	sung
sink	sank	sunk
sleep	slept	slept
spend	spent	spent
spill	spilt	spilt
steal	stole	stolen
swear	swore	sworn
teach	taught	taught
wear	wore	worn
win	won	won

WORDLIST

adj = adjective, *adv* = adverb, *n* = noun, *v* = verb, *pv* = phrasal verb, *prep* = preposition, *exp* = expression

Note: the numbers show which page the word or phrase first appears on in the unit.

Unit 1

adventurous *adj* (13) willing to try new or difficult things, or exciting and often dangerous things

ambitious *adj* (12) having a strong wish to be successful, powerful or rich

artistic *adj* (13) able to create or enjoy art

bossy *adj* (12) describes someone who is always telling people what to do

bother *v* (11) to make someone feel worried or upset

cautious *adj* (13) describes someone who avoids risks

challenging *adj* (11) difficult, in a way that tests your ability or determination

cheeky *adj* (13) slightly rude or showing no respect, but often in a funny way

childish *adj* (12) (disapproving) If an adult is childish, they behave in a way that would be expected of a child.

client *n* (11) a customer or someone who receives services

competitive *adj* (13) wanting very much to win or be more successful than other people

dash *n* (11) When you run somewhere very quickly, you 'make a dash for it'.

depressing *adj* (11) making you feel unhappy and without hope for the future

emotional *adj* (13) having and expressing strong feelings

energetic *adj* (13) having or involving a lot of energy

exhausted *adj* (11) extremely tired

fascinating *adj* (11) extremely interesting

foolish *adj* (13) unwise, stupid or not showing good judgement

grab *v* (11) to take the opportunity to get, use or enjoy something quickly

greedy *adj* (13) wanting a lot more food, money, etc. than you need

head for *pv* (11) to go in a particular direction

irritating *adj* (9) making you feel annoyed

make up for *pv* (11) to take the place of something lost or damaged or to compensate for something bad with something good

optimistic *adj* (12) hopeful; believing that good things will happen in the future

peak *n* (11) the highest, strongest or best point, value or level of skill

query *n* (11) a question, often expressing doubt about something or looking for an answer

refreshed *adj* (11) less hot or tired

roll *v* (11) to move somewhere easily and without sudden movements; to move somewhere by turning in a circular direction, or to make something move this way

schedule *n* (11) a list of planned activities or things to be done showing the times or dates when they are intended to happen or be done

sensitive *adj* (12) easily upset by the things people say or do, or causing people to be upset, embarrassed or angry; understanding what other people need, and being helpful and kind to them

sympathetic *adj* (13) describes someone who shows, especially by what they say, that they understand and care about someone's suffering

task *n* (8) a piece of work to be done

thoughtful *adj* (12) kind and always thinking about how you can help other people

unsurprisingly *adv* (11) used to say that something is not unusual or unexpected

Unit 2

at ease *exp* (17) relaxed

at first sight *exp* (21) when you first see someone or something

balanced diet *n* (17) a combination of the correct types and amounts of food

bargain *n* (17) something on sale at a lower price than its true value

be attracted to *exp* (21) If you are attracted by or to someone, you like them.

break off *pv* (21) to end a relationship

break somebody's heart *exp* (21) to make someone who loves you very sad, usually by telling them you have stopped loving them

catering *n* (18) the activities involved in preparing and providing food and drink

chop *v* (18) to cut something into pieces with an axe, a knife or other sharp instrument

consume *v* (18) to eat or drink, especially a lot of something

get on somebody's nerves *exp* (21) to annoy someone a lot

go off *pv* (18) If food or drink goes off, it is not good to eat or drink any more because it is too old.

heat up *pv* (17) to make something hot or warm, or to become hot or warm

in season *exp* (18) If fruit and vegetables are in season, they are being produced in the area and are available and ready to eat.

junk food *n* (17) food that is unhealthy but is quick and easy to eat

keep somebody company *exp* (21) to stay with someone so that they are not alone

leave somebody alone *exp* (21) to stop speaking to or annoying someone

live on *pv* (17) to only eat a particular type of food

lose touch *pv* (21) to stop communicating with someone, usually because they do not live near you now

portion *n* (17) the amount of a particular food that is served to one person, especially in a restaurant or a shop which sells food ready to be eaten

propose to *pv* (21) to ask someone to marry you

ripe *adj* (18) (of fruit or crops) completely developed and ready to be collected or eaten

skip *v* (17) not to do or not to have something that you usually do or that you should do

slice *v* (18) to cut something into thin, flat pieces

son-in-law *n* (21) your daughter's husband

starving *adj* (17) very hungry

take somebody/something for granted *exp* (21) If you take situations or people for granted, you do not realise or show that you are grateful for how much you get from them.

tough *adj* (18) describes food that is difficult to cut or eat

Unit 3

ashamed of *exp* (29) feeling guilty or embarrassed about something you have done

capable of *exp* (29) having the ability, power or qualities to be able to do something

conscious of *exp* (26) aware that a particular thing or person exists or is present

cruise *n* (24) a journey on a large ship for pleasure, during which you visit several places

familiar with *exp* (29) knowing something or someone well

fed up with *exp* (29) bored, annoyed or disappointed, especially by something that you have experienced for too long

get away *pv* (26) to go somewhere to have a holiday, often because you need to rest

have nothing to do with *exp* (29) to have no connection or influence with someone or something

in connection with *exp* (29) on the subject of something

in need of *exp* (29) having to have something that you do not have

in place of *exp* (29) instead of someone or something

in relation to *exp* (29) in connection with something

in response to *exp* (29) as an answer or reaction to something

in terms of *exp* (29) used to describe which particular area of a subject you are discussing

in view of *exp* (29) because of a particular thing, or considering a particular fact

involved in *exp* (29) included in something

means of transport *exp* (27) a way of travelling

obliged to *exp* (29) forced to do something or feeling that you must do something

obsessed with *exp* (29) unable to stop thinking about something; too interested in or worried about something

prepared to *exp* (29) willing, or happy to agree to do something

required to *exp* (29) when it is necessary for you to do something

sensitive to *exp* (29) easily upset by the things people say or do

sort of *exp* (29) one of a group of things which are of the same type or which share similar qualities

be supposed to *v* (29) to be expected to be something; to be considered by many people to be something; intended or expected to

the trouble with *exp* (29) used to say what is wrong with someone or something

tour operator *n* (26) a company that makes arrangements for travel and places to stay, often selling these together as package holidays

trekking *n* (24) the activity of walking long distances, usually over land such as hills, mountains or forests

voyage *n* (24) a long journey, especially by ship

wander *v* (24) to walk around slowly in a relaxed way or without any clear purpose or direction

with regard to *exp* (29) in connection with

Unit 4

absurd *adj* (38) stupid or unreasonable; silly in a humorous way

bizarre *adj* (38) very strange and unusual

bother *v* (35) to make the effort to do something

breathtaking *adj* (38) extremely exciting, beautiful or surprising

cast *n* (32) the actors in a film, play or show

count on *pv* (33) to be confident that you can depend on someone

delightful *adj* (38) very pleasant, attractive or enjoyable

depend on *pv* (33) to trust someone or something and know that they will help you or do what you want or expect them to do

dreadful *adj* (38) very bad, of very low quality, or shocking and very sad

entertaining *adj* (32) funny and enjoyable

exceptional *adj* (38) much greater than usual, especially in skill, intelligence, quality, etc.

fine *adj* (38) excellent or much better than average

focus on *pv* (33) to give a lot of attention to one particular person, subject or thing

go on *pv* (35) to continue

impressive *adj* (38) If an object or achievement is impressive, you admire or respect it, usually because it is special, important or very large.

log on *pv* (33) to connect a computer to a computer system by typing your name, so that you can start working

lyrics *n* (32) the words of a song, especially a pop song

moving *adj* (38) causing strong feelings of sadness or sympathy

mysterious *adj* (38) strange, not known or not understood

outstanding *adj* (38) excellent; clearly very much better than what is usual

plot *n* (37) the story of a book, film, play, etc.

poor *adj* (32) not good, being of a very low quality, quantity or standard

regret *v* (35) to feel sorry about a situation, especially something sad or wrong or a mistake that you have made

rely on *pv* (32) to need a particular thing or the help and support of someone or something in order to continue, to work correctly, or to succeed

remarkable *adj* (38) unusual or special and therefore surprising and worth mentioning

scene *n* (32) a part of a play or film in which events happen in one place

set *v* (32) If a story, film, etc. is set in a particular time or place, the action in it happens in that time or place.

shot *n* (32) a short piece in a film in which there is a single action or a short series of actions

solo *n* (32) a musical performance done by one person alone, or a musical performance in which one person is given special attention

soundtrack *n* (32) the sounds, especially the music, of a film, or a separate recording of this

superb *adj* (38) of excellent quality; very great

tend *v* (35) to be likely to behave in a particular way or have a particular characteristic

tense *adj* (38) If a situation is tense, it causes feelings of worry or nervousness.

theme *n* (38) the main subject of a talk, book, film, etc.

tremendous *adj* (38) very great in amount or level, or extremely good

work *n* (32) something created as a result of effort, especially a painting, book or piece of music

Unit 5

academic *adj* (40) relating to schools, colleges and universities, or connected with studying and thinking, not with practical skills

commerce *n* (44) the activities involved in buying and selling things

consultant *n* (47) someone who advises people on a particular subject

current *adj* (43) of the present time

demanding *adj* (43) needing a lot of time, attention or energy

duty *n* (44) something that you have to do because it is part of your job, or something that you feel is the right thing to do

earnings *plural n* (44) the amount of money that someone is paid for the work they do

gain *v* (43) to increase in weight, speed, height or amount

graduate *n* (40) a person who has a first degree from a university or college

highly *adv* (43) very, to a large degree, or at a high level

institution *n* (44) a large and important organisation, such as a university or bank

inventor *n* (41) someone who has invented something or whose job is to invent things

lecturer *n* (41) someone who teaches at a college or university

management *n* (43) the group of people responsible for controlling and organising a company; the control and organisation of something

manufacturing *n* (44) the business of producing goods in large numbers

motivated *adj* (43) wanting to do something well

novelist *n* (41) a person who writes novels

operator *n* (41) someone whose job is to use and control a machine or vehicle

overtime *adv* (44) (time spent working) after the usual time needed or expected in a job

position *n* (43) a job

production *n* (44) the process of making or growing goods to be sold

qualify *v* (40) to successfully finish a training course so that you are able to do a job; to have or achieve the necessary skills, etc.

roughly *adv* (43) approximately

seminar *n* (40) an occasion when a teacher or expert and a group of people meet to study and discuss something

shortly *adv* (43) soon

supplier *n* (41) a company, person, etc. that provides things that people want or need, especially over a long period of time

take on *pv* (43) to accept a particular job or responsibility; to employ

take out a loan *exp* (43) to borrow a sum of money, often from a bank, which has to be paid back, usually together with an extra amount of money that you have to pay as a charge for borrowing

take over *pv* (43) to get control of a company by buying most of its shares

thesis *n* (40) a long piece of writing on a particular subject, especially one that is done for a higher college or university degree

take up *pv* (43) to start doing a particular job or activity

tutor *n* (40) a teacher who works with one student or a small group, either at a British college or university or in the home of a child

unlike *prep* (43) different from someone or something

Unit 6

competitive *adj* (54) involving competition

diving *n* (52) the sport of jumping into water or swimming under water

eat up *pv* (51) to eat all the food that you have been given

facility *n* (54) a place, especially including buildings, where a particular activity happens

helmet *n* (52) a strong hard hat that covers and protects the head

illness *n* (48) a disease of the body or mind

infection *n* (48) a disease in a part of your body that is caused by bacteria or a virus

injury *n* (48) physical harm or damage to someone's body caused by an accident or an attack

medal *n* (51) a small metal disc, with words or a picture on it, which is given as a reward for winning a sports competition

pitch *n* (52) an area painted with lines for playing particular sports, especially football

slope *n* (52) a surface or piece of land that is high at one end and low at the other

smell *n* (48) the ability to notice or discover that a substance is present by using your nose

speak up *pv* (51) to speak in a louder voice so that people can hear you

spectator *n* (53) a person who watches an activity, especially a sports event, without taking part

sum up *pv* (51) to describe or express the important facts or characteristics about something or someone

taste *n* (48) the flavour of something, or the ability of a person or animal to recognise different flavours

thermometer *n* (48) a device used for measuring temperature, especially of the air or in a person's body

touch *n* (48) the ability to know what something is like by feeling it with the fingers

treatment *n* (48) the use of drugs, exercises, etc. to cure a person of an illness or injury

use up *pv* (51) to finish a supply of something

wound *n* (48) a damaged area of the body, such as a cut or hole in the skin or flesh made by a weapon

Unit 7

acid rain *n* (56) rain which contains large amounts of harmful chemicals as a result of burning substances such as coal and oil

alternative *n* (59) something that is different from something else, especially from what is usual, and offering the possibility of choice

bear in mind *exp* (61) to remember a piece of information when you are making a decision or thinking about a matter

chemical *n* (59) any basic substance which is used in or produced by a reaction involving changes to atoms or molecules

climate change *n* (56) the way the world's weather is changing

conservation *n* (56) the protection of plants and animals, natural areas, and interesting and important structures and buildings, especially from the damaging effects of human activity

cut down on *pv* (59) to do less of something or use something in smaller amounts

device *n* (58) an object or machine which has been invented for a particular purpose

disposal *n* (59) when you get rid of something, especially by throwing it away

extreme *adj* (56) very severe or bad

freezing *adj* (56) extremely cold

frost *n* (56) a period of time in which air temperature is below the freezing point of water, or the white, powdery layer of ice which forms in these conditions, especially outside at night

generate *v* (59) to cause something to exist

global warming *n* (56) a gradual increase in world temperatures caused by polluting gases such as carbon dioxide which are collecting in the air around the Earth and preventing heat escaping into space

hi-tech/high-tech *adj, n* (58) using the most advanced and developed machines and methods

in all *exp* (61) with everything added together to make a total

in doubt *exp* (61) If the future or success of someone or something is in doubt, it is unlikely to continue or to be successful.

in due course *exp* (61) at a suitable time in the future

in practice *exp* (59) in reality rather than what is meant to happen

in progress *exp* (61) happening or being done now

in the long term *exp* (61) for a long period of time in the future

in the meantime *exp* (61) until something expected happens, or while something else is happening

industrial waste *exp* (56) unwanted matter or material caused by the process of producing things in a factory

mild *adj* (56) describes weather that is not very cold or not as cold as usual

mist *n* (56) thin fog produced by very small drops of water collecting in the air just above an area of ground or water

play a part in *exp* (61) to help to achieve something

poisonous *adj* (59) very harmful and able to cause illness or death

process *v* (59) to prepare, change or treat food or raw materials as a part of an industrial operation

regulation *n* (59) an official rule that controls how something is done

severe *adj* (56) causing very great pain, difficulty, worry, damage, etc; very serious

shelter *n* (56) (a building designed to give) protection from bad weather, danger or attack

solar power *n* (56) electricity produced by using the energy from the sun

substance *n* (59) material with particular physical characteristics

substitute *n* (59) a thing or person that is used instead of another thing or person

toxic *adj* (58) poisonous

tropical storm *n* (56) an extreme weather condition with very strong winds and heavy rain that forms over tropical oceans

Unit 8

absorb *v* (67) to take something in, especially gradually

anti-virus *adj* (69) produced and used to protect the main memory of a computer against infection by a virus

application *n* (69) a computer program that is designed for a particular purpose

atom *n* (66) The smallest unit of any chemical element, consisting of a positive nucleus surrounded by negative electrons. Atoms can combine to form a molecule.

bookmark *n* (69) a record of the address of an Internet document on your computer so that you can find it again easily

breakthrough *n* (66) an important discovery or event that helps to improve a situation or provide an answer to a problem

broadband *n* (64) a system that makes it possible for many messages or large amounts of information to be sent at the same time and very quickly between computers or other electronic devices

browse *v* (69) to look at information on the Internet

bug *n* (69) a mistake or problem in a computer program

carbon dioxide *n* (66) the gas formed when carbon is burned, or when people or animals breathe out

carbon monoxide *n* (66) the poisonous gas formed by the burning of carbon, especially in the form of car fuel

casually *adv* (65) in a way that shows you do not find something difficult or important

cell *n* (66) the smallest basic unit of a plant or animal

charge *v* (69) to put electricity into an electrical device such as a battery

crash *v* (69) If a computer or system crashes, it suddenly stops operating.

data *n* (69) information, especially facts or numbers, collected to be examined and considered and used to help decision-making, or information in an electronic form that can be stored and processed by a computer

database *n* (64) a large amount of information stored in a computer system in such a way that it can be easily looked at or changed

desktop *n* 64) a type of computer that is small enough to fit on the top of a desk

element *n* (66) a simple substance which cannot be reduced to smaller chemical parts, e.g. hydrogen

faint *adj* (69) not strong or clear; slight

instant messaging *n* (64) a type of service available on the Internet that allows you to exchange written messages with someone else who is using the service at the same time

interact *v* (64) to communicate with or react to

launch *v* 69) to send something out, such as a new ship to sea or a rocket into space

prove *v* (69) to show that something is true

run *v* (69) If you run a computer program, you use it on your computer.

satellite *n* (69) a device sent up into space to travel round the Earth, used for collecting information or communicating by radio, television, etc.

social networking *n* (64) the activity of sharing information and communicating with groups of people using the Internet, especially through websites that are specially designed for this purpose

spreadsheet *n* (64) a computer program, used especially in business, which allows you to do financial calculations and plans

test tube *n* (66) a small glass tube, with one closed and rounded end, which is used in scientific experiments

theory *n* (69) a formal statement of the rules on which a subject of study is based or of ideas which are suggested to explain a fact or event or, more generally, an opinion or explanation

times *adv* (69) multiplied by

tone of voice *n* (65) a quality in the voice which expresses the speaker's feelings or thoughts, often towards the person being spoken to

undo *v* (65) to remove the good or bad effects of an action or several actions

update *n* (67) new information

wave *n* (67) the pattern in which some types of energy, such as sound, light and heat, are spread or carried

Unit 9

broadcasting *n* (72) when programmes are sent out on television or radio

commercial *n* (72) an advertisement which is broadcast on television or radio

current affairs *plural n* (72) political news about events happening now

editor *n* (72) a person who corrects or changes pieces of text or films before they are printed or shown, or a person who is in charge of a newspaper or magazine

episode *n* (72) one of the single parts into which a story is divided, especially when it is broadcast on the television or radio

gossip column *n* (72) the part of a newspaper in which you find stories about the social and private lives of famous people

headlines *plural n* (72) the lines of words printed in large letters as the title of a story in a newspaper, or the main points of the news that are broadcast on television or radio

make a name for oneself *exp* (75) to become famous or respected by a lot of people

microphone *n* (74) a piece of equipment that you speak into to make your voice louder, or to record your voice or other sounds

network *n* (72) a large system consisting of many similar parts that are connected together to allow movement or communication between or along the parts or between the parts and a control centre

presenter *n* (72) someone who introduces a television or radio show

press *n* (72) newspapers and magazines, and those parts of television and radio which broadcast news, or reporters and photographers who work for them

privacy *n* (75) someone's right to keep their personal matters and relationships secret

producer *n* (72) a person who makes the practical and financial arrangements needed to make a film, play, television or radio programme

publication *n* (72) the act of making information or stories available to people in a printed form

publicity *n* (75) the activity of making certain that someone or something attracts a lot of interest or attention from many people, or the attention received as a result of this activity

quiz show *n* (72) a TV or radio programme based on a game or competition in which you answer questions

reality TV show *n* (72) a television programme about ordinary people who are filmed in real situations, rather than actors

role model *n* (75) a person who someone admires and whose behaviour they try to copy

scriptwriter *n* (72) a person who writes the words for films or radio or television broadcasts

set designer *n* (72) a person who decides which pictures, furniture, etc. will be used when a film or play is performed or recorded

tabloid *n* (72) a type of popular newspaper with small pages which has many pictures and short simple reports

Unit 10

bargain *n* (80) something on sale at a lower price than its true value

be out of *v* (85) to have no more of something

brand *n* (81) a type of product made by a particular company

casual *adj* (80) describes clothes that are not formal or not suitable for special occasions

catalogue *n* (81) a book with a list of all the goods that you can buy from a shop

consumer *n* (80) a person who buys goods or services for their own use

debit card *n* (82) a small plastic card which can be used as a method of payment, the money being taken from your bank account automatically

designer label *n* (80) something made by a famous company that makes expensive clothes, bags, etc.

exchange *v* (80) to take something back to the shop where you bought it, and change it for something else

export *v* (80) to send goods to another country for sale

false *adj* (80) not real, but made to look or seem real

genuine *adj* (80) If something is genuine, it is real and exactly what it appears to be.

guarantee *n* (82) a promise that something will be done or will happen, especially a written promise by a company to repair or change a product that develops a fault within a particular period of time

ideal *adj* (86) without fault; perfect, or the best possible

import *v* (80) to buy or bring in products from another country

in stock *exp* (80) available to buy

loose *adj* (80) (of clothes) not fitting closely to the body

massive *adj* (86) very large in size, amount or number

on offer *exp* (82) If goods in a shop are on (special) offer, they are being sold at a lower price than usual.

out of stock *exp* (80) not available to buy

purchase *n* (80) something that you buy

reflect *v* (80) to show, express or be a sign of something

run out *pv* (85) to finish, use or sell all of something so that there is none left

sale *n* (80) an occasion when goods are sold at a lower price than usual

sales *n* (80) the number of products sold

sell out *pv* (85) If a supply of something sells out, there is no more of that thing to buy.

shopkeeper *n* (80) a person who owns and manages a small shop

sophisticated *adj* (80) having a good knowledge of culture and fashion

stunning *adj* (86) extremely beautiful or attractive

suit *v* (80) (usually of a colour or style of clothes) to make someone look more attractive

throw out *pv* (85) to get rid of something that you do not want any more

tight *adj* (80) Clothes or shoes that are tight fit the body too closely and are uncomfortable.

trolley *n* (82) a small vehicle with two or four wheels that you push or pull to transport large or heavy objects

try out *pv* (81) to use something to discover if it works or if you like it

turn out *pv* (85) to happen in a particular way or to have a particular result, especially an unexpected one

vivid *adj* (86) very brightly coloured

ANSWER KEY

Unit 1

LISTENING

Part 1

2 **1** one male radio journalist reporting from the street
2 the focus is place

3 **C** is the correct answer: *there isn't anybody in* means the people who live there are not at home, and *by the look of the place* indicates that the reporter is outside the house.

B is the wrong answer: the reporter says *away … at a luxury hotel in the city centre*, so he is not there.

A is the wrong answer: he uses the conditional *would be* about someone else (the *TV crews*).

4 **2** one female talking about travelling by train every day; focus: feelings/attitude

3 one female making a phone call; focus: purpose

4 one male talking about reading books at home; focus: reason

5 female and male (probably) talking in a holiday resort; focus: person

6 one male talking about staying healthy; focus: something he's doing

7 one female talking about where she lives; focus: place / type of home

8 female and male (probably) talking about finding something; focus: feelings

Exam task answers

2 A **3** B **4** B **5** C **6** C **7** B **8** B

Recording script

You will hear people talking in eight different situations. For questions 1–8, choose the best answer (A, B or C).

1 *You hear a reporter talking on the radio.*

I'm standing here in Church Avenue with about thirty other media people, but by the look of the place there isn't anybody in. Nobody's quite sure if he'll be back later this afternoon – or whether he's spending the weekend away, perhaps at a luxury hotel in the city centre. What does seem clear, though, is that he's unlikely to play in Sunday's big match – otherwise these TV crews would be waiting at the gates of the club's training ground to film him, not here.

2 *You hear a woman talking about travelling to work every day.*

The traffic into town is getting worse all the time so the train was the obvious alternative. I'd kind of assumed I'd be able to sit back and relax with a newspaper and a cup of coffee, maybe chat with my fellow passengers and so on, but actually most mornings it's standing-room only with everyone squashed together, the conversation usually limited to 'excuse me'. Somebody is always pushing and you spend half your time trying to avoid falling over, so that by the time you arrive you feel as though you've already done half a day's work.

3 *You overhear a woman talking on the phone.*

Well, I'm very sorry but I'm just not prepared to pay for items I didn't receive. As you say, I ordered the DVDs a fortnight ago, and when I did so I gave your sales department all the details they needed to deliver them to the right address, and it's not my fault if they sent them somewhere else. The only mistake I made was in dealing with your company in the first place. Next time I want things like that, I'll buy them online instead. Like most people do these days.

4 *You hear a man talking about reading books.*

I'm an editor in a publishing company and this month I'm working particularly hard on a rather long novel, so it may seem a little surprising that my favourite way of relaxing in the evenings is to sit down somewhere quiet with a good book. Whenever I can, I go into the study and settle down to read for as long as possible. I just wish I could do so more often as I'm the kind of person who needs to get away from other people for a while, but these days I'm usually just too busy helping out with the housework, and the kids.

5 *You overhear a conversation in a holiday resort.*

Man: The weather's been awful this summer, hasn't it? I'm not surprised people are looking so miserable. Those who haven't already gone home, that is. Non-stop rain spoils everything at the seaside.

Woman: I know. If I were a tourist I would've left too. The place is half-empty and I've already had to reduce the number of staff.

Man: Really? Is it that bad?

Woman: Yes, with so few customers I just couldn't afford to keep paying their wages. I hated having to let them go, especially as I used to be a waitress myself. But what else could I do?

Man: You had no choice. The same thing's happening everywhere round here.

6 You hear a man talking about staying healthy.

I was getting a bit worried about my unhealthy lifestyle, so I started spending a few hours each week at the local gym, but it was pretty boring and I haven't been for a while. Then someone suggested I should try going to the office on foot rather than taking the car, and I took her advice. I live a long way out in the suburbs and in fact I go right past the gym every day, but it's really helping me get in shape. And the funny thing is that with all this exercise I get more hungry and I'm actually having bigger meals now, but I'm told it doesn't matter because I'm using up a lot more energy.

7 You hear a woman talking about her home.

I'm staying at a friend's apartment downtown, but I'll move back into my place when they finish repainting it, probably on Friday. It's pleasant enough here, though I miss my garden with its beautiful bushes and trees. It's almost like being in the countryside there, even though it's actually on the outskirts of town. It's right on top of a hill, so from my upstairs window you can see the city-centre office buildings in one direction and a rural area not far away in the other. And a south-facing room gets lots of sunshine, too.

8 You overhear two people talking about finding something.

Woman: Yes, it's just as well that memory stick turned up when it did. If it'd been missing any longer, I'd be getting a bit worried by now.

Man: I knew it must be somewhere in the living room. If you remember, I suggested looking there the other day.

Woman: Actually, that wasn't where I found it.

Man: No? Where was it?

Woman: It was in the spare room, plugged into that old laptop of yours.

Man: Was it? Oh, I remember now, I was using it last year to copy some files. Sorry about that.

Woman: It doesn't matter now. Forget it.

Grammar

Review of present tenses

1 **1** c **2** b **3** f **4** a **5** g **6** d **7** e

2 **1** you understand **2** having fun **3** you like **4** 'm/am waiting **5** I prefer **6** have **7** 'm/am standing

3 **1** 's/is writing (something happening right now)
2 are rising (a situation that is changing or developing)
3 quite often goes (a routine or habit)
4 are always shouting (something irritating or surprising)
5 belongs (stative verb)
6 'm/am staying (a temporary situation)
7 sets (something which is always true)
8 's/is having (something happening right now)

Present simple in time clauses

4 yes, present simple

5 **1** 'll get, go **2** 'll wait, come **3** ends, 'll catch **4** won't, start **5** arrive, 'll be **6** 'll talk, get

6 Suggested answers
1 I get home. **2** I go on holiday. **3** I have enough money. **4** I'm thirty. **5** I pass Proficiency. **6** I finish my homework.

READING AND USE OF ENGLISH

Part 7

2 **1** four **2** one text in four sections **3** four people's daily lives **4** which person does or thinks particular things **5** ten **6** yes

3 **1** B Assistant Sales Manager **2** A University student **3** C Website Designer **4** D Tour Guide
earliest B, latest C

4 **B:** Correct – if lunch is the first meal of the day for her, she can't have eaten breakfast.
A: If there's time he has tea and toast, so it's not true to say he never has breakfast.
D: Usually she skips (misses) breakfast, but not always – she sometimes has 'cereal or something'.

5 Exam task answers
1 C **2** A **3** C **4** B **5** A **6** D **7** A **8** B **9** D **10** B
Underlining
A
(5) 'Assuming I don't oversleep, which can happen
(7) I do the uphill walk into town, which wakes me up and enables me to plan what I'm going to do in the morning and afternoon
(2) I sometimes head for the gym, but not as often as I should
B
(4) a dash to the station to catch the 7.15
(10) dealing with client queries, which for me is one of the most interesting, challenging and worthwhile aspects of the job
(8) At first I found working here pretty stressful, but I'm used to it now and it doesn't bother me.
C
(3) the previous evening. 'If I have a creative peak,' he says, 'that's when it is
(1) having a 20-minute lie-down after lunch. Then, when I wake up

D

(9) It's the custom here to have a sleep after lunch, but I haven't got time for that. In any case, I'm not tired then

(6) can be a bit irritating if I end up doing unpaid overtime

Adjectives ending in *-ed* and *-ing*

6 **1** -ed **2** -ing

7 **1** relaxed **2** amusing **3** worried **4** depressing **5** motivated **6** terrified **7** astonishing **8** puzzling

SPEAKING

Part 1

1 **1** your town
2 what you like about your town
3 your family
4 your favourite season, and why
5 what you like doing on holiday
6 what you use the Internet for
(all questions are about you)
You would use the present simple to reply, although in some cases you may also need to use the present continuous, for example to say a relative is studying abroad.

2 Suggested answers
1 One-word answer. He gives examples when asked *in what ways*, but he could have done this without being prompted.
2 The verb form should be *I stay*.
3 She doesn't give a reason. She could reply as she does after the examiner asks *why* without being prompted.
4 The verb form should be *I go*.
5 Not polite. He could say *Could you repeat that, please?*
6 He doesn't give a reason for not liking newspapers. He could say something like *because there's too much in them about politics*, or *I listen to the radio news, so I don't need to*.

3 **1** at the end (*hardly ever* goes before the verb)
2 hardly ever
3 from time to time / now and then

Character adjectives

7 **1** thoughtful **2** optimistic **3** childish **4** bossy **5** practical **6** impatient **7** ambitious **8** sensitive **9** decisive **10** unpredictable **11** reasonable **12** disorganised

READING AND USE OF ENGLISH

Forming adjectives

1 reasonable (*also* unpredictable), practical, disorganised, thoughtful, optimistic, impatient, childish, decisive, sensitive, ambitious, unpredictable, bossy

2 (un)adventurous, aggressive, anxious, artistic, cautious, cheeky, competitive, (un)emotional, energetic, (un)enthusiastic, foolish, greedy, (un)helpful, dishonest, pessimistic, impolite, unpopular, (un)reliable, (dis)respectful, (un)sympathetic

Part 3

3 **1** charming **2** impolite **3** healthy **4** disorganised **5** sociable **6** stressful

4 **1** optimistic **2** challenging **3** depressed **4** unsympathetic **5** refreshed **6** unenthusiastic

5 **1** eight
2 a word formed from the word in capitals at the end of the same line
3 mainly vocabulary (especially prefixes and suffixes)

6 The purpose of the text is to show how different people from the same family can be.
paragraph 1: to introduce the topic
paragraph 2: to describe one of the daughters
paragraph 3: to describe the other daughter
paragraph 4: to describe the son

7 **1** an adjective **2** what causes a feeling (to friends of the family) **3** *-ing* **4** drop the final *e*
Exam task answers
1 personalities **2** motivated **3** ambitious **4** unemotional **5** sensitive **6** sympathetic **7** adventurous **8** anxious

WRITING

Part 2 informal letter

1 **1** an English friend / Alex
2 write back saying: how important friends are to you, who your best friend is, what you like about him or her
3 informal
a *I've, don't, I'd, Who's* **b** *kid, do* **c** *So, and*
d exclamation mark **e** *Looking forward to hearing from you*

2 **1** yes
2 no
3 *Dear Alex, Best wishes*
4 Introduction: she thanks Alex for his/her message and comments on this.
Conclusion: she talks about the future and asks Alex to write back soon and give her more information.
5 Yes: the importance of friends in the first main paragraph, who her best friend is in the second main paragraph, a description of her friend's personality in the third main paragraph.
6 Informal expressions such as *thanks, just down the road, mates, a bit*; dash and exclamation marks; contracted forms: *they're, who's, we've, she's*; linkers: *and, but*; friendly expressions: *It was great to hear from you, Write soon*
7 *indecisive, practical, bossy, thoughtful, sympathetic*
8 *tell each other, can be … at times, whenever I … she's always, cheer me up, sense of humour, have the chance*, etc.

5 Model answer

> Hi Alex,
>
> It's always great to hear from you!
>
> You're absolutely right about how much friendship matters. Life just wouldn't be the same if we didn't have friends, would it?
>
> My very best friend is called Luis and we've grown up together, really. We first met at primary school and he's been my best mate ever since.
>
> We're quite similar in a lot of ways. For instance, we're the same age, almost exactly the same height and weight, and we're both crazy about sports, especially basketball and swimming.
>
> Like me, he can be rather shy at times, though he's perhaps a little more talkative than me. He's also someone you can rely on to help you if you're in trouble or worried about something. He's a fantastic friend and I'm sure you'd get on really well with him.
>
> Hope to hear from you again soon!
>
> Bye for now,
>
> Enrique

Revision

1 **1** 'm/am staying, 'm/am working
2 usually eat, 're/are having
3 'm/am waiting, seems
4 is changing, are getting
5 is, 's/is always complaining
6 own, don't live
7 gets, 'm/am thinking

2 **1** greedy **2** dishonest **3** artistic **4** impolite **5** energetic **6** cautious **7** pessimistic

3 **1** unpredictable **2** sympathetic **3** unreasonable **4** challenging **5** thoughtful **6** decisive

4 **1** relaxing **2** reliable **3** practical **4** terrifying **5** astonished **6** aggressive **7** competitive **8** childish **9** puzzling **10** exhausted

Unit 2

READING AND USE OF ENGLISH

Part 6

2 **1** an article with six sentences removed
2 the missing sentences
3 no – only six of them

3 **1** He was feeling unhealthy.
2 He began to feel better and his appearance improved.

4 *At that time* and *Before long* are time links (see Writing in this unit) that in this case indicate a progression. The use of *though* shows there is a contrast in meaning, *those* refers back to *ready meals*, and *cooking for myself* contrasts with *heat up ready meals*.
C couldn't fit gap 2 because *those* is plural and *(junk) food* is uncountable. It would not make any sense referring to *meals*.

5 Exam task answers
2 F **3** G **4** E **5** B **6** A

6 **2** At first / But after a few months, I couldn't believe / realise it was true, unhealthy appearance / in bad shape
3 I took time … / In the same way, I got to know the best times to … when to / These changes
4 But / On the more positive side, took some reorganising and a commitment to set aside time / doing all this
5 throw the whole thing in the oven / Cooking it that way, fish or chicken portions … vegetables / tasty meal
6 I'd let … abandoned / I hadn't (past perfect: see Grammar in this unit)

7 **1** heat up **2** snacking **3** junk food **4** skipping meals **5** living on **6** balanced diet **7** portions **8** starving **9** filling **10** pick up a bargain

LISTENING

Part 2

2 **1** noun, probably a person; a close relationship, perhaps a relative or friend
2 Suggested answers
2 noun **3** date **4** noun (phrase) **5** noun (phrase) **6** noun **7** adjective **8** noun (phrase) **9** adverb **10** noun

Exam task answers
1 (elder) sister **2** a (professional) footballer **3** 2001 **4** head chef **5** restaurant owner **6** film/movie stars **7** local **8** variety **9** freshly **10** fish

Recording script

You will hear a restaurant chef talking about his work. For questions 1–10, complete the sentences.

Max

It's difficult to say when exactly I made up my mind I wanted to cook for a living, because I'd always been interested in cooking. As a child I used to watch my parents preparing meals at home, and I would imagine myself cooking something delicious for the family. But (1) it wasn't until my elder sister showed me how to create some really original dishes that I realised I wanted to make a career of it. Though she wasn't a chef and in fact I very nearly wasn't either because my dad had other ideas.

He was an engineer but in his younger days he would've loved to be (2) a footballer, so when he saw I could play a bit he tried to persuade me to take it up professionally and forget about cooking. But by then I knew I was better with a frying pan than a ball, and I didn't take any notice.

It would be a while before I actually began work, though. First I went to catering college, in the autumn of 1999, and studied there until (3) 2001. Towards the end of that year I was offered work at a hotel in London, and I accepted straightaway. That job was tough at first, extremely tough. I was working very long hours when I was there and it was always unbelievably hot in the kitchens, but (4) it was the head chef who really got me down. He treated us like slaves, and I hated him so much I hardly noticed the working conditions. As soon as I could, I moved to France.

Some people were surprised by my decision to do that, but I'd been thinking of going to Paris for some time before I actually went. And although I hardly knew any of the language (5) I had a very useful contact there: the owner of one of the city's top restaurants. I'd met him when he was staying at the hotel in London, and fortunately he was very impressed by the meal I'd made for him. And the rest, as they say, is history.

I worked there for five years, developing my skills and sometimes preparing dishes for celebrities. (6) They included film stars, unlike at the London hotel where they tended to be big-name sportspeople, or rock stars.

Nowadays I have a restaurant of my own, and our regular customers also include quite a few well-known faces. It's popular with people from both home and abroad, and I have a team of four chefs from different countries. Even so, (7) I try to ensure, wherever possible, that all our vegetables, fruit and meat comes from local farms. It gives them business, and it makes environmental sense, too. In terms of the cooking, I suppose what makes it special is (8) the variety of dishes on the menu, actually, rather than any one type such as vegetarian or fish dishes. That's what I really take pride in, because it's not something that's easy to achieve.

Unlike in many other restaurants, we only cook when we receive orders from (9) customers. So to ensure that their food is freshly made, we need to keep all the ingredients ready for anything they might choose from the menu. And that's difficult because there are so many things that can go wrong. Starting with deliveries. They can turn up late, as the meat did on Friday, or even disappear altogether, which is what happened to (10) a van heading here last July. I still wonder what the thieves did with several hundred kilos of fish at the hottest time of the year.

Grammar

Review of past tenses

1 **1** d past simple **2** e past continuous **3** a past perfect **4** f past perfect continuous **5** b *used to / didn't use to* **6** c *would*

2
1. he'd / he had left his bike
2. Anita was crying
3. we'd / we had organised *or* we'd / we had been organising for weeks
4. I was a member
5. the house had been empty
6. someone was walking
7. people didn't use to worry
8. because I'd / I had decided

3 **1** C **2** A **3** B **4** C **5** B **6** C

4 Example answers
1. was walking along the road.
2. used to go away with my family.
3. had been crying.
4. was doing a summer job.
5. would play lots of games.
6. had gone home.

SPEAKING

Part 2

1 **2** other **3** similar **4** similarity **5** both **6** same **7** both **8** different **9** difference **10** other

2 **a** different **b** different **c** same **d** similar **e** different **f** different

4 **Photographs 1 and 2**

A Talk for a minute, comparing their two photos. Say what they think could be enjoyable about having a meal there.

B Say whether they like to eat in restaurants.

Photographs 3 and 4

B Talk for a minute, comparing their two photos. Say why they think people choose to eat there.

A Say which of the two kinds of place they prefer to go to.

READING AND USE OF ENGLISH

Fixed phrases

1 **1** at ease **2** get on my nerves **3** lose touch **4** at first sight **5** is attracted to **6** propose to her **7** leave me alone **8** keep me company **9** break my heart **10** takes me for granted

Part 2

2 **1** eight **2** one **3** no – you must think of them for yourself

3 **1** The title means 'a formal agreement to a marriage; the agreement did not last long'. In the last paragraph it is clear that Emily ended that agreement.

2 an extract from a biography or biographical article

Exam task answers

1 those **2** first **3** to **4** had **5** getting **6** at **7** taking **8** off

4 fixed phrases: 2, 3, 5, 6, 7; past tenses: 0, 4

WRITING

Linking expressions

1 **1** at first **2** between those two times **3** as soon as **4** very surprisingly **5** immediately **6** at the same time

Part 2 article

2 **1** young people who read an international website

2 the past

3 140–190

3 **1** yes

2 Neutral. Although the model answer uses some informal features such as conversational expressions to address the reader, words such as *fun*, *kid* and *sure*, and exclamation marks, there are no contracted forms and it is written in complete sentences, some of them quite complex.

3 The mystery of who is at the door arouses their curiosity / creates suspense.

4 The person who sent the text was someone mentioned in the previous paragraph.

5 I sat at home watching TV, how delighted I was, meeting people, invited me out for dinner

4 **1** Have you ever felt, You can imagine, I think you will agree

2 past continuous: *was going*; past perfect: *had given, had been*; past perfect continuous: *had been talking*

3 **a** the moment **b** before long **c** eventually

5 Model answer

Out at night

I've had several great nights out in my life, but one that sticks in my memory is when I did actually have a great night out – and I mean out!

I was sixteen years old. My parents couldn't afford holidays abroad, so they encouraged me to go camping overnight with three friends. I'd never been camping before and we immediately got off to a bad start. We couldn't read a map, so we lost our way. Then my feet began to hurt, so we arrived late and in the dark at the place where we had decided to camp.

You might think that the whole trip was a disaster but as soon as we put the tents up, things changed. We cooked a meal on our stove and made a hot drink. Then Lorenzo got out his guitar and we started singing. Can you imagine singing 'Starry Starry Night', lying on your back and looking at the stars above you? We never got into our sleeping bags. It was a great night out!

Revision

1 **1** was eating **2** had arranged **3** used to go **4** would spend **5** went **6** met **7** gave **8** 'd been waiting **9** was starting **10** 'd sent **11** 'd forgotten **12** did **13** suggested **14** 'd given up **15** ran

2 **1** at first sight **2** I lost touch **3** at ease **4** keep you company **5** Josef's heart **6** take you for granted **7** it gets on my nerves **8** leave me alone

3 **1** Eventually **2** meantime **3** Once **4** moment **5** long **6** amazement

4 **Across**

5 dish **6** filling **8** propose **9** skip **14** tough **15** portion **16** consume

Down

1 slice **2** adopt **3** chop **4** snack **7** ripe **9** starving **10** widow **11** bargain **12** divorce **13** junk

Unit 3

LISTENING

Part 3

1 to: cruise, explore, tour, wander

to go: hitchhiking, sailing, sightseeing, trekking

to go on a/an: cruise, expedition, flight, tour, trip, voyage

2 1 **1** Petra **2** Uyuni **3** Masai Mara **4** Forbidden City **5** Uluru

2 Suggested answers:
Uyuni – spectacular, like another planet; cold, high up
Uluru – hot, desolate place; spectacular, mysterious sight
Petra – ancient rock carvings, amazing skills; hot
Masai Mara – many kinds of animal, some dangerous; safari; hot
Forbidden City – ancient, beautiful design, big area to see

3 Suggested answers
B not take, enough water; little/short, etc., should carry, more
C large animal, attack; tiger/crocodile/lion, etc., chase/catch/ escape/eat, etc.
D vehicles, not allowed; car/bus/lorry, etc., mustn't / can / can't / have to
E expensive, enter; cost/charge/cheap/value, etc., admission/ entry
F respected, wishes, local people; ignored/agreed/reason, etc., ask/request, inhabitants/live
G guidebook, carrying, useful; guide, on/with me, useless/ practical
H All, people, tourists; Everyone/Everybody/Nobody; visitors/inhabitants/local

Exam task answers
1 B **2** D **3** F **4** G **5** A

Recording script

You will hear five different people talking about going to famous places. For questions 1–5, choose from the list (A–H) what each speaker says about their visit to each site. Use the letters only once. There are three extra letters which you do not need to use.

Speaker 1

Last August in Bolivia we saw the incredible Salar de Uyuni, the world's biggest salt flat, nearly 4,000 metres up in the Andes. We were on a five-day expedition which also took in volcanoes, old mining towns and the astonishing multicoloured lakes there. The views were stunning, and although it was winter and well below freezing at night, the midday sun was really strong. Everything was well organised and good value for money, though bottled water was running a little short by the fourth day. It wasn't easy to find water up there and we should have carried more with us, really. We spent a night in a hotel made entirely of salt and met some of the local people, who were really friendly.

Speaker 2

We approached the Jordanian town of Petra on the Desert Highway, but we had to leave our hire car on the outskirts as the only means of transport you can use there are four-legged: horse, donkey or camel. I suppose we could have walked, but it was hot so we decided to go by camel with a local guide. He spoke excellent English and explained the historical background as we admired the magnificent buildings cut from the rock many centuries ago. It must have been around 40 degrees there and we'd forgotten to take any drinking water with us, but that didn't matter as there were plenty of cafés serving cool drinks along the way.

Speaker 3

When I actually saw Uluru, the huge red rock in central Australia, it took my breath away. Also known as Ayers Rock, it towers 350 metres above the flat surrounding desert, and has religious significance to the native inhabitants who live in and run the Uluru National Park. In fact, when you arrive there and buy an inexpensive two-day pass, they ask you very politely if you would mind not walking on the rock itself, and for that reason we decided to go round it instead. That turned out to be over ten kilometres, rather more than the guidebook said, but we had plenty of water with us. As we left, we saw tourists climbing Uluru, but we were glad we'd chosen not to.

Speaker 4

Visiting the Forbidden City was definitely the highlight of our stay in Beijing. It's a massive place, and I don't know what we would've done without the pocket guide I had with me. You have to pay an admission fee of about six euros, but I thought it was worth it bearing in mind there are nearly a thousand buildings there. We loved the use of the royal colour yellow and I was fascinated by the complex design of everything, but you can't keep walking all day without a break so in the afternoon we stopped at a café that was full of local people. Remarkably, there's now a Starbucks actually inside the Forbidden City!

Speaker 5

We had an absolutely fantastic week in the Masai Mara National Reserve in Kenya. We saw all the big animals you'd expect there: elephants, giraffes, crocodiles and so on, all for just 30 euros a day entry fee. We didn't need to drive, either, because a guide picked us up in a safari vehicle at the hotel each morning. Actually, that's the only way you can get about, because you mustn't go anywhere on foot within the Reserve, presumably because you might meet a hungry lion if you do. And the local guides were great at pointing out animals which on your own you might have missed.

4 Distraction in the recording:

1 good value for money, local people
2 we could have walked, a local guide, we'd forgotten to take any drinking water with us
3 inexpensive, you would mind not walking / we'd chosen not to, guidebook, plenty of water
4 admission fee of about six euros, worth it, local people
5 30 euros a day entry fee, guide

Grammar

Review of modal verbs

1 **1** correct: *could have walked* (past possibility); *could walk* is for past ability
2 correct: *mustn't* (prohibition); *don't have to* is for no obligation
3 correct: *might have dropped* (past possibility); *had to drop* is for past obligation
4 correct: *must* (obligation by the speaker); *have to* is for external obligation
5 correct: *don't have to* (not necessary); *shouldn't* is for something that is the wrong thing to do
6 correct: *may have been* (past possibility); *must have been* is for certainty about the past
7 correct: *needn't have got* (did something unnecessarily); *didn't need to get* is for something not done because it was unnecessary
8 correct: *shouldn't have* (the wrong thing to do in the past); *can't have* is for a past impossibility

2 **1** *had to buy* (wrong past form of modal verb)
2 *was able to find* (one occasion)
3 *should have been* (it didn't actually happen)
4 *mustn't drive* (not allowed, not unnecessary)
5 *didn't need to call* (wrong past form of modal verb)
6 *don't have to spend* (wrong negative modal verb)
7 *may/might have to stand* (possibility, not ability)
8 *may/might have already heard* (past possibility)

3 **1** must have missed **2** could have got in **3** might have left **4** can't have done **5** had to walk **6** must have switched off **7** might even have forgotten **8** must have had

4 Suggested answers

1 They must be twins.
2 You should have gone to bed earlier last night.
3 We didn't have to wear a uniform.
4 Someone must have stolen it.
5 You could have saved some money.
6 You shouldn't do that.
7 You can't have done!
8 You might have spent/lost it.

READING AND USE OF ENGLISH

Part 5

2 **1** a single article
2 direct questions, incomplete statements, questions on reference words, questions on the meaning of particular words
3 three

3 The writer's main purpose is: D.

4 **B** is correct: the main factors are still the right experience, the right price and convenient departure schedules.
A Francis wishes this *were* the case, but it isn't.
C This isn't the *only* thing they are interested in.
D Francis doesn't mention global warming.

Exam task answers
1 B **2** A **3** B **4** D **5** B **6** B

6 **1** travelling public **2** departure schedules **3** fly **4** get away **5** destination **6** tour operators **7** brochure **8** accommodation-only **9** means of transport

SPEAKING

Adverbs of degree

2 **1** pretty (*also* fairly, quite)
2 slightly (*also* a bit, a little)
3 rather (*also* quite, a bit, a little, extremely, very, really)
4 quite (*also* rather)
5 really
6 a bit (*also* slightly, a little, quite)
7 rather (*also* quite, really)
8 quite (*also* absolutely)
9 totally (*also* quite, absolutely, completely, really)
10 absolutely (*also* quite, completely, really, totally)
11 fairly (*also* pretty, rather, quite)
12 extremely (*also* really, very)

Recording script

Lucas: So how was the trip to the coast?

Sarah: It was pretty good, overall. The bus was slightly late, though only ten minutes, and I was rather tired after quite a long day, but once we got out of town I really started to relax.

Lucas: Yes, sometimes I'm a bit surprised to find that I rather enjoy bus journeys, though the train's much quicker.

Sarah: Yes, you're quite right, but it was totally impossible to get a cheap ticket.

Lucas: I know what you mean. I was absolutely astonished to see how much the train costs on a Friday evening. But anyway, it sounds like the bus was fairly comfortable.

Sarah: Actually, it was extremely comfortable! I slept most of the way.

Part 3

3 **1** the other candidate
2 about three minutes
3 a booklet with written prompts: a diagram containing a question plus various options

4 Your town wants to attract more tourists.
1 You have to talk to your partner about how the things in the diagram can help bring in more tourists.
2 You have to decide which two things would attract most visitors to the town.

5 **1** yes
2 yes
3 They both choose the carnival, but whereas Laura's second choice is the art gallery, Jonas's is the boat rides.

6 **1** shall I **2** that could be **3** how about **4** we could **5** what about **6** it might not be **7** Let's look at **8** I'd go for

Recording script

Teacher: Now, I'd like you to talk about something together for about two minutes. I'd like you to imagine that your town wants to attract more tourists. Here are some things that may help make a town more attractive to visitors. Talk to each other about how these things could help bring in more tourists. You now have some time to look at the task. *[15-second pause]*
Could you start now, please?

Jonas: Right, shall I start?

Laura: Yes, go ahead.

Jonas: Well, first there's the theatre. I think that could be quite a good one, because it would attract some fairly rich people, and they would spend more in the town.

Laura: Yes, but there's only one theatre. Don't you think we'd need lots of them to make much difference to the number of visitors to the town?

Jonas: That's true.

Laura: So how about the next one – the carnival? Think of all the people who go to the one in Rio. Maybe we'd get crowds like that here. Or a bit like them, anyway.

Jonas: Er, well, at least the weather here is fairly good in summer, almost like Brazil. And it'd be really good fun to set up, too.

Laura: Talking about summer, we could have the boat rides, too. So people can cool off a bit in all that tropical heat. That would look pretty good in the town's brochure: smiling couples in rowing boats, picnics next to the lake. Stuff like that.

Jonas: Yes, maybe. And what about including the bus tour? That's open-air, too.

Laura: I'm not sure. It's only a small town, so it'd be rather a short tour. Or else they'd have to keep going round and round it. Either way, it might not be very popular with visitors.

Jonas: The marathon might be better. There's some absolutely stunning countryside round here, and we could get some great photos of people running through it.

Laura: Yes, I agree. Though from what I've seen of marathons in other cities and countries, it tends to be the local people who come out to watch them, rather than tourists.

Jonas: Hmm, you may be right. OK, that's five of them done. Let's look at the last one, the art gallery.

Laura: I quite like that one. It'd show the cultural side of the town, and there are some pretty good local artists.

Jonas: Yes, and some of them have painted landscapes of the countryside we were talking about just now.

Laura:	Right.
Teacher:	Thank you. Now you have a minute to decide which two things would attract most visitors to the town.
Laura:	OK, I'll start this time if you like.
Jonas:	Fine.
Laura:	Which two shall we choose? I'd go for the art gallery and the carnival. I think that'd make a lot of people want to come to the town. And you?
Jonas:	Definitely the carnival. But instead of the art gallery, I'd choose the boat rides. They would be much more popular, I think.
Laura:	OK, so we agree on one but not the other. That's fine.
Jonas:	I agree.
Teacher:	Thank you.

READING AND USE OF ENGLISH

Dependent prepositions

1 word/phrase + *to*: in relation, in response, obliged, prepared, required, sensitive, supposed, with regard (*also* about, belong, bound, compared, object, opposed, tend, thanks)

word/phrase + *with*: familiar, fed up, in connection, involved, (have) nothing to do, obsessed, the trouble (*also* agree, along, associated, beginning, compared, disappointed, have a word, pleased, satisfied)

word/phrase + *of*: ashamed, capable, conscious, in need, in place, in terms, in view, informed, sort (*also* afraid, approve, aware, jealous, no sign, proud, take care)

2 **1** D **2** C **3** A **4** D **5** B **6** A

Part 1

3 **1** eight
2 four
3 All four are the same kind of word with some kind of link in meaning.

4 Suggested answers
what happens in the Barranquilla Carnival, Colombia
or
what makes Colombia's Barranquilla Carnival so good
Exam task answers
1 D **2** A **3** C **4** B **5** D **6** A **7** A **8** B

WRITING

Part 1 essay

1 **a** First of all, For one thing, In the first place
b For another thing, Next
c Lastly
d On balance, To conclude

2 **1** you have had a discussion in an English class and you have been asked to write an essay; the advantages and disadvantages of taking holidays near home rather than travelling abroad
2 your teacher
3 whether it is better to have holidays near home rather than travel abroad
4 which is cheaper, which is better for the environment, and your own idea
5 reasons for your point of view

3 **1** holidays abroad
2 2nd: cheaper, 3rd: better for the environment, 4th: own idea
3 to begin with, secondly, finally, to sum up
4 first of all, next, then, lastly, in conclusion, to conclude, on balance, etc.

4 **1** should not **2** however **3** locations **4** inexpensive (*also*: budget, economical) **5** can be done **6** cannot **7** I am absolutely convinced (that)

6 Model answer

These days many people are choosing not to travel abroad for their holidays. There are several reasons for this.

The main reason is financial. In the current economic climate, people have less money for their leisure pursuits. Holidays abroad are not cheap. Additional expenses include the purchase of a visa for some countries, and the need to buy travel insurance and foreign currency.

Another important reason for holidaying at home is the effect foreign travel has on the environment. Air travel produces more pollution than any other form of transport, so is the least green.

People also feel safer in their own country. They are used to the food and water, so they feel they are less likely to become ill. And, if necessary, they can more easily return home.

This year I have decided to stay at home. In fact, I'm going to sleep in my own bed every night. There are many beautiful places in my country which foreign visitors come to see. I want to enjoy these places too. And some of them, I can visit by bike!

Revision

1 **2** mustn't hit **3** must have ridden *or* must have been riding **4** shouldn't have spent **5** can't have seen **6** mightn't / might not have taken **7** needn't have cooked

2 **2** have to check in (*or* need to)
 3 must've / must have gone home early
 4 didn't need to go to college
 5 had to wear life jackets
 6 should've / should have put petrol in the car
 7 might've / might have had the wrong address (*or* may've / may have *or* could've / could have)

3 **1** D **2** A **3** B **4** B **5** C **6** C

4 **1** with **2** of **3** of **4** with **5** at **6** of **7** to **8** of **9** with **10** of

Unit 4

READING AND USE OF ENGLISH

Part 6

3 B

4 **1** D (reaction)
 2 this
 3 After saying the reaction was understandable, the writer supports this by saying *Who hasn't been to …* , claiming that everyone has had a similar experience.

Exam task answers

1 D **2** B **3** A **4** F **5** G **6** C

Phrasal verbs with *on*

6 **1** depends on **2** continued **3** stand on **4** continued

7 **2** log on **3** carried on **4** depends on **5** sit on **6** played on **7** turn on **8** based on **9** count on **10** focuses on

LISTENING

Part 4

2 Suggested answers
 1 most want – main interest, girl – child
 2 B – *colour paintings were* her *main interest then*
 3 A – she *worked on sculptures*, but later, *when I grew up* and was *at art college*
 C – referring to drawing in the interviewer's question, she says *I tended to see it as just the first step in creating colour paintings*

Recording script

You will hear part of a radio interview with Sonia Evans, an artist whose work first became popular on the Internet. For questions 1–7, choose the best answer (A, B or C).

Interviewer: My guest today is artist Sonia Evans, whose drawings have become popular on the Internet and elsewhere. Tell me, Sonia, have you always been keen on drawing?

Sonia: Yes, but as a child I tended to see it as just the first step in creating colour paintings, which were my main interest then. When I grew up I realised I didn't really have an eye for colour, and although at art college I worked on sculptures for a while I eventually went back to doing pictures, though this time just with a pencil. And that's what I've been doing ever since.

3 Suggested answers
 2 disappointed, exhibition **3** decided, Internet, because **4** Sonia's video, different **5** feel, how many, looked **6** result, success **7** react, negative comments

Exam task answers

2 A **3** A **4** C **5** A **6** B **7** C

Recording script

You will hear part of a radio interview with Sonia Evans, an artist whose work first became popular on the Internet. For questions 1–7, choose the best answer (A, B or C).

Interviewer: My guest today is artist Sonia Evans, whose drawings have become popular on the Internet and elsewhere. Tell me, Sonia, have you always been keen on drawing?

Sonia: Yes, but as a child I tended to see it as just the first step in creating (1) <u>colour paintings, which were my main interest then</u>. When I grew up I realised I didn't really have an eye for colour, and although at art college I worked on sculptures for a while I eventually went back to doing pictures, though this time just with a pencil. And that's what I've been doing ever since.

Interviewer: So when did you first display any of your work?

Sonia: Quite some time ago, at the art gallery in my home town. I was really excited when they agreed to show some of my drawings, though that feeling didn't last when I realised the so-called exhibition was taking place in a tiny place outside the main building. Of course, it was never my aim to sell any of them, but (2) <u>it would have been nice if more than a handful of visitors to the gallery had actually realised they were there</u>. The fact that the art critic in the local paper was quite impressed didn't help much, as he didn't write about them until the day after the exhibition had ended.

Interviewer: That must have been quite annoying.

Sonia: Yes, it was. I didn't bother trying to have anything else shown there after that.

Interviewer: And what made you decide to put your work online?

Sonia: A photographer friend of mine had the idea first, though he never actually got round to doing it. And (3) <u>as the only alternative was to move to a big city and try to get noticed there, something that didn't appeal to me at all, I felt that going online was the best thing to do</u>.

Interviewer: And how did you actually go about it?

Sonia: I made a short video of myself drawing. Of course, there were already lots like that on YouTube – there were too many to count, in fact – but (4) <u>mine was unique at the time in that I left the drawing unfinished</u>. So although others were often by people who could handle a video camera better than me, and probably had just as much artistic ability too, it was mine that made viewers want to come back three days later to find out what the subject actually was.

Interviewer: And that created a lot of interest, did it?

Sonia: Well, yes, probably because I'm quite good at disguising what I'm drawing. Anyway, an astonishing number of people viewed the second video. There were literally tens of thousands of hits from all over the world. And the strange thing was that I should have been delighted by figures like those, or at least relieved that at last my work was out there, but instead (5) <u>I had the uneasy sensation that there were too many hits</u>.

Interviewer: How long did that feeling last?

Sonia: I got over it quickly enough once I'd done a few more videos. In fact, I started going to the opposite extreme.

Interviewer: How do you mean?

Sonia: When I realised how well they were doing, I started to become a bit too obsessed with the number of hits they were getting – logging on to check them dozens of times a day, and getting really stressed whenever they slowed down a little. I found myself (6) <u>staying up later and later</u> to keep an eye on them, because of course many of the hits were from different time zones, <u>and getting up earlier and earlier the next day</u>. So then I'd find it hard to stay awake in the daytime, to the point where I didn't have enough time to do my work properly.

Interviewer: Not so good.

Sonia: No, and it got even worse when I started reading reviews of my videos on those websites that specialise in criticising online videos.

Interviewer: They were bad, were they?

Sonia: Some of them, yes. There were attacks on the quality of my work, and some quite personal stuff, too.

Interviewer: What was your reaction?

Sonia: Well, fortunately I'm not someone who suffers from depression or anything like that, but (7) <u>I decided to keep well away from those sites</u>. They just made me feel angry and want to write back to the people who wrote those things, but of course I didn't. And nowadays I never even think about them. Especially since my work started to appear in other media.

Interviewer: Yes, I'm sure quite a few of our listeners will recognise your name from magazines, and now from radio, too. Thank you, Sonia.

Sonia: Thank you.

Grammar

Verbs followed by *to* + infinitive or *-ing*

1 **1** *to* + infinitive: **b** agree, **f** start
-ing: **c** (not) bother, **d** get round to, **e** start
2 *start* with no change in meaning

2 *to* + infinitive: appear, expect, learn, manage, offer, promise, refuse, seem, threaten, want
-ing: avoid, dislike, enjoy, finish, imagine, insist on, keep (on), mind, miss, suggest

3 **1** a-ii (continued the same activity), b-i (changed activity)
2 a-ii (as an experiment), b-i (it was impossible)
3 a-ii (you're sorry about a past action), b-i (you're sorry about what you're going to have to say)
4 a-i (something that stays in your memory for a long time), b-ii (something you should do)
5 a-ii (you haven't wanted to speak to them since then), b-i (you were walking but you stood still and spoke to them)
6 a-i (remember something from the past), b-ii (remember to do something in the future)

4 **1** agreed to help **2** suggested buying **3** forgot to ask **4** remember being **5** mind working **6** go on behaving

5 **1** to show **2** to indicate **3** going **4** to spend **5** to see **6** rising

SPEAKING

too and *enough*

1 **a** too **b** too **c** enough **d** too **e** enough
1 before, no **2** after, before **3** *to* + infinitive

2 **1** too lazy **2** too many people **3** enough leisure time **4** early enough **5** The streets here are too narrow **6** very bad news

3 **2** This computer is too slow for me to watch films on.
This computer isn't fast/quick/powerful enough for me to watch films on.
3 It was too noisy for us to hear what was going on.
It wasn't quiet enough for us to hear what was going on.
4 That book was too long for me to read in a week.
That book wasn't short enough for me to read in a week.
5 That bed was too uncomfortable for me to sleep on.
That bed wasn't comfortable enough for me to sleep on.

Part 4

4 **1** *Asking for opinions*: What's your opinion?, What do you think?, What are your feelings about this?, How do you feel about … ?
2 *Asking for reasons*: Why do you think so?, Is that because … ?, Could you tell me why?, Any particular reason?
3 *Giving reasons*: because … , for one thing … , so … , The main reason is that …
4 *Giving examples*: for example … , for instance … , like … , such as …

5 The teacher asks questions 1, 4 and 6. Daniela does this part of the Speaking text better – because she gives fuller answers, responding to what Julian says in her comments, giving reasons and examples. She also asks her partner for his opinions, and the reason for them.

Recording script

Teacher: Julian, what are the advantages and disadvantages of having lots of leisure time?

Julian: Er, you can do many things, like go to the cinema, or look at things on the Internet. And the disadvantages are that you can get quite bored if there isn't much to do, and maybe spend too much time watching TV.

Daniela: Yes, you can waste your time, especially if you don't plan your free time well. But everyone needs to have leisure time because often they do too much work and it's not good only to work or study all the time. You can use it to learn to do new things, too.

Teacher: Which hobby or interest would you most like to take up, Daniela?

Daniela: Dancing, I think. Probably salsa dancing. The main reason is that it's pretty simple to learn, and it's lots and lots of fun. The music is fantastic too. I've always liked it, particularly the salsa music from Colombia.

Teacher: And which hobby or interest would you most like to take up, Julian?

Julian: I'd like to have a big dog and take it out for long walks in the country. I've wanted to have a dog for a while. But I can't keep one at home. *[short pause]*

Daniela: Could you tell me why?

Julian: Well, we've just moved to a smaller flat and although I haven't asked my parents yet, I think they'll say there isn't enough room, that it wouldn't be fair to keep a big dog there. I suppose I'll have to wait until I get my own house.

Teacher: Daniela, do you think people these days read fewer books than previous generations did?

Daniela: I'm not sure. In the past in my country not many people read books, but all that has changed now. There are more novels specially for young people, about modern society, so more people buy them, I think. Also it is very easy to find any book you like on the Internet, in online bookshops or auction sites, and they will send it to you quickly by post. If you have a credit card, of course! So no, I don't believe that people read less now. What do you think?

Julian: Well I don't think people read less these days, but maybe not so many books. I mean, there are so many magazines and newspapers and articles that you can read on the Internet. There's isn't enough time to read books too.

Daniela: Maybe people read books at different times. For instance, on the Metro, or on the beach. You can't really take your computer there with you. Also, some people say that reading from a screen all the time is very bad for your eyes, that a book is much better. What's your opinion?

Julian: Actually, that may be true. I know my eyes have been getting sore since I began reading a lot of texts online last year. I've already had to start using reading glasses.

Teacher: Thank you, that's the end of the test.

6 because … , The main reason is that … , Could you tell me why?, so … , What do you think?, for instance … , What's your opinion?

READING AND USE OF ENGLISH

Review of present perfect

1 **1** **a** past simple, **b** present perfect continuous, **c** present perfect
2 **a** already, **b** for, **c** yet, **d** since, **e** just

2 **1** I've been living **2** what I did last month **3** for a month *or* since a month ago **4** I've / I have already printed **5** We've been waiting **6** hasn't ended yet

Part 4

3 **1** for
2 past simple to present perfect (negative)
3 *last* is not used
4 haven't / have not been there = 1 mark, for = 1 mark

4 Exam task answers
1 light enough | (for me) to (*because* + *so* → *enough* + *for*)
2 carried on | reading (verb + infinitive → phrasal verb + *-ing*)
3 haven't done ballet | since (verb + *-ing* → negative present perfect + *since*)
4 too complicated | for any of (*so … that* + *none* → *too … for* + *any*)
5 've/have been learning Chinese | for (present perfect + *since* → present perfect continuous + *for*)
6 count on | winning (*will* + infinitive → phrasal verb + *-ing*)

WRITING

Part 2 review

1 **1** international readers of an English-language magazine
2 information on the setting, story and main characters, and your recommendation to other readers on whether they should read the novel or not
3 between 140 and 190

2 **1** paragraph 1: c, paragraph 2: d, paragraph 3: b, paragraph 4: a
2 quite formal: no contracted forms; some long, less common words; formal structures (e.g. *in which*); complex sentences (e.g. second sentence of third paragraph)
3 **a** plot, **b** fast-paced, **c** gripping, **d** convincing, **e** impressive, **f** themes, **g** tense
4 Yes. *If you enjoy a tense thriller which is quick and easy to read, I suggest you choose this one.*

3 dreadful, poor, predictable, slow-moving

4 *To recommend something*:
This … is really worth … because …
This is one of the best … I have ever… , so I suggest …
Anyone who likes … will really enjoy this …
To say not to do something:
My advice is to avoid this … and instead …
I would advise everyone to … a better … than this, such as …

5 Model answer

The Strange Case of Dr Jekyll and Mr Hyde

The famous novel *The Strange Case of Dr Jekyll and Mr Hyde* was written in the late nineteenth century by the Scottish author Robert Louis Stevenson. It is set in the foggy London of the time, which helps to give many of the scenes a mysterious atmosphere.

The story is told by Gabriel Utterson, a lawyer friend of Henry Jekyll, a wealthy doctor who has an interest in unusual scientific experiments. Jekyll's behaviour becomes increasingly weird as the plot develops. The other main character is Edward Hyde, an ugly, violent man whose repulsive appearance and manner make people react with horror and fear.

When Hyde commits a series of brutal crimes, Utterson and Hastie Lanyon, another close friend of Jekyll, become concerned about the apparent links between Hyde and the doctor. Eventually, following Hyde's death, Utterson discovers that Dr Jekyll had in fact drunk a liquid that totally changed his personality, turning him into the absolutely evil Mr Hyde.

Even though it was written so long ago, this is one of the best science-fiction novels I have ever read. I would strongly recommend reading it.

Revision

1 1 regret not | going
2 has been doing gymnastics *or* has been a gymnast | since
3 insisted on | paying for *or* insisted (that) he | paid for
4 keeps on | breaking
5 too difficult for | all pianists *or* any pianists
6 hasn't sung here | for

2 1 How long have you been learning English? I've / I have been learning English for X years.
2 How many times have you been to the theatre? I've / I have been to the theatre X times. *or* I've / I have never been to the theatre.
3 Have you had your evening meal yet? Yes, I've / I have had my evening meal (already). *or* No, I haven't / have not had my evening meal yet.
4 Have you been listening to the radio for the last hour? Yes, I've / I have been listening to the radio for the last hour. *or* No, I haven't / have not been listening to the radio for the last hour.
5 Have you just spoken to your partner? Yes, I've / I have just spoken to him/her. *or* No, I haven't / I have not just spoken to him/her.

3 **1** listening **2** to do **3** to do **4** having to **5** to do **6** to play **7** hearing **8** not doing

4 **Across**
1 scene **2** live **4** work **5** fine **7** superb **8** theme **10** plot **12** shot **13** critic **14** lyrics **15** gig
Down
1 script **3** venue **6** gripping **7** set **9** moving **11** poor **12** solo **13** cast

Unit 5

LISTENING

Part 2

1 **1** USA (Harvard) **2** New Zealand (Canterbury at Christchurch) **3** UK (Cambridge) **4** Australia (John Curtin School of Medical Research, Canberra)

2 **1** secondary **2** qualify **3** Bachelor's **4** undergraduates **5** lectures **6** seminars **7** tutor **8** graduate **9** postgraduate **10** Master's **11** academic **12** thesis

Recording script

The higher education systems in some English-speaking countries such as the UK, Australia and New Zealand are similar in some ways. Pupils at secondary school take examinations at the age of 18, and those who qualify for university then usually begin their Bachelor's degree courses, which normally last three or four years. At this stage students are known as undergraduates, and they learn about their subject by attending lectures in large groups. These are often followed by discussion in seminars, involving a much smaller group of students and a tutor who asks questions and encourages them to talk about the topic. When they successfully finish their first degree, students graduate and may then go on to do a postgraduate course such as a Master's degree. For most students, the highest academic achievement is to obtain a doctoral degree by writing a thesis based on research.

3 1 A student talks about going from Europe to university in New Zealand.
2 Suggested answers: to go to a good university, to do a particular course, to experience a new culture, to improve her English, to meet new people, to become more independent, to be near the sea and mountains, etc.
3 Suggested answers: advantages – different academic system, different country, new challenges, travel, make new friends; disadvantages – distance from home country, time difference, adapting to new culture, having to make new friends, possible language difficulties, different food

4 Suggested answers
1 person **2** sport or hobby **3** noun (phrase) **4** noun (phrase) **5** noun (phrase) **6** verb (+ noun) **7** verb **8** place or noun **9** date **10** noun (phrase)

Exam task answers

1 cousin **2** (rock) climbing **3** approach to learning **4** first name(s) **5** textbooks **6** problem solving / solving problems **7** teach **8** Australia **9** twelfth/12(th) November / November 12(th) / November (the) twelfth **10** whales

Recording script

You will hear European student Alba Ortega talking about going to university in New Zealand. For questions 1–10, complete the sentences.

Alba

What made me want to come to New Zealand? Well, my teacher at school told me about the high academic standards here, and one of my friends had already decided to study in Perth, Australia. But (1) the person who influenced me most was my cousin, who did her first degree here and loved every minute of it. She was in Wellington, but often came down to the South Island for the scenery and sports.

That was something that attracted me to Christchurch in particular, though whereas she came for the winter sports (2) it was the opportunities for rock climbing that really appealed to me. Although now I've actually seen those fantastic mountains I think I'll give skiing a try sometime.

As for the university itself, I mentioned the academic standards as something that's important to me, and (3) something I hadn't experienced before was the approach to learning here. I was used to much more formal teaching: memorising facts, using material from textbooks in essays, things like that. But the way things are done here is much better.

Some people might find it hard to adapt, but I took to it straightaway. (4) The only thing that really took some getting used to was being on first-name terms with tutors and lecturers. That would never have happened with my teachers at school. And the academic staff here are great. I mean, as well as being friendly, they're really professional. They often include the latest research findings in their lectures, and (5) nearly all of them have had textbooks published. So they really are experts in their field.

Someone asked me recently in what way I thought studying here had benefited me most. I thought about it, and replied that throughout my schooldays I was always pretty good at revising and passing exams so that hasn't changed much, but (6) there's been a vast improvement in my problem solving skills.

I will have graduated, I hope, by the end of this year, and I'm meeting my personal tutor on Wednesday to talk about my plans for the future. I know she'd like me to do research here, but (7) I've already made up my mind I'm going to teach locally. I'll be doing that for about a year, I should think.

Sometimes I think back to when I first arrived, and how easy I found it to settle here, but there were certainly a few things that surprised me about living in New Zealand. For instance, I knew it was a long way from Europe, nearly 20,000 kilometres, and I'd already worked out it was almost 10,000 going east to South America. But (8) what I hadn't reckoned on was that it's over 2,000 to Australia, which somehow you'd always thought was close by. And being twelve hours ahead causes its own problems, like when you call someone on their birthday but forget it's the middle of the night over there.

And of course the seasons are the other way round, though right now I'm very happy about the fact that it's nearly summer. My exams started on October 28th and they finish a week from now, which means (9) we're on vacation from November 12th until February 21st. In December in previous years I've gone to Europe to see my family, but to be honest it's not much fun travelling all that way and then finding it's cold and wet when you get there. (10) So I've arranged to spend a few days at a place along the coast from here where you're almost certain to spot whales at that time of the year. I'm really looking forward to it.

Grammar

Review of future forms

1 **1 c** present continuous **2 e** future continuous **3 d** *going to* future **4 a** future simple **5 f** present simple **6 b** future perfect

2 **1** arrives **2** *correct; also* will be meeting *or* is going to meet **3** I'll have just finished **4** *correct* **5** *correct* **6** I'm going *or* I'm going to go **7** *correct* **8** 'll/will go

3 Suggested and example answers

2 When are you going to do your homework?
I'm going to do it tonight.

3 Who are you meeting next weekend?
I'm meeting my cousins, on Saturday.

4 In which month does the next school term start?
It starts in January.

5 By what age do you think you will have finished studying?
I think I'll have finished by the time I'm 22.

6 How many children do you think you will have?
I don't think I'll have any.

7 Where will you probably be working ten years from now?
I'll probably still be working here.

Noun suffixes: *-or*, *-ist*, *-ian*, *-er*, *-ant*

4 **1** -ant: assistant, (flight) attendant, consultant, accountant, (civil) servant
2 -ian: musician, politician, electrician, historian, mathematician
3 -ist: novelist, guitarist, economist, physicist, psychologist
4 -or: inventor, operator, inspector, investigator, investor
5 -er: dealer, lecturer, banker, philosopher, researcher

Changes
1 drop the final *e* **2** drop the final *s, y* or *ity* **3** drop the final *s, cs* or *y* **4** drop the final *e* **5** drop the final *y*, keep the final *e*

5 the *givers* (or *providers*) are trainer, employer, payer, interviewer, examiner; the *receivers* (or *victims*!) are trainee, employee, payee, interviewee, examinee

6 **1** a participant **2** an instructor **3** a chemist **4** a presenter **5** a specialist **6** a librarian **7** a survivor **8** a motorist **9** a supplier **10** a refugee

READING AND USE OF ENGLISH

Part 7

2 **1** people talking about their careers, four
2 young trainees
3 which person says what about their job, their past and their future

3 Suggested answers
2 company, bought **3** pleasantly surprised, conditions **4** enthusiasm, determination, success **5** difficult, at first, on time **7** paid, financial, simpler **8** liked, started **9** understand, new things, quickly **10** unsure, how much, will earn

4 Exam task answers
1 D 2 C 3 A 4 B 5 C 6 B 7 A 8 B 9 C 10 D

Underlining

A

(3) Before I started here I'd expected to have to work very long hours, but nowadays there's a maximum of 48 hours per week for doctors. There is of course shift work, but the days of junior doctors having to live in and be on call all night are, I was happy to find, long gone.

(7) a clearly laid-down salary structure in this profession, and that makes it easier to think ahead – for instance, if you're intending to take out a loan for house purchase, you know roughly what you'll be able to afford

B

(8) took to the work straightaway

(6) That will mean taking on a lot of added responsibilities such as building lasting business relationships with clients, but I'm sure I'll manage.

(4) If, like me, you're highly motivated, in this firm your career can really take off.

C

(9) there was a tremendous amount to take in all at once

(5) in those early days I had a little trouble meeting deadlines

(2) rumours that a major international corporation is considering taking the firm over

D

(1) I would like to have studied Law at university but I didn't have the grades, so I went straight from school into a law firm.

(10) The salary here is reasonable, although in the present economic climate, with such huge cuts to public spending, that may not be the case for much longer.

Phrasal verbs with *take*

6 **1** took up **2** taking over **3** taken on **4** took to **5** take in **6** take out **7** take off **8** taking on

7 **1** take on **2** take to **3** taken over **4** taken on **5** taken off **6** take up **7** take out **8** take … in

SPEAKING

Countable and uncountable nouns

1 **1** countable nouns **2** uncountable nouns

2 **1** transport **2** a lot of information **3** furniture **4** much news *or* a lot of news **5** work **6** a little money **7** software **8** some spare time *or* a little spare time *or* a lot of spare time **9** unemployment is increasing **10** little experience

3 *countable*: deal, discovery, duty, earnings, institution, opportunity, position, profession, qualification, responsibility
uncountable: advertising, advice, commerce, education, homework, knowledge, leisure, manufacturing, production, research, technology

Part 1

4 c, e, f

5 *countable*: (an) engineering course, (a) research degree
uncountable: (some) spare time, (for) pleasure, (doing) overtime, (in) management

Recording script

Examiner: OK, could you tell us something about your family, Alisa?

Alisa: Yes, I live with my mother, who's a scientist, and my younger brother Nikolai. He's starting at the same university as me this September.

Examiner: And your family, Francesco?

Francesco: There's my mother and father, and my two sisters, Giorgia and Sara. They all live at home, but these days I have my own flat.

Examiner: Alisa, what kind of things do you do in your free time?

Alisa: I have to do a lot of homework, but when I have some spare time I like to go to the theatre or a concert. Or I read, at home. Either to increase my knowledge, or just for pleasure. That's what I'll be doing later this evening, actually.

Examiner: And what about your free time, Francesco? What sort of things do you do?

Francesco: I spend quite a lot of time on my computer, reading newspapers in English and looking at interesting websites, things like that. Though sometimes I go out with friends in the evening. If I'm not doing overtime, that is!

Examiner: And what kind of work do you do?

Francesco: I work in manufacturing. I started out as an ordinary employee, but now I'm in management. I have a lot of responsibilities, but I'm sure there will be some good opportunities in the future if I work hard.

Examiner: Tell us about your studies, Alisa.

Alisa: I'm in my second year of an engineering course, and when I graduate I'm going to do a research degree. That's partly because I enjoy studying, but also because these days I think it's very important to get as many qualifications as possible. I'm hoping I'll have finished my studies by the time I'm 26.

Examiner: OK. Thank you.

READING AND USE OF ENGLISH

Part 3

1 **1** biologist **2** responsibilities **3** production **4** interviewee **5** knowledge **6** employers **7** advice **8** advertising **9** politicians

2 Suggested answers
most – medicine and dentistry, least – technology

3 **1** verb **2** noun **3** *-ment* **4** uncountable, no *-s*

4 Exam task answers
1 earnings **2** researchers **3** availability **4** qualification **5** scientists **6** management **7** consultants **8** engineers

WRITING

Part 2 formal letter of application

1 **1** the International Student Fair
2 assistants
3 giving directions and offering advice
4 you must like helping people, have experience of choosing a place of study, and be willing to work evenings
5 Ms Ross, in a formal style
6 convince her / the organisation that you are suitable for the job

2 **2** I would like to apply for the post of
3 as advertised in the newspaper on 2 January
4 I have always enjoyed assisting others, I looked at the advantages and disadvantages of many academic institutions, I would be available to work evenings as all my lectures are in the afternoons
5 Could you please tell me how much I would be paid, and whether training would be necessary?
6 last year I worked as a volunteer at a book fair
7 my curriculum vitae, which I enclose
8 If you need any further information, please do not hesitate to contact me.
9 I would be able to attend an interview any morning.

5 Model answer

Dear Ms Ross,
I am writing to apply for the position of assistant at the International Student Fair this summer, as recently advertised in the press.
I have recently begun an undergraduate course in chemistry at the university here, after carefully considering a number of possible higher-education institutions. I therefore feel I have some relevant experience, and I would very much like to pass this on to others.
In addition, over the last twelve months I have done a considerable amount of voluntary work, in particular with inner-city youth groups. I have always felt that the most rewarding kind of job to have is one that involves helping others.
As most of my work with the youth groups took place between 6 and 8 pm I am quite accustomed to working in the evenings. I would, however, be grateful if you could tell me which days and at what times I would be required to work, if I were offered the post.
I enclose my curriculum vitae, and I look forward to receiving your reply.
Yours sincerely,
Maria Karalis

Revision

1 **1** B **2** A **3** D **4** B **5** D **6** C **7** C **8** B

2 **2** little experience **3** few opportunities **4** a little research **5** few professions **6** a little overtime

3 **1** I'll help **2** takes **3** won't mind **4** I'm seeing **5** will have been working **6** I'll be surfing

4 **1** discoveries **2** graduation **3** economist **4** accountant **5** librarian **6** electrician **7** attendant **8** employee

Unit 6

READING AND USE OF ENGLISH

Medical vocabulary

1 **a** people: nurse, patient, porter, specialist, surgeon

b injuries and illnesses: ache, bruise, disease, fever, fracture, graze, infection, pain, sprain, temperature, wound

c treatment: bandage, injection, medicine, operation, plaster, prescription, stitches, tablets, thermometer

4 **1** sight, probably before she was born **2** yes

5 Suggested answers

2 *from* Dr Percival closed … *to* … and stared at the light

3 *from* she turned her face away … *to* … I don't know what I mean

4 *from* Over the next few weeks … *to* … how close they were

5 *from* But Dr Percival was patient … *to* … they worked well

6 Exam task answers

1 B **2** A **3** C **4** B **5** C **6** B

LISTENING

Part 1

1 You hear a woman telling a neighbour in the street about a <u>road accident</u> she has just seen. <u>What happened?</u>

1 an event **2** a woman and a neighbour **3** in the street **4** to describe the accident **5** very recently

2 **1** C **2** A **3** B

3

Recording script

You hear a woman telling a neighbour in the street about a road accident she has just seen.

It all happened so quickly. A car came racing out of that side street without stopping, and the poor cyclist had no chance. He came off and fell onto the road really hard, I thought he must have broken an arm or a leg. I've had some medical training so <u>I would've given him first aid if he'd needed it, but amazingly he didn't, and there didn't seem any point in calling an ambulance, either</u>. The cyclist really told the driver what he thought of him, though, because he could have been badly hurt. And I don't think he would've been able to ride that bike anywhere: it was pretty badly damaged in the crash.

4 **A:** *there didn't seem any point in calling an ambulance, either* – it didn't actually happen

B: *I would've given him first aid if he'd needed it, but amazingly he didn't* – she didn't actually need to give first aid, so we can infer he was not hurt. Plus *I thought he must have broken an arm or a leg* and *he could have been badly hurt*, neither of which were actually the case but could be misunderstood.

C: *I would've given him first aid if he'd needed it*

Correct answer: **B**

5 question 2 *woman, street, Where, now*; 1 place, 2 woman to friend, 3 in the street, 4 no information on *why*, 5 now

question 3 *patient, phone, What, dislike, hospital*; 1 opinion/attitude, 2 patient to someone on the phone, 3 hospital, 4 to complain, 5 no information on *when*

question 4 *two, doctor's, How, feel, now*; 1 feelings, 2 two people, 3 doctor's waiting room, 4 to express feelings, 5 now

question 5 *young woman, race, What, agree*; 1 agreement, 2 young woman to friend, 3/5 to discuss a race, 4/5 no information on *where* or *when*

question 6 *woman, phone, Why*; 1 purpose, 2 woman to someone on the phone, 3/5 no information on *where* or *when*

6 Exam task answers

1 B **2** C **3** B **4** C **5** A **6** A

Recording script

You will hear people talking in six different situations. For questions 1–6, choose the best answer (A, B or C).

1 You overhear a man in a restaurant talking to a colleague about his work.

The other day I saw a teenager who spends all his time doing sports and he had a whole series of problems: stiff knee, swollen ankles, sore elbow, and so on. <u>I think he expected me to give him painkillers or a prescription</u> for something that would instantly sort everything out, and was obviously disappointed when <u>I told him no such magic cure existed</u>. I suggested instead that he should try doing less training and take a day off each week, as he was clearly overdoing it. It was tricky because many young men in Newtown, where he grew up, are involved in crime. The only ones who aren't are those who are mad about sports, and I didn't want to put him off.

2 You hear a woman talking to a friend in the street.

I'm afraid I can't stop long. I've got to pick up something for this evening and they close in half an hour. I was on my way back from seeing Nathan, who's in hospital, and suddenly I remembered there's nothing in the fridge for the kids. They're going into town to see a film that begins at seven and I can't send them off with empty stomachs, so I had to get off the bus a couple of stops early and head this way. Fortunately Nathan is due out of hospital on Monday, which is wonderful news, so tomorrow should be my last visit there.

3 You hear a patient talking on the phone.

I know there's a lot in the papers about things going wrong in hospitals, doctors making mistakes and patients catching infections and things like that, but I can't say I have any complaints in that respect. Even the meals they give you aren't as bad as everyone says, certainly no worse than what I cook for myself at home! I would like a bit more peace and quiet, though. There always seems to be something going on 24/7, and in a place like this sound travels a long way. Still, the nurses say I should be out of here by the weekend, so I'll soon be back at the house.

4 You overhear two people talking in a doctor's waiting room.

Man: Actually I was here last week after my daughter's pet rabbit bit me.

Woman: Really? I thought rabbits were supposed to be friendly animals.

Man: Me too, until Bunny sank his teeth into my arm. When I told a friend of mine about it he couldn't stop laughing, but I didn't really see the funny side of it and I got a bit cross with him at the time.

Woman: And what did the doctor do?

Man: She gave me an injection and told me to come back if there were any signs of infection, but so far there haven't been, I'm glad to say. I've kept away from Bunny, though, just in case he gets nasty again.

5 You hear a young woman talking to a friend about a cross-country race.

Man: My knee still hurts, and I've got that cross-country race coming up in two weeks.

Woman: Maybe it'd be best to miss it this time. There might be something seriously wrong with your knee.

Man: I don't think so. My own feeling is that it'll have cleared up in time for the race.

Woman: It won't if you keep training so hard every day.

Man: I realise that. But I don't want to lose fitness in the meantime.

Woman: So why don't you do something different? Go down to the pool, for instance? That's just as good for keeping fit.

Man: I think you're probably right. I'll do that each evening, instead of going out running.

6 You overhear a woman on the phone.

I had an appointment with the dentist on Friday morning but without any warning at all I've just received an email saying that it's been put off till Monday, and I just can't make that. I'm actually going away on Saturday for a fortnight, and I certainly don't intend spending my entire holiday with toothache. I'm now going to have to ring up my old dentist and ask her if she can see me this week, but even if she can give me an appointment at such short notice it means a ten-mile journey to and from her surgery, and that really is quite inconvenient.

Grammar

Phrasal verbs with *up*

1 *grew up* means 'became an adult', *coming up* means 'getting nearer in time', *cleared up* means 'got better'

2 **1** eat, d **2** use, j **3** tidy, i **4** speak, b **5** speed, c **6** split, a **7** healed, h **8** ran, g **9** dug, f **10** sum, e

Relative clauses

3 **1** b only has one sister, a has more than one
2 b had never seen a match before, a had only seen boring matches before
3 *which* could be left out in a because it is a defining relative clause, and the relative pronoun is the object of the clause

4 **1** defining **2** non-defining **3** non-defining; immediately before the relative pronoun, and possibly also at the end of the relative clause

5 **2** , which was set in a school, was
3 , when the World Cup was held in South Africa, Spain
4 , who were in an accident,
5 , whose mother had also been a top swimmer, won a medal
6 , where the final was about to take place, everyone was

6 **1** which **2** *comma before* which, Davos **3** when, June **4** who/that, people **5** whose, man **6** *commas before* who *and* saw, Mark **7** where, a gym

SPEAKING

Sports vocabulary

1 course – golf
court – basketball, squash, tennis
gym – gymnastics
pitch – baseball, football, hockey, rugby
ring – boxing
rink – ice skating
sea – diving, sailing, surfing
slope – skiing, snowboarding
track – athletics, cycling, motorcycling

2 do – athletics (athlete), boxing (boxer), gymnastics (gymnast)
play – baseball (baseball player), basketball (basketball player), football (football player *or* footballer), golf (golfer), hockey (hockey player), rugby (rugby player), squash (squash player), tennis (tennis player)
go – cycling (cylist), diving (diver), ice skating (ice skater), motorcycling (motorcyclist), sailing (sailor), skiing (skier), snowboarding (snowboarder), surfing (surfer)

3 Suggested answers
A baseball player uses a (baseball) bat.
A surfer uses a (surf)board.
A golfer uses a (golf) club.
A boxer wears (boxing) gloves.
A motorcyclist wears a helmet.
A tennis player uses a (tennis) racket.
An ice skater wears (ice) skates.
A skier uses skis.

Agreeing and politely disagreeing

4

Recording script

Man: I think you're probably right.
Man: I don't think so. My own feeling is …

5 **a** absolutely **b** so **c** agree **d** just **e** what **f** sure **g** know **h** keen

Recording script

Agreeing

a Yes, you're absolutely right.
b I think so, too.
c Yes, I agree with that.
d That's just what I was thinking.

Politely disagreeing

e Perhaps, but what about …?
f I'm not so sure. Don't you think …?
g I don't know about that.
h I'm not really so keen on …

Part 3

6 **1** gymnastics **2** motorcycling *3* rugby, snowboarding **4** boxing

7 **1** c **2** g **3** d **4** a **5** f **6** b **7** e
The speakers do not use h.

Recording script

Teacher: Now, I'd like you to talk about something together for about two minutes. Here are some sports that can be dangerous. Look at the task and talk to each other about what can happen to people doing these sports if they are not careful. You now have some time to look at the task. *[15-second pause]*
Could you start now, please?

Tomasz: Is it OK if we start with rugby?

Eva: Yes, let's begin with that.

Tomasz: Well, I think you have to be very careful in this sport, because it's quite violent and they don't have any protection like in American football.

Eva: (c) Yes, I agree with that. They don't wear a helmet to protect their head, so they can have some serious injuries. Also to their arms and legs.

Tomasz: It's the same for the motorcycling. Even though they wear a helmet and some body protection, it's still very dangerous if they fall off when they're going fast.

Eva: It's much more dangerous than car racing, I think. The drivers are a lot safer because of the way they make the cars these days, but if you crash a motorbike you will probably still get injured.

Tomasz: And what about diving? What can happen there?

Eva: Well, when you're deep in the water I suppose the biggest risk is that for some reason you can't breathe. Such as getting trapped under the water and your air runs out. Or something goes wrong with the oxygen thing.

Tomasz: Or a shark attacks you. That's another danger.

Eva: (g) I don't know about that. In films, maybe. But it's not very common in real life, is it? Anyway, let's go on to the next one.

Tomasz: Yes, gymnastics. Now that's definitely not as dangerous as some of the others. I mean, even if you're really careless, normally the worst thing that can happen is that you get hurt a bit, nothing very bad.

Eva: (d) That's just what I was thinking really. It can't be very nice if you fall, but at least the ground is soft. It's not like landing on a racetrack, or even a rugby pitch.

Tomasz: Though people can get hurt snowboarding, and they do that on snow, which is pretty soft. Probably because they go so fast.

Eva: Especially if they go off the proper slopes. If they do that in bad weather they can't see where they're going, and they can hit a tree, or rocks.

Tomasz: I suppose hitting rocks is the biggest risk for people who go surfing, too. They might be just under the surface but you don't know until a wave pushes you onto them.

Eva: (a) Yes, you're absolutely right. I think you have to know the place where you are going surfing, to make sure there aren't any dangerous ones near you. And always have a surfing buddy with you, someone who knows where you are all the time.

Tomasz: Yes, that makes it much safer.

Eva: Next there's boxing. What do you think of that? To me it's not really a sport – it's just fighting, hitting someone's head. That's really stupid, and it must damage them in the end.

Tomasz: (f) I'm not so sure. Don't you think that wearing gloves makes it safer?

Eva: Well, actually last week I read that boxers hit each other much harder with gloves on, because without them they would hurt their hands.

Teacher: Thank you. Now you have a minute to decide which two are the most dangerous sports.

Tomasz: Shall I start?

Eva: Yes, go on.

Tomasz: OK. So which two of these sports do we think are the most dangerous? I'd say the motorcycling simply because it's so fast and the surface is so hard.

Eva: (b) I think so, too. And also boxing. They should ban it completely, starting with the next Olympic Games. Don't you agree that it's one of the most dangerous sports in the world?

Tomasz: (e) Perhaps, but what about rugby? Or snowboarding?

Eva: Boxing.

Tomasz: OK, we have different opinions about this, but let's leave it at that.

Eva: Yes, that's fine.

Teacher: Thank you.

READING AND USE OF ENGLISH

Part 2

2 jobs – checking tickets, handing out uniforms, showing spectators to their seats, tidying after events have finished
advantages – helping to make the Games a success for everyone, training (though may not be paid)
disadvantages – unpaid, no accommodation, no travel expenses, giving up two weeks of their summer holidays, spending three days being trained

4 Exam task answers
1 whose **2** who **3** which **4** own **5** where **6** from **7** up **8** that *or* which

WRITING

Purpose links

1 **1** to **2** in order that **3** so that **4** In order to **5** so as to **6** both possible **7** both possible **8** so that

2 Suggested answers

2 to / in order to / so as to watch sports *or* so that / in order that they can watch sports

3 to / in order to / so as to get medicine *or* so that / in order that they can get medicine

4 to / in order to / so as to lose weight *or* so that / in order that they can lose weight

5 to / in order to / so as to win *or* so that / in order that they can win

6 to / in order to / so as to give them a good time *or* so that / in order that they can have a good time

Part 2 letter

3 **1** a letter

2 an Irish penfriend, Linda; she's coming to your country in the summer and will see you

3 give her some advice on sports she can do while she's in your town

4 informal: *tips*, *write back soon*; contracted forms (*I'm*); informal punctuation (dash, exclamation mark); informal linkers (*and*, *so*).

4 **1** **a** indoor sports: 3rd paragraph **b** sports they can do together: 4th paragraph **c** outdoor sports: 2nd paragraph

2 **a** *Hi, Thanks, lots of, Now that, nice, how about, get, Anyway, let me know, Bye for now*; contracted forms (*I'm, you're, you'll, you'd, there's, it'd, I'll,*); informal punctuation (dash, exclamation mark); short sentences

b sports you can do, a really good one which, an Olympic-size pool where

c so that we have more time, to make sure we get a court

6 Model answer

> Dear Linda
>
> Many thanks for your letter. It was good to hear from you.
>
> I'm pleased to hear that you want to keep fit while you're here. I like sport too, so I'm sure there are lots of things we can do together.
>
> Do you like playing tennis? There are courts in the park, so we could play tennis. Two friends of mine are very keen tennis players, so we could make up a four. That would be fun! Let me know so that I can warn my friends in advance.
>
> I hope you enjoy cycling. I've got a bike and you could borrow my sister's. We could cycle to the river and go swimming there. It's about an hour's ride.
>
> I hope the weather's fine while you're here. You never know these days! If it rains, there's a hotel near our house which has a gym, a sauna and a small swimming pool. I've never been there, but I could make enquiries if you're interested.
>
> Let me know if you have any other questions.
>
> Looking forward to seeing you soon!
>
> Erika

Revision

1 **Across**

1 pitch **3** track **7** sailor **9** ache **11** nurse **12** bruise **14** court **16** patient **17** course

Down

2 helmet **4** athlete **5** fracture **6** sprain **7** sight **8** cyclist **10** wound **12** bat **13** slope **15** ring

2 **2** , when I was born, … who *or* that

3 whose … that *or* which

4 where … who *or* that

5 whose … that *or* which

6 who *or* that … , which

You can leave out *that* or *which* in sentence 5, and *who* or *that* in sentence 6.

3 **1** order **2** who *or* that **3** if **4** whose **5** which **6** same **7** to **8** so

4 **1** in order that it **2** who grew up **3** so as not to get *or* so that he didn't / did not get **4** up the rubbish that was *or* which was **5** in order not to **6** whose name is

Unit 7

LISTENING

Part 3

1 acid rain, animal conservation, carbon emissions, climate change, global warming, industrial waste, melting icecaps, oil spills, renewable resources, solar power
good – animal conservation, renewable resources, solar power
harmful – acid rain, carbon emissions, climate change, global warming, industrial waste, melting icecaps, oil spills

2 **1** heatwave **2** extreme rainfall **3** tropical storm **4** tornado

3 Suggested answer
extreme weather events the speakers have seen, and what happened

4 Suggested answers
- **A** injured, going on (during, at the same time)
- **B** glad, by train (pleased, disappointed; rail)
- **C** swim, safety (water, drown; escape, danger)
- **D** stayed, all the time (didn't move, watched; throughout, during)
- **E** help people, while (gave, offered; during, at the same time)
- **F** fortunate, found, shelter (lucky, just as well; discovered, came across; safety, protection)
- **G** more severe, previous years (worse, stronger; summer before)
- **H** wasn't sure, do (didn't know, wasn't used to; go, run)

5 no, because Speaker 1's sentence refers to something that didn't happen, with imaginary results, whereas F describes a real event

6 Exam task answers
1 H **2** G **3** D **4** A **5** E

Recording script

You will hear five different people talking about extreme weather events that they have seen. For questions 1–5, choose from the list (A–H) what each speaker says about what happened. Use the letters only once. There are three extra letters which you do not need to use.

Speaker 1

It was a fine spring day and I was out walking in the fields, when suddenly everything went dark and I noticed this dark column in the sky. It seemed to be getting bigger and then I realised it was a tornado, heading my way. I'd seen them on TV, of course, but there'd never been one round here so this wasn't something I was used to. If there had been shelter around I would've used it, but there just wasn't any. Then hailstones and bits of rubbish started to fall around me, so I just ran, anywhere. The tornado came closer and closer, but at the very last moment it turned left. If it hadn't changed direction, I wouldn't be here now.

Speaker 2

The forecast had mentioned extreme rainfall, but I'd heard that before in June and it usually meant that everything got very wet and that was about it. But this time it just kept pouring down, hour after hour. I knew that if the river reaches a certain level it bursts its banks, so I walked up through the village. That was a mistake, because I suddenly saw this mass of water and mud racing down the main street towards me. If I'd stayed there I would've been in big trouble, so I turned and ran, desperately looking for shelter. Through shop windows I saw terrified people, but the doors were closed and I had to keep running until I was out of the village. I was unhurt, but if it happened again, I'd find somewhere safe much sooner.

Speaker 3

So far this year we've had hardly any rainfall, and unless it rains soon, most of the crops will die. As they did last year, when the same thing happened. We had a heatwave in May that left the countryside dry as a bone, and not surprisingly there have been bush fires, including one right here. From my upstairs window I saw the smoke in the distance, and then watched, horrified, as the flames came closer and closer, before thankfully stopping just short of my house. Some people were trapped in a valley near here, and there could've been a tragedy if they hadn't found a cave where they could shelter until the worst of the fire had passed. They had a few minor burns, but were otherwise none the worse for their experience.

Speaker 4

We'd had a very mild winter on the island, with just the occasional sea mist and nothing stronger than light breezes. Then one evening the wind started to pick up, and huge waves began crashing onto the beach, until by midnight it was clear we were being hit by a tropical storm. From my house I saw a large tree fall onto the street, and a car crash into it. I dashed outside to help, but as I got close I saw the driver and passenger had had a lucky escape and could manage on their own. By then there were branches flying everywhere, so I ran back indoors, avoiding all but one of them on the way. I had some cuts and bruises, but it might've been a lot worse if it'd been a bigger branch.

Speaker 5

We'd had days of freezing temperatures last month, with frost on the car windows every morning, but I'd decided to drive home for Christmas anyway. All went well until the mountain pass, when a snowstorm suddenly struck. Within minutes some vehicles were in trouble, unable to go any further uphill. And I was stuck behind them. If I had a bigger car, I could have slept in it. But it's tiny and I'm very tall. So it was a miserable, sleepless night, even though I had several blankets with me. Actually, I got out and offered a couple to the family in the car behind and they were very grateful for them, which was nice. But I know one thing for sure: if I have to travel next Christmas, I'll take the train.

Grammar

Review of conditionals 1–3

1 **a** simple present, *will* future **b** past simple, *would* + infinitive **c** past perfect, *would* + *have* + past participle
a no, likely **b** unlikely, no **c** no, no

2 **1** c first **2** e third **3** b second **4** a first **5** d second

3 **1** I would try **2** I would have written **3** If I lived **4** we will have **5** I would spend **6** If I had known

4 Suggested and example answers

1 is, will you go; If the weather is fine, I'll / I will go to the beach.

2 became, would you do; If the summers where I live became much hotter, I'd / I would move to the mountains.

3 you were able (*or* you could), would the seasons be; If I were able to control the weather, spring would be longer *or* summer would be warmer *or* autumn would be shorter and winter would be snowier.

4 would you have done, had prevented; If bad weather had prevented me going out, I'd have / I would've / I would have stayed at home and read. *Also*, with *had not prevented*: If bad weather hadn't / had not prevented me going out, I'd have / I would've / I would have gone to the beach.

Mixed conditionals

5 **1** **a** past event (it changed direction) with present result (she's here now)
b permanent situation (she has a small car) with past result (she couldn't sleep in it)

2 yes, yes

3 no, no

6 **1** you hadn't brought your coat
2 could have gone skiing with my friends last week
3 wouldn't be stuck in the snow
4 hadn't polluted the air for many years
5 wouldn't be so high
6 I weren't from Australia

7 Example answers

1 If I had grown up in the north of Russia, I would know how to ski very well.
If I'd grown up in Britain, I'd probably work in an office.
If I'd grown up in the Caribbean, I wouldn't go away on holiday.

2 If I were British, I would've had to get used to a much warmer climate, a different culture and language, etc.

READING AND USE OF ENGLISH

Part 6

1 Suggested answers
store them away, put them in the bin, take them to recycling points, return them to the shop; they end up in landfill, they are broken up for recycling, they are exported

2 the first four describe the problem, the last two describe possible solutions

3 Suggested answers
C Compared with that, it **D** Much of this (*though sentence not needed*) **E** There **F** Add to that **G** The other

4 Exam task answers
1 E **2** F **3** C **4** G **5** B **6** A
Linking words: The issue (2); But (3); This (4); In practice (5); This (6)

6 substances + materials, globally + worldwide, flow + stream, reduce + cut down on, forcing + putting pressure on, poisonous + toxic, alternatives + substitutes, duty + responsibility, dumped + thrown away, enormous + vast

7 **a** devices **b** chimneys **c** hi-tech **d** regulation **e** recycling **f** generate **g** greenhouse gas **h** chemicals **i** disposal **j** processed

SPEAKING

Comparative forms

1 **1** than **2** as **3** so **4** less

2 **2** less hard than these
3 harmful as the old ones
4 less successfully than big companies *or* worse than big companies
5 as sensible as the second (one) *or* as sensible as the other one
6 so negatively as driving a car *or* as negatively as driving a car

Part 2

4 In task 1, A has to compare the photographs and say what they think could be good or bad about living there. B has to say which place they would prefer to live in.
In task 2, B has to say why they think people have chosen to take part in these activities. A has to say which of the activities will do more to help the environment.

READING AND USE OF ENGLISH

Phrases with *in*

1 **1** i **2** d **3** e **4** c **5** a **6** j **7** b **8** f **9** h **10** g

2 **1** in progress **2** play a part in **3** In practice **4** in due course **5** in all **6** in doubt **7** In the meantime **8** in the long term

Part 4

3 **1** present simple + infinitive becomes second conditional, *your* becomes *my*

2 *my job* = 1 mark, *if I were* = 1 mark: each of the two phrases gets one mark when correctly formed

4 **1** conditional (third) **2** comparative adverb **3** phrase with *in* **4** conditional (third) **5** phrase with *in* **6** conditional (third) **7** comparative adjective **8** conditional (mixed)

Exam task answers

1 would've / would have called | if I **2** drive so well | as **3** aren't / are not | in favour **4** would have / would've / 'd have arrived | in **5** probably not as | harmful as **6** would work | if we'd / we had

WRITING

Contrast links

1 **1** Even though **2** whereas **3** In contrast, **4** Despite the fact that **5** Despite **6** On the other hand,

Part 1 essay

2 **1** the class has done a project on the environment

2 the teacher

3 whether we are doing enough to protect our world

3 **1** yes – it's a little over the maximum but this normally doesn't matter, yes

2 **1** d **2** e **3** b **4** c, a

3 **a** Despite, in contrast, On the other hand, Nevertheless

b Firstly, In addition

c *we should do more … if we really want* (modal conditional), *unless richer nations give up … our planet will in the long term face* (first conditional)

d the problems are getting worse, do more than just talk, we use more … than ever before, lead a greener way of life, unless richer nations

6 Model answer

We are often told that we must do more to look after the environment, that the Earth will be damaged forever unless we take steps now to save it. But how true is this?

First of all, there can be no doubt that the rapidly increasing numbers of cars, factories and houses are polluting our towns and countryside. In addition, growing populations consuming more products are using more and more of the Earth's scarce resources and, at the same time, are creating huge amounts of waste.

Nevertheless, people's greater awareness of the dangers means that we are now turning to alternative, cleaner forms of energy such as wave power. Moreover, in our personal lives we are recycling more instead of throwing things out, using less electricity and starting to go by bicycle instead of by car. Technology, too, is playing a part, as homes become greener and electric vehicles a reality.

To sum up, although the increasing pressure on the environment is certainly a challenge, I believe that we are now beginning to respond to it successfully.

Revision

1 **1** than **2** further/farther **3** more **4** as **5** as **6** far *or* much **7** less **8** so *or* as **9** as **10** less

2 **1** B **2** B **3** B **4** C **5** A **6** A **7** C **8** D

3 Suggested and example answers

1 Where will you go next summer if it's very hot? I'll go to the seaside if it's very hot.

2 What would you most like to see if you went to Antarctica? If I went to Antarctica, I'd most like to see the penguins.

3 If it had snowed last month, would you have gone skiing then? No, if it'd snowed last month, I wouldn't have gone skiing then.

4 What will happen to the rainforests if we don't protect them? The rainforests will no longer exist if we don't protect them.

5 If you didn't have any electronic items, would you miss them? Yes, if I didn't have any electronic items, I'd miss them.

6 Do you think you would have done better in your last exam if you had revised more? No, I don't think I would've done better in my last exam if I'd revised more.

7 What would life be like today if we hadn't invented the car? Life would be much more pleasant today if we hadn't invented the car.

4 **1** quite so dirty | as **2** if we | hadn't / had not eaten **3** in | the long term **4** I'd / I had remembered | to take **5** if | I were you **6** if | they hadn't / had not helped *or* had | they not helped

Unit 8

READING AND USE OF ENGLISH

Communications vocabulary

1 **1** emailing **2** blogging **3** instant messaging **4** texting **5** social networking **6** video conferencing.

2 computer: bookmark, broadband, database, desktop, keyboard, spreadsheet, website
mobile phone: handset, ringtones
both: password

Part 5

4 Suggested answer
In some particular ways it has driven people apart, but overall it has brought the world closer together.

5 **a** 4 **b** 3 **c** 1

6 Exam task answers
1 B **2** C **3** A **4** D **5** D **6** C

LISTENING

Science vocabulary

2 **1** living **2** substances **3** energy **4** liquid, gas, solid **5** oxygen, carbon dioxide, carbon monoxide **6** laboratories, test tubes, experiments **7** atom, element, cell **8** discovery, invention, breakthrough

Recording script

1 Biology is the study of living things.

2 Chemistry is the study of substances and how they react or combine with each other.

3 Physics is the study of matter and energy, and their effect on one another.

4 Oil is a liquid, steam is a gas, and copper is a solid.

5 People breathe in oxygen and breathe out carbon dioxide. Cars give off carbon monoxide.

6 Scientists working in laboratories often use glass test tubes to carry out experiments.

7 An atom is the smallest unit that an element can be divided into, and a cell is the smallest unit of a plant or animal.

8 The discovery of electricity, which led to the invention of the light bulb, was a huge breakthrough in scientific knowledge.

Part 2

4 thirty-first, nineteen eighty-nine, four hundred and sixty-three, three point five five, twelfth, sixty per cent, one/a third, twelve thousand three hundred, thirty-five degrees, twenty-second, twenty fifteen *or* two thousand and fifteen, three-quarters

5 **1** age **2** year **5** fraction/percentage **6** number **10** date

6 Exam task answers
1 17 **2** 2009 **3** electricity **4** careers **5** two-thirds / ⅔ **6** 312 **7** coffee **8** explanation **9** communication skills **10** March (the) eleventh / March 11th / March 11 *or* the eleventh of March / 11th March / 11 March

Recording script

You will hear a journalist reporting on a prize for young scientists and engineers. For questions 1–10, complete the sentences.

Ryan

The National Science and Engineering Competition is aimed at young scientists and engineers who have developed new ideas completely of their own. They may be school projects or something they've done as a hobby, and the winners are awarded prizes and named Young Scientist and Young Engineer of the Year. Anyone aged 18 or under can take part, although (1) the science category was won by a 17-year-old last year, as was the engineering one. The competition covers every area of science, technology, engineering and mathematics, and is intentionally broadly based so as to encourage as many young people as possible to enter.

It's been going for a few years now. In fact, (2) it's been an annual event since 2009, although it became much bigger in 2010 once more people became aware of it. And then the media started to take an interest in the Big Bang Fair, where the winners are announced. From that year on, there have been lectures by top speakers, and shows put on by national television channels.

The Big Bang Fair is a three-day fair for school students interested in science and engineering, with lots of things to do like interactive science quizzes, games and activities. For instance, one boy had set up a non-moving bicycle, like those you find in a gym, and was pedalling away energetically. But (3) this was about electricity rather than exercise, with a challenge to anyone present to generate more than he could, as measured by the attached equipment. Nobody managed to, at least while I was around.

So they have a good time there, with plenty of fun things to do. But its real purpose is more serious: (4) to promote careers in those subjects, especially where there is a national skills gap in particular areas. This is done in a wide range of ways, and a study into how this can be extended is currently being carried out by the Centre for Science Education.

The fair is becoming increasingly popular. The total number of people at the most recent one was over 22,500, of whom (5) at least two-thirds, according to the figures I have, would have been of secondary-school age, with teachers and parents making up rather less than a quarter between them. Over 110 public and private organisations from across the country were represented, and it was clear that everyone there had a genuine desire to raise awareness of young people's achievements in science and technology.

Naturally, the number of young people actually involved in the competition was smaller. They can enter either as individuals or as part of a team, so that whereas in total 193 projects were presented, (6) there were actually 312 competitors working in the fields of science, technology, mathematics and engineering.

And there were some great projects. In one I particularly liked, the team built quite complicated structures in the shape of road bridges … entirely in chocolate. Most were surprisingly strong, though of course any that collapsed could simply be eaten. In another, a team managed to (7) convert coffee into a gas that then became the source of energy for a car, successfully covering the 300 kilometres to the fair. Finding alternatives to petrol as a fuel was a common theme, not surprisingly, with many entries aimed at reducing the amount of carbon monoxide and carbon dioxide being released into the atmosphere.

The final is held at the Big Bang Fair, where the number of entries is reduced to a shortlist of six. Neither individuals nor teams need to make a formal presentation to a big audience, but they are expected to be able to give a clear (8) explanation, going into some detail about their project so that it can be properly assessed by the five judges.

They may well be asked things about it, too, partly to see how well they respond to questions. Although the quality of the work they do is the main thing, (9) their communication skills are also taken into account as the winners may have the chance to speak in public, including on TV, on behalf of young scientists and engineers. And that, not surprisingly, appeals to quite a lot of teenagers.

Everyone's keen to know who's won this year, but it's quite a long process and although all entries had to be in by October the thirty-first, we'll have to wait until nearly the spring to find out. It'll actually be (10) on the first day of the next Big Bang Fair, which runs from March the eleventh to the thirteenth. I'm sure that will be followed with a lot of interest.

GRAMMAR

Review of passive forms

1 is done, can be extended, is (currently) being carried out
1 be **2** past participle (of the main verb)

2 **1** The equipment has been broken.
2 Firstly, the liquid is heated up.
3 Safety glasses must be worn in the laboratory.
4 This year's Science Competition was won by a very young student.
5 Dr Liu is said to be a brilliant scientist. / It is said that Dr Liu is a brilliant scientist.
1 b **2** a **3** d **4** e **5** c

3 **1** was invented **2** is being made **3** will be asked **4** painted **5** *correct* **6** used to be taught **7** had been born **8** *correct*

4 **1** a meal is warmed up **2** radio waves are absorbed by the food **3** the meal is being cooked **4** the food has been heated up **5** the radio waves will not have been absorbed by these materials **6** microwaving can be described **7** the microwave is often thought of **8** it was invented **9** they were already being used by restaurants **10** over a million had been sold

6 **2** is believed that there is water on that distant planet
3 are known to be dangerous
4 are thought to have made a breakthrough
5 is considered essential to have a mobile phone
6 is reported that doctors have found a cure

SPEAKING

Articles

1 **1** a/an **2** the **3** no article

2 **1** from flu (illness) **2** the telephone (invention) **3** the army (only one) **4** the greatest (superlative) **5** a 7.8 per cent (number) **6** the piano (musical instrument) **7** an engineer (job) **8** a very interesting job (first time mentioned)

3 **1** – **2** the **3** a **4** – **5** the **6** a **7** the **8** – **9** a **10** the **11** – **12** – **13** the

Recording script

Lena: I think geology would be the most interesting science to study. It's a pity we don't do it at school because I like the idea of becoming a geologist.

Felix: I think the one that appeals to me most is zoology. It'd be fantastic to get a job in the countryside in Africa studying animals like the lion or leopard.

Part 4

4 Lena 3, Felix 2; as well as that, and not only that, and there's another thing, and also

> **Recording script**
>
> Teacher: Lena, how important is it that people study science?
>
> Lena: It's quite important, I think, because the country will need a lot of scientists in the future. As well as that, people need to understand science so they can make the right choices when they buy things. And not only that, they can also make better decisions on how to protect the environment.
>
> Felix Yes, I agree. And there's another thing: they can make more sense of the world around them, learning things like how electricity works and which chemicals are dangerous, and that can make people safer. And also how the human body works, which can help them lead healthier lives.

READING AND USE OF ENGLISH

Collocations

1 attach a file, browse websites, carry out an experiment, charge a mobile phone, prove a theory, run a program, store data, undo a change

2 **1** A (voice) **2** D (computer) **3** A (screen) **4** B (PC) **5** C (two numbers) **6** C (of two things) **7** D (computer)

Part 1

3 in the text: tell people where they are, helping in emergencies/accidents, search and rescue, weather forecasting, seeing into space, phone calls, the Internet, TV

also: mapping the ground, searching for archaeological sites, pollution monitoring

4 **1** positioning (systems) **2** emergency **3** space **4** space **5** ten, more clearly than **6** phone calls **7** the Internet **8** TV programmes

Exam task answers

1 A 2 B 3 A 4 A 5 B 6 D 7 C 8 D

WRITING

Reason and result links

1 **1** result **2** why **3** owing **4** account **5** Consequently/Therefore **6** reason **7** Since/Because **8** view **9** because **10** consequently/therefore

Quite formal: owing to, on account of, consequently, in view of the fact that, therefore

Part 2 article

2 **1** readers of an international magazine

2 you may win a prize

3 give reasons why the most important piece of technology you have is so important to you, say how it could be improved

3 Suggested answers

1 neutral: it uses contracted forms, e.g. *couldn't*, and one informal word (*lappy*), but is not generally conversational in tone. It is written in complete sentences, some of them fairly complex, and uses passive forms. It uses full reason and result links, but not the more formal ones.

2 good things: first and second; problems and improvements: third and fourth

3 a title that catches the eye, expressing enthusiasm for the subject; the possibility of linking the mind directly to the laptop, and what that could lead to

4 **a** since, As a result, because of, that is why, for that reason

b I couldn't imagine a world without laptops; Without my lappy, my life would crash

c they can't always be connected, batteries are needed

6 Model answer

> Cool technology
>
> It was invented half a century ago, though it hasn't changed much since then. We all seem to have one because it makes life so much easier, yet we hardly notice it's there. So what is it?
>
> It's the freezer, that unexciting-looking box in the kitchen that keeps the fridge company. But whereas food in the fridge only stays fresh for a few days, the freezer allows it to be kept for weeks or even months.
>
> Consequently, food can be bought in large amounts, saving both time and money. As well as that, any food left over from meals can be stored for another day, rather than having to be thrown out.
>
> My favourite use of my freezer is for frozen fruit and vegetables. These, believe it or not, are particularly good for you, as they are frozen just when they are ripe. Fresh fruit and vegetables, in contrast, are often picked too early.
>
> The only improvement I would make to my freezer is to make it bigger, so I can keep even more icecream in it!

Revision

1 **Across**

1 cell **3** backup **4** undo **6** run **7** global **9** data **12** update **14** browse **15** crash

Down

1 charge **2** launch **3** blog **5** faint **8** outer **10** access **11** atom **13** prove **14** bug

2 **1** times **2** charge **3** outer **4** access **5** video **6** exploration

3 **1** the **2** a **3** – **4** – **5** the **6** the **7** an **8** a **9** the **10** a **11** the **12** the **13** – **14** the **15** – **16** the **17** – **18** – **19** a **20** the

4 **1** might not | have been **2** are expected | to fall suddenly **3** it is | even suggested (that) **4** is believed that | carelessness was **5** is said | to have been **6** are being | changed constantly / constantly changed

Unit 9

LISTENING

Media vocabulary

1 *television and radio*: broadcasting, commercials, episode, network, remote control, satellite dish
newspapers and magazines: circulation, gossip column, illustrations, print version, publication, tabloids, the press
both: news items, the headlines

2 Suggested answers
comedies, current affairs programmes, drama series, documentaries, live sports, news bulletins, quiz shows, soap operas, talent shows

3 camera operator: person who films a programme (*also* 'cameraman' or 'camerawoman')
editor: person who corrects or changes parts of a programme before it is shown
interviewer: person who asks the questions during TV interviews, especially with celebrities
investigative journalist: reporter who tries to discover hidden information of public interest
newsreader: person who reads out the news in a news bulletin (*also* newscaster, especially US English)
news reporter: person who obtains information about news events and describes them for TV
presenter: person who introduces a TV show
producer: person who controls how a programme is made
scriptwriter: person who writes the words for programmes
set designer: person who is responsible for the visual aspects of a programme

Part 4

4 **1** an interview **2** Kirsty Ross, a television presenter **3** her work

5 **1** occupation *or* what **2** activity *or* how **3** opinion **4** activity *or* how **5** feelings **6** attitude **7** opinion
Exam task answers
1 C 2 C 3 A 4 A 5 B 6 B 7 A

Recording script

You will hear part of a radio interview with Kirsty Ross, who works as a television presenter. For questions 1–7, choose the best answer (A, B or C).

Interviewer: Now I have a guest whose voice will be familiar to many listeners: TV presenter Kirsty Ross. Good morning Kirsty, and welcome to radio!

Kirsty: Good morning!

Interviewer: To start off, why did you choose presenting as a career? Had you done media studies or something like that at university?

Kirsty: Actually (1) <u>I'd been working in entertainment ever since I left school. I was the keyboard player in a band</u>. I was having loads of fun but it wasn't leading anywhere and what really fascinated me was television. I'd thought of trying acting and getting into TV that way, but I think I felt I wanted to be myself in front of the camera, and that's why I decided on presenting.

Interviewer: And how did you manage to get into it? There must be thousands of people out there with the same ambition.

Kirsty: Yes, I knew there would be a lot of competition for the few jobs going, and that just watching TV all day long and trying to imitate those doing the presenting wouldn't bring success. I looked at specialist courses for would-be presenters but they were all too expensive, so instead (2) <u>I spent six months doing work experience. It was a difficult time because of course I wasn't earning anything, but being right inside a major TV organisation taught me a lot</u>.

Interviewer: What did you do after that finished?

Kirsty: I made a short film of myself, about three minutes long, showing off what I felt to be my strongest points.

Interviewer: What are they?

Kirsty: People say I'm good at looking straight into the camera and talking, and I've always enjoyed getting into conversation with a live audience, but (3) being able to ask guests the right questions and get good answers out of them is what I take most pride in. Though I'm probably awful as an interviewee – sitting here being asked all these questions is making me nervous! Anyway, in those days people used to record their own films on video and post them to the production company.

Interviewer: Did you do that?

Kirsty: I was going to, but then I had this sudden fear about mail getting lost and it was so important to me that (4) I took it round to their office myself. Of course, if I were starting out these days I'd send it electronically as an attachment as everyone does now.

Interviewer: And how did they respond?

Kirsty: They asked me if I would go in for a test the next week.

Interviewer: That must have been good news for you.

Kirsty: Yes, you'd have thought I'd be delighted, wouldn't you? Though actually I'd been hoping that once they'd seen my film I'd be offered a job straightaway, so (5) when I heard I'd have to go there and perform live in front of the bosses, I began to worry about what might go wrong. At the same time, though, I knew I could rise to the challenge.

Interviewer: Which I imagine you did.

Kirsty: It went quite well, yes. Though they made it clear I had a lot to learn before they'd actually put me in front of live TV cameras.

Interviewer: What kind of things?

Kirsty: Well, they said I'd need to practise memorising scripts, but of course I'd spent years learning music and lyrics off by heart so I was used to that kind of thing. (6) What was trickier was knowing where you're supposed to be looking at any given point when you have cameras either side of you and right in front. Fortunately you get some guidance from the producer, who's in touch with you through the earpiece, a small listening device that fits in your ear, so she can give you precise instructions while you're going out live.

Interviewer: And what would you say a presenter most needs to be able to do?

Kirsty: Well it helps a lot if you have a good working relationship with the others in the studio: the producer, the camera operators, the make-up people – everybody, in fact. And on the other hand it's good if you can work on your own, Googling the people you're going to interview, for instance, and the topics you'll be talking about. But (7) none of this matters unless you and everybody around you knows that whatever happens you won't panic. They have to be able to trust you to carry on as normal, even if something truly awful occurs.

Interviewer: Has anything ever gone badly wrong while you were presenting live?

Kirsty: Yes, it's happened recently. Last week my guest suddenly walked out because …

Grammar

Review of reported speech and reporting verbs

1 **a** I have a guest whose voice will be familiar.
b Sitting here being asked all these questions is making me nervous.
c It's happened recently. Last week my guest suddenly walked out.

2 present simple → past simple, *will* future → conditional, present continuous → past continuous, present perfect → past perfect, past simple → past perfect

3 I → he, here → there, these → those, me → her, last week → the week before, my → her
demonstratives: this → that; personal pronouns I → she, we/you → they; possessive adjectives: our/your → their, my → his; reflexive pronouns: myself → herself, etc.; time expressions: today → the previous day, next week → the following week, etc.

4 **1** Jaime said he didn't want to watch that programme then *or* at that time.
2 Louise told me over the phone she was going out when her boyfriend got there.
3 On Monday Joey said he'd / he had seen the match at his friend's house the night before *or* the previous night.
4 My sister said (that) later that evening she'd / she would be talking to her favourite TV star.
5 Anna told the presenter (that) she'd been working in entertainment ever since she left school. (tense stays the same)
6 Julia said she'd / she had always wanted to be on TV, and the day after *or* the next day *or* the following day she would be.

5 **a** if/whether she had done / she'd done that
b how they had / they'd responded
To make questions: we use the same word order as in a statement, without *do* or *did*, making the same tense etc. changes as for reported statements. We add *if* or *whether*.

6 **2** suggested **3** told **4** apologised **5** admitted

7 **a** *to*: decide, promise, refuse, threaten
b object + *to*: advise, invite, order, persuade, remind, tell, warn
c *-ing*: admit, deny, recommend, suggest
d (*that*) + clause: decide, deny, explain, promise, recommend, tell, threaten, warn
e preposition + *-ing*: advise (against), apologise (for), insist (on)

8 **1** refused to listen | to me **2** reminded us | to bring our **3** invited Jo to meet | her **4** denied doing *or* denied having done | anything wrong **5** advised her | against going **6** suggested going *or* suggested we go | that way

READING AND USE OF ENGLISH

Part 7

2 **1** people who have become famous in their country
2 four people
3 celebrities for different reasons

3 Suggested key-word answers
1 expensive **2** regrets **3** media, aggressive **4** set an example **5** advise **6** most, enjoy **7** impossible, secret, media **8** more important **9** suspicious, other celebrities **10** wishes, hadn't said
Exam task answers
1 A **2** D **3** B **4** C **5** A **6** D **7** D **8** C **9** B **10** C

5 (note: *that* is possible after the reporting verbs)
2 Jake said he was meeting some big stars, and he was doing worthwhile things, too.
3 Jake said he had to leave extra-large tips in case they recognised him. *or* Jake complained …
4 Rachita said she'd / she had made good friends on that show.
5 Rachita said she was happy as she was.
6 Elka said winning that gold medal had changed her life.
7 Marcos said it was a pity he hadn't / had not realised sooner. *or* Marcos admitted …
8 Marcos said that the press would always find out every personal detail. *or* Marcos complained …

6 **1** guest **2** agent **3** film rights **4** being in the public eye **5** microphones **6** show off **7** look down on **8** inspire **9** role model **10** publicity **11** privacy **12** making a name for themselves

SPEAKING

Keeping going

1 all except 7
2 another difference is, There's also the fact that, As well as that

Recording script

Well, both are about the media, but one of them is taking place in a studio and the other outdoors. There are two people in the studio and they are sitting while those in the street are standing, and another difference is that the TV presenter has some notes to refer to whereas the reporters are simply listening as the woman gives an explanation of what happened. She has a sad expression on her face and the reporters look quite serious too, but in the studio both the people there are smiling and seem relaxed. Of course, that interview is for entertainment and the other one is for a news story. There's also the fact that their appearance is different, not just because those in the studio are younger, also because they're wearing indoor clothes. As well as that, there are some other people in the street though they aren't taking any notice of them, but in the studio there's probably an audience who are enjoying the interview.

3 Suggested answers
both probably for TV, both show cameras and camera operators, both show people concentrating on their work, both programmes probably being recorded, probably hot in both situations, TV crew have to keep quiet in both situations, outdoors *and* in studio, one person *and* four people, crew sitting and hiding *and* crew standing and clearly visible, dressed for outdoor heat in shorts, etc. *and* dressed for urban indoors, subjects are animals *and* subjects are actors, unaware they are being filmed *and* aware they are being filmed, potentially dangerous situation *and* safe situation

Part 2

5 In task 1, A has to compare the photographs and say what they think people find interesting about each type of programme. B has to say which of these kinds of programme they would prefer to watch.
In task 2, B has to compare the photographs and say which situation they think celebrities may like or dislike more. A has to say whether they would like to work as a reporter or a press photographer.

READING AND USE OF ENGLISH

Noun suffixes

1 **a** appear + -ance **b** explain + -ation (explain *drops* i) **c** entertain + -ment **d** express + -ion **e** differ + -ence

2 -ance: disappearance, maintenance (ai *changes to* e)
-ation: expectation, identification (y *changes to* i, *adds* c), recommendation, variation (y *changes to* i)
-ment: arrangement, requirement
-ion: contribution (*drops* e), intention (d *changes to* t), introduction (*drops* e, *adds* t)
-ence: existence, preference

3 **1** explanation (explain) **2** advertisement (advertise) **3** suggestions (suggest) **4** requirements (require) **5** reduction (reduce) **6** solutions (solve)

Part 3

4 **2** choice, choose **3** height, high **4** proof, prove **5** depth, deep

5 No, he does not believe it has reached its peak.
Exam task answers
1 publication **2** organisation **3** length **4** advertisements/adverts **5** variety **6** viewers **7** choice **8** belief

WRITING

Part 2 report

1 **1** recommendation **2** conclusion **3** step **4** sum **5** challenge **6** carried out **7** purpose

2 **1** a group of English-speaking people
2 they are planning to visit your town next winter
3 information about the television and radio there
4 which kinds of programme you think the group might enjoy watching and listening to

3 **1** five
2 yes
3 neutral or fairly formal
4 the sports, nature and arts programmes on TV, films and drama series in English with subtitles, 24-hour music radio stations
5 **a** The aim of this report is to, I strongly recommend, To sum up
b In addition, also, while, too, and, To sum up, even if
c Many tourists have said they were able to enjoy …

5 Model answer

The local media
The purpose of this report is to provide information about the broadcast media in this town, and to make recommendations for visitors.
Radio
The main national stations are: Radio 1, which broadcasts news and discussion programmes; Radio 2, offering pop music and lifestyle features; and Radio 3, which mainly plays classical music. In addition, there are several local stations. These provide coverage of news stories from the area, chat about topical issues, and regular phone-ins.
Television
As with radio, there are both local and national broadcasts, while the main international channels are available in most homes and hotels via cable or satellite TV. There are also several channels that show the latest films, although these normally require payment.
Recommendations
Visitors will find local radio and TV stations of particular interest for traffic updates, weather forecasts and details of what's on in sport and culture. For music and live sports coverage, national radio is highly recommended. For the latest news, both TV1 and TV2 broadcast regular bulletins covering national and international events, accompanied by well-informed discussion and analysis.

Revision

1 **1** talent show **2** satellite dish **3** gossip column **4** investigative journalist **5** drama series **6** camera operator
The unused compound nouns are *current affairs*, *remote control*, *set designer* and *soap opera*.

2 **1** he looked **2** he was **3** was wrong **4** (that) he had / he'd lost his job the previous **5** if/whether he had / he'd told his **6** he couldn't **7** her (that) his dad was in prison **8** his mum was **9** (that) she had / she'd disappeared the week **10** him what he would do **11** (that) he didn't know **12** (that) he was thinking

3 **1** promised to talk | to her **2** warned us | not to touch **3** how deep | the river was **4** apologised for | interrupting my **5** asked (her) whether/if | she knew **6** their hands where | he could

4 **1** readers **2** illustrations **3** depth **4** entertainment **5** humorous **6** recommendations **7** powerful **8** editors

Unit 10

READING AND USE OF ENGLISH

Clothing and shopping vocabulary

1 casual – formal, clashing – matching, cool – unfashionable, loose – tight, patterned – plain, simple – sophisticated, smart – untidy

2 brightly, casually, formally, plainly, simply, unfashionably, untidily (*and possibly* coolly)

5 **1** *out of stock* – not available in a shop; *in stock* – available in a shop
2 *a bargain* – on sale for less than its real value; *poor value for money* – costs more than it is worth
3 *exchange* – take it back to the shop where you bought it and change it for something else; *a refund* – money given back to you because you are not happy with something you have bought
4 *launched* – made available to customers for the first time; *sold out* – no more left to buy
5 *imports* – buys products from other countries; *exports* – sends goods to other countries for sale
6 *false* – not real; *genuine* – real
7 *budget* – very cheap; *uncompetitive* – worse than other prices, services or salaries
8 *consumers* – people who buy goods or services for their own use; *dealers* – people who trade in something
9 *shopkeepers* – people who own or manage a small shop; *suppliers* – companies that sell something
10 *purchases* – things people buy; *sales* – number of items sold

6 Suggested answers
designers, models, stylists, hairdressers, make-up artists, buyers

Part 6

7 **1** f **2** e **3** a **4** c **5** d **6** b

8 **B** like that **C** This **D** This means **E** That (+ it, it's) **F** in that way **G** Consequently, like those

9 Exam task answers
1 D **2** G **3** E **4** B **5** A **6** F

Position of adverbs of manner and opinion

11 it quickly takes off and sells really well
they won't let us stock them, unfortunately
Obviously, you need to be really enthusiastic and motivated.
think carefully about the target customer
Most of them, sadly, fail in their first year.

12 **1** do not speak English well
2 I very much like doing sports *or* I like doing sports very much
3 I had carefully read the store's catalogue. *or* I had read the store's catalogue carefully.
4 thankfully they believed me *or* , thankfully, they believed me *or* they believed me, thankfully
5 get to know the city better
6 send an email very quickly to the seller *or* send an email to the seller very quickly *or* very quickly send an email to the seller
7 naturally I have *or* , naturally, I have *or* I have a bicycle, naturally
8 I learned that I hadn't passed the examination, unfortunately *or* I learned that unfortunately I hadn't passed the examination *or* I learned, unfortunately, that I hadn't passed the examination

LISTENING

Part 3

1 **1** mall **2** trolley **3** brand **4** on offer **5** off **6** checkout **7** debit **8** debt **9** catalogue **10** guarantee

Recording script

I always try to get everything I need for the week down at the shops and supermarket at the big shopping mall on the outskirts of town. At the supermarket, I fill up my trolley with my favourite items of food, sometimes choosing a different brand from the one I usually buy if it happens to be on offer, for instance 'Buy 2 and get 1 free', or '20% off'. At the checkout I normally pay cash or by debit card rather than by credit card, as I don't want to get into debt by spending more than I can afford. Sometimes I call in at one of the other shops to buy something for the house, though for a big item I usually look it up in the catalogue first. I always check it has a good guarantee in case anything goes wrong after I've bought it.

3 Suggested answer
their experiences when shopping

4 **A** more, than, intended **B** good value **C** someone else, angry **D** make, for me **E** Internet, first time **F** tried, money back **G** advertisement, not, truthful **H** glad, alternative, paying
Exam task answers
1 F 2 B 3 D 4 A 5 H

Recording script

You will hear five different people talking about shopping experiences. For questions 1–5, choose from the list (A–H) what each speaker says. Use the letters only once. There are three extra letters which you do not need to use.

Speaker 1

I was in the computer shop looking for a new printer when a fantastic-looking laptop caught my eye. It was a completely new model, and although it was no bargain I bought it there and then instead of the printer, paying by cheque. The day after, though, I saw exactly the same model on sale in the supermarket, but for 150 euros less! I'd hardly used mine, so I took it back to the shop and asked for a refund, but the staff said they couldn't do that. I thought of stopping the cheque but that would've made them angry, and in the end I decided to keep the laptop. It runs well and I wouldn't be without it now, though I wish I still had those 150 euros, too.

Speaker 2

I always pick up a few things at the weekly street market, and last Wednesday I saw some interesting-looking items on a stall there and asked the seller how much they were. One in particular, a beautiful patterned vase, seemed very expensive and I didn't have enough cash on me, but the friend I was with lent me some, saying I could pay her back later. Delighted with my purchase, though worried in case I'd paid too much, I took it home and looked carefully at it. To my surprise there was a signature on the base, and when I looked it up I realised I had a genuine antique, worth far more than the man had charged me. I bet he'd be quite upset if he knew.

Speaker 3

I'd been looking for a cabinet that would fit the shape of the bathroom wall, so when I saw one advertised at the furniture store I raced round and paid cash for it. But I wish I'd been more careful measuring the wall because when I got home I found the cabinet was actually half a centimetre too wide. Furious with myself, I went back to the store and asked the salesman whether they had a slightly smaller one in stock, but they didn't. I could've got my money back but I knew that it was just the kind of cabinet I needed, so when he suggested having one made to fit exactly I agreed straightaway, though it meant handing over more money.

Speaker 4

I'd bought loads of stuff online before without any problems, so I wasn't pleased when I received an email saying that I still owed a seller for three blouses. She was quite reasonable about it, but I knew I'd only ordered one and it hadn't arrived yet anyway. I was just about to send her an angry reply saying she could keep the blouse and I'd keep my money, when there was a knock at the door. The postman handed me a large package, and inside were the three most gorgeous blouses I'd ever seen. I tried one on, and it fitted me as if I'd had it made to measure. I knew instantly that I wouldn't be sending any of them back, and later I sent the seller a payment for all three.

Speaker 5

By the time I reached the checkout queue I'd spent over an hour shopping and my trolley was full of the usual stuff. For once I hadn't seen any special offers but everything I'd picked up was essential, though I should've realised the total bill would be a bit higher this time. Because when at last I'd got to the counter and all my fish and fruit and veg and everything had gone through, my debit card was declined. It was just as well I had cash on me or else I would've held up all the other customers waiting behind me, and I know how annoying that can be. Just the other day I was saying how I wish people would check they have enough money before they go shopping.

Grammar

Review of *wish* and *if only*

1 **1** b (past perfect simple) **2** c (*would*) **3** a (present simple) **4** all of them

2 **1** wish you'd / you had been **2** could find *or* would find **3** wish I'd / I had bought **4** wished I hadn't answered **5** If only I had known **6** you would come **7** wish I could spend **8** wish I hadn't decided to wear

3 Example answers

2 I wish I'd bought the shirt on Friday. If only I hadn't waited until Monday.

3 I wish I hadn't come here on a Saturday. I wish people would stop pushing.

4 If only I didn't have to go to work tomorrow. I wish I could go to the sales.

5 I wish she wouldn't keep borrowing my things. I wish she would ask me before borrowing my things.

Review of causative *have* and *get*

4 **1** no **2** *have* **3** past participle

5 **1** have … repaired *or* get … repaired **2** having … wasted **3** 'll/will have … cut *or* 'll/will get … cut **4** have … cleaned *or* get … cleaned **5** have … tested *or* get … tested **6** have … delivered *or* get … delivered

6 Example answers

have my hair styled differently every week, have an expensive suit made, have my room tidied, have some exotic dishes cooked, have my appointments booked

SPEAKING

Parts 3 and 4

1

> **Recording script**
>
> To bring the conversation towards a conclusion, you can say *Which do you think would be best?* or *So which shall we choose?*, and to try to reach a decision you can use expressions such as *Well, are we both in favour of this one?* or *Shall we go for those two, then?* If you both decide on the same one or ones, say something like *Right, we're agreed* or *OK, those are the ones we'll go for*, but if you can't reach a decision, just say to your partner *Let's just agree to disagree* or *Let's leave it at that*.

2 six things

1 talk together about what might be good or bad about buying things in each of these shops

2 decide which two are the best to go shopping in

READING AND USE OF ENGLISH

Phrasal verbs with *out*

1 **1** finished the supply of, none left **2** get rid of **3** have none left **4** see what it's like **5** get **6** doesn't come into the house **7** are found **8** be unavailable, no more to buy

2 **1** breathe out **2** rushed out **3** cross (it) out **4** back out **5** shut out **6** worn out

Part 4

3 *I should've (gone)* → *wish I'd* (*wish* + past perfect), *gone for a ride on it* → *tried out* (phrasal verb with *out*): *I'd / I had | tried out*

4 **1** *wish* **2** causative *have* **3** *wish* + phrasal verb **4** *if only* + phrasal verb **5** causative *get* **6** *wish* + causative *have*

Exam task answers

1 wishes she hadn't / had not | spent **2** may have your luggage | searched **3** I hadn't / had not | stayed out **4** hadn't / had not | (been) sold out or run out **5** I'll get it | sent **6** 'd had / had had his tyres | checked

WRITING

Extreme adjectives

1 angry – furious, big – massive, bright – vivid, pleasant – delightful, silly – absurd, strange – bizarre, suitable – ideal, surprising – breathtaking

2 all 'very good' except *disgraceful, dreadful, severe*

3 **1** furious **2** vivid **3** absurd, bizarre **4** ideal **5** breathtaking, stunning, superb **6** dreadful **7** severe **8** stunning, fine

Part 1 essay

4 **1** You have been talking in your English class about the advantages and disadvantages of buying things on the Internet rather than getting them in the shops.

2 write an essay for your English teacher

3 which is cheaper, and easier

5 **1** disagrees, 5th paragraph

2 Note 1: 3rd paragraph – young people may not have debit or credit cards, card details can be stolen

Note 2: 2nd paragraph – goods may be late or not arrive, buyer has to post faulty or unsuitable items back

Note 3: 4th paragraph – going to the shops can be fun, you can try clothes on

3 **a** also, In conclusion

b however, On the other hand, though, in contrast

c Increasingly, Certainly, Worse still

d massive, enormous, tremendous

e having your purchases delivered, having your card details stolen

6 Model answer

> I don't agree that shopping online is better than going to the shops. It is certainly not easier for anyone without a computer or for those with limited computer skills. However, I do feel that sometimes shopping online is the only real option.
>
> When choosing clothes and books, I don't always know exactly what I want to buy beforehand. I like to browse before making my choice. In clothes shops, you can try things on. And in bookshops, you can browse the shelves and displays, and choose something that appeals to you. I accept that shopping online is generally cheaper, but in my view the extra expense I may incur is worthwhile.
>
> So when is online shopping the only option? Here's an example. My father loves opera. However, the major music store in my city has recently closed down and the others only have a small selection of opera CDs. My father has had no choice but to buy his CDs online.
>
> In conclusion, I would always choose to go shopping if this option is available to me.

Revision

1 **1** 'd bought **2** were **3** 'd waited **4** didn't **5** lived **6** hadn't **7** would **8** wouldn't

2 **1** I hadn't / had not | thrown out *or* thrown away **2** wish they wouldn't | try **3** have this skirt | completely altered *or* altered completely **4** hadn't / had not | run out of **5** could have my clothes | ironed **6** only we'd / we had | been able

3 *Get* is also possible in all these answers.

   2 You should have it mended. *or* Why don't you have it mended? *or* How about having it mended?

   3 You should have it filled. *or* Why don't you have it filled? *or* How about having it filled?

   4 You should have it (dry) cleaned. *or* Why don't you have it (dry) cleaned? *or* How about having it (dry) cleaned?

   5 You should have it cut. *or* Why don't you have it cut? *or* How about having it cut?

   6 You should have them taken. *or* Why don't you have them taken? *or* How about having them taken?

4 **Across**

1 item **4** off **8** dealer **9** loose **10** label **13** stock **16** casual **17** match **15** debit

Down

2 mall **3** bargain **5** false **6** cool **7** trolley **8** debt **11** bright **12** launch **13** sales **14** brand **15** plain

WRITING GUIDE ANSWER KEY

Part 1

Essay

1 1 your English class has been discussing studying and jobs
2 whether it is better to go into higher education rather than get a job straight from school
3 your teacher
5 which has immediate advantages, which is better for your career, your own idea

2 1 fairly formal – no contracted forms, formal linking expressions, impersonal tone (until the conclusion)
2 short introduction, arguments 'for' getting a job straight from school in one main paragraph, arguments 'for' going into higher education in another, concluding paragraph
3 1 second paragraph
2 first part of third paragraph
3 second part of third paragraph
4 in favour of going into higher education

Part 2

Letter

Exam task A

1 1 an email from your penfriend; informal
2 an email in reply; your favourite kind of food, where you would like to eat, where you would like to go afterwards
3 your penfriend Lena

2 1 yes – informal: *Hi*, expressions such as *Many thanks*, conversational *Yes*, exclamation marks, contracted forms, informal ending, etc.
2 yes
3 accepts invitation: first paragraph; says what her favourite kinds of food are: second paragraph; says which kind of restaurant: third paragraph; suggests somewhere to go afterwards: fourth paragraph

Exam task B

1 1 a job advertisement; (fairly) formal
2 a job application; whether you: are interested in clothes and fashion, have a good level of English, have experience of selling in shops
3 Mr James O'Neill, the manager

2 1 yes – formal: *Dear Mr*, no contracted verb forms, complete and complex sentences, *Yours sincerely*, etc.
2 yes
3 says she is interested in clothes and fashion: second paragraph; says she has a good level of English: fourth paragraph; says she has experience of selling in a shop: third paragraph

Article

1 1 an interesting place / a place worth visiting
2 travel magazine, readers of that magazine
3 describe the place, say what you most remember about your visit there

2 1 neutral – use of contracted forms but also complex complete sentences
2 the first two paragraphs describe the place, the last two deal with the writer's visit
3 the location, appearance and dimensions of the rock; how long people have lived near it; legends surrounding it; the route to the top of it; the variations in temperature, flora and fauna; the views from the top
4 He appears to find it very interesting, though at the end he wonders if the legend had a basis in fact.

Report

1 1 a public park near your home
2 your teacher
3 give a brief description of the park, say what people can do there, recommend some improvements

2 1 formal – no contracted verb forms, passive verb forms, complex sentences
2 Main features – brief description of the park, Leisure facilities – what people can do there, Conclusion – recommend some improvements
3 the park should be looked after a little better, more sporting activities should be made available

Review

1 1 a swimming pool in your area
2 an English-language website, visitors to your country
3 describe the pool, say what you think of it, say whether you would recommend it to other people

2 1 b 2 a 3 d 4 c

ACKNOWLEDGEMENTS

Author Acknowledgements

The author would like to thank Neil Holloway and Liz Driscoll for all their input, efficiency and good humour. Many thanks to Matt Stephens (production project manager), Chloe Szebrat (permissions controller), Alison Prior (picture researcher), Leon Chambers (audio producer), Alicia McAuley (proof reader).

Publisher acknowledgements

Development of this publication has made use of the Cambridge English Corpus (CEC). The CEC is a computer database of contemporary spoken and written English, which currently stands at over one billion words. It includes British English, American English and other varieties of English. It also includes the Cambridge Learner Corpus, developed in collaboration with Cambridge English Language Assessment. Cambridge University Press has built up the CEC to provide evidence about language use that helps to produce better language teaching materials.

This product is informed by the English Vocabulary Profile, built as part of English Profile, a collaborative programme designed to enhance the learning, teaching and assessment of English worldwide. Its main funding partners are Cambridge University Press and Cambridge English Language Assessment and it aims to create a 'profile' for English linked to the Common European Framework of Reference for Languages. English Profile outcomes, such as the English Vocabulary Profile will provide detailed information about the language that learners can be expected to demonstrate at each CEF level, offering a clear benchmark for learners' proficiency. For more information, please visit www.englishprofile.org

The Cambridge Advanced Learner's Dictionary is the world's most widely used dictionary for learners of English. Including all the words and phrases that learners are likely to come across, it also has easy-to-understand definitions and example sentences to show how the word is used in context. The Cambridge Advanced Learner's Dictionary is available online at dictionary.cambridge.org. © Cambridge University Press, Third edition (2008), reproduced with permission.

Text Acknowledgements

The authors and publishers acknowledge the following sources of copyright material and are grateful for the permissions granted. While every effort has been made, it has not always been possible to identify the sources of all the material used, or to trace all copyright holders. If any omissions are brought to our notice, we will be happy to include the appropriate acknowledgements on reprinting.

Studentcook.co.uk for the text on p. 17 adapted from 'How I cooked for myself at University: A Case Study' by Meg Russell, 25.08.2010. www.studentcook.co.uk. Reproduced with permission;

The Independent for the text on pp. 26–27 adapted from 'Leave only your footprints' by Aoife O'Riordain, The Independent 30.03.2010, for the text on pp. 32–33 adapted from 'Quiet please: rock gig etiquette' by Fiona Sturges, The Independent 02.11.2010, for the text on pp. 58–59 adapted from 'The Big Question: How big is the problem of electronic waste, and can it be tackled?' by Michael McCarthy, The Independent 24.02.2010, for the text on pp. 64–65 adapted from 'The first decade: Has the internet brought us together or driven us apart?' by Johann Hari, The Independent 08.12.2009, for the text on p. 81 adapted from 'I want your job: fashion buyer' by Lindsey Friedman, The Independent 13.09.2007. Copyright © The Independent, 2007, 2009, 2010;

Cambridge University Press for the text on p. 49 from Windows of the Mind by Frank Brennan, © Cambridge University Press 2001, reproduced with permission.

Photo Acknowledgements

p. 8 (TL): Getty Images/© BrandX/Verity Jane Smith; p.8 (CL): Getty Images/© London Eye; p.8 (CR) Alamy/© Wavebreak Media; p.8 (BL): Getty Images/© Betsie van der Meer; p.8 (BR): Alamy/© Image Source; p.9 (T): iStockphoto/© Manuel Burgos; p.10 (T): iStockphoto/© ajt; p.10 (TL): Alamy/© Tetra Images; p.10 (TC): Glow Images; p.10 (TR) Alamy/© Zak Waters; p.10 (CR): Getty Images/© Daniel Grill; p.12 (T): iStockphoto/© spet p.12 (BR): Getty Images/© Leander Barenz; p.12 (B): Getty Images/© AFP; p.12 (BL): Shutterstock/© Creatista; p.13 (T): iStockphoto/© ajt; p.14 (T): iStockphoto/© bluestocking; p.15 (T): iStockphoto/© SorenP; p.15 (B): Shutterstock/© Piotr Marcinski; p.17: Alamy/© Neil & Molly Jansen; p.18 (T): Getty Images/© BrandX/Verity Jane Smith; p.18 (B): Getty Images; p.19 (T): iStockphoto/© Manuel Burgos; p.19 (B): Shutterstock/© Pinky Pills; p.20 (T): iStockphoto/© spet; p.20 (CL,CR): Alamy/© Radius Images; p.20 (BL): Getty Images/Bloomberg/© Antoine Antoniol; p.20(BR): Glow Images/© Blend Images; p.21 (T): iStockphoto/© firebrandphotography; p.22 (T): iStockphoto/© bluestocking; p.23 (T): istockphoto/© SorenP; p.23:Shutterstock/© Ollyy; p.24 (T): Getty Images/© BrandX/Verity Jane Smith; p.24 (1): Thinkstock/© Ingram Publishing; p.24 (2): Alamy/© Look Die Bildagentur; p.24 (3): Shutterstock/© Dennis Donohue; p.24 (4): Glow Images/© Aflo Diversion; p.24 (5): Alamy/© Manfred Gottschalk; p.25 (T): iStockphoto/© Manuel Burgos; p.25 (BL): Press Association/Demotix/© Erik Teer; p.25 (BR): Alamy/© JHP News; p.26 (T): iStockphoto/© ajt; p.26 (B): Alamy/© Superstock; p.27: Getty Images/© Mike Harrington; p.28 (T): iStockphoto/© spet; p.29 (T): iStockphoto/© firebrandphotography; p.29 (B): Reuters/© Daniel Munoz; p.30 (T): iStockphoto/© bluestocking; p.31 (T): iStockphoto/© SorenP; p.31 (B): Corbis/© Ralph Lee; p.32 (T): iStockphoto/© ajt; p.32 (1): Shutterstock/© Kamira; p.32 (2): Alamy/© David Pearson; p.32 (3): Alamy/© Jeff Greenberg; p.32 (4): Shutterstock/© Stocklite; p.34 (T): Getty Images/ BrandX/© Verity Jane Smith; p.35 (T): iStockphoto/© Manuel Burgos; p.35 (B): Shutterstock/© Monkey Business Images; p.36 (T): iStockphoto/© spet; p.37 (T): iStockphoto/© firebrandphotography; p.38 (T): iStockphoto/© bluestocking; p.38 (B): The Sugar Glider/Neilsen R, CUP B2 English Reader/© Cambridge University Press; p.39 (T): iStockphoto/© SorenP; p.39 (B): Getty Images/© Kemeter; p.40 (T): Getty Images/ BrandX/© Verity Jane Smith; p.40 (1,2): Thinkstock/© iStockphoto; p.40 (3): Alamy/© Arcaid Images; p.40 (4): Shutterstock/© Fraser Young; p.41 (T): iStockphoto/© Manuel Burgos; p.41 (B): Getty Images/© Carlo A; p.42 (T): iStockphoto/© ajt; p.42 (TR): Thinkstock/© iStockphoto; p.42 (BR): Glow Images/© Corbis RF; p.42 (BL): Getty Images/© The Image Bank/© Peter Dazeley; p.42 (TL): Corbis/© Betsy Winchell; p.44 (T): iStockphoto/© spet; p.45 (T): iStockphoto/© firebrandphotography; p.45 (B): Alamy/© Andrew Fox; p.46: iStockphoto; p.47 (T): iStockphoto/© SorenP; p.47(B): Shutterstock/© Michael Kowalski; p.48 (T): iStockphoto/© ajt; p.49: Alamy/© Organics Image Library; p.50 (T): Getty Images/ BrandX/© Verity Jane Smith; p.51: iStockphoto/© Manuel Burgos; p.52: iStockphoto/© spet; p.53: iStockphoto/© firebrandphotography; p.54: iStockphoto; p.55:iStockphoto/© SorenP; p.56 (T): Getty Images/© BrandX/Verity Jane Smith; p.56 (1): Thinkstock/© Hemera; p.56 (2): Shutterstock/© Portokalis; p.56 (3): Glow Images/© Stock; p.56 (4): Alamy/© A.T. Willett; p.57: iStockphoto/© Manuel Burgos; p.58: iStockphoto/© ajt; p.58 (C): Rex Features/© Denis Coulson; p.58 (B): Getty Images; p.59: Shutterstock/© K J Pargeter; p.60 (T): iStockphoto/© spet; p.60 (B): Alamy/© Blend Images; p.61: iStockphoto/© ajt; p.62: iStockphoto; p.63: iStockphoto/© SorenP; p.64: iStockphoto/© ajt; p.66 (T): Getty Images/ BrandX/© Verity Jane Smith; p.66 (B):Glow Images; p.67 (T): iStockphoto/© Manuel Burgos; p.67 (B): Alamy/© AgefotoStock; p.68 (T): iStockphoto/© spet; p.69 (T): iStockphoto/© ajt; p.69 (B): Glow Images; p.70: iStockphoto; p.71: iStockphoto/© SorenP; p.72 (T): iStockphoto/© spet; p.72 (L): Alamy/© Image Brokers; p.72 (C): Glow Images/© BlendRM; p.72 (R): Rex Features/© Ken McKay; p.73: iStockphoto/© Manuel Burgos; p.74(T): iStockphoto/© ajt; p.74 (B): Corbis/ Alison Langley/© Aurora Photos; p.75 (T): Shutterstock/© Snow White Images; p.75 (C,B): Getty Images; p.76 (T): iStockphoto/© spet; p.76 (CL): Getty Images/© 2011 Kevin Winter/Tonight Show; p.76 (CR): Shutterstock/© Ints Vikmanis; p.76 (BL): Rex Features/© ITV: p.76 (BR): Getty Images/© Caspar Benson; p.77: iStockphoto/© ajt; p.78: iStockphoto; p.79: iStockphoto/© SorenP: p.80 (T): iStockphoto/© ajt; p.80 (1): Getty Images/© Image Source; p.80 (2): Getty Images/© David Lees; p.80 (3): Getty Images/© Mimi Hadden; p.80 (4): Getty Images/© Tim Robberts; p.80 (5): Alamy/© Tetra Images; p.80 (6): Alamy/© Image Source Plus; p.82: iStockphoto/© spet; p.83: iStockphoto/© Manuel Burgos; p.84: iStockphoto/© spet; p.85 (T): iStockphoto/© ajt; p.85 (B): Getty Images/© AFP; p.86: iStockphoto; p.87: iStockphoto /© SorenP; p.88: iStockphoto; p.94: Getty Images/© BrandX/Verity Jane Smith; p.97: iStockphoto/© spet; p.101 (TL): Thinkstock/© Hemera; p.101 (TR): Alamy/© Steven May; p.101 (BL): Rex Features/© Sipa Press; p.101(BR): Getty Images/© UIG; p.102(TL): Getty Images/© NBC; p.102 (TR): Rex Features/© ACTION; p.102(BL): Rex Features; p.102 (BR): Rex Features/© Sipa Press; p.103: iStockphoto/© Manuel Burgos.

Illustrations

Maxwell Dorsey (NB Illustration) p.48; Richard Jones (Beehive Illustrations) pp. 34, 53, 57, 61, 82, 83; Laszlo Veres (Beehive Illustrations) pp. 16, 21, 50, 64, 79